D0758522

CONFESSIONS OF AN ISLAMOPHOBE

CONFESSIONS OF AN ISLAMOPHOBE

ROBERT SPENCER

BOMBARDIER
BOOKS

A BOMBARDIER BOOKS BOOK
An Imprint of Post Hill Press

Confessions of an Islamophobe

ISBN: 978-1-68261-490-7
ISBN (eBook): 978-1-68261-491-4

Cover Design by Dan Pitts

Post Hill Press
New York • Nashville
posthillpress.com
Published in the United States of America

This book is offered, with immense respect and gratitude,
to all those who dare to speak truly about
the nature and magnitude of the jihad threat,
despite the character assassination that inevitably ensues.

CONTENTS

ACKNOWLEDGEMENTS

THE CHARGE OF "ISLAMOPHOBE," when attached to any honest analyst of the jihad terror threat, is a nasty smear that has destroyed reputations, besmirched noble initiatives and important research, and poisoned the public discourse. I am humbled and honored to work with and be associated with many of the foremost warriors for freedom who have been defamed in this way, including David Horowitz, Pamela Geller, Steve Emerson, and Frank Gaffney. If free societies prevail, the constant abuse to which they and others who have borne the label "Islamophobe" have suffered will be remembered as a manifestation of hysteria reminiscent of the Salem Witch Trials, and they will be hailed as the heroes they are.

This book could not have been written if I didn't have so much help to maintain our daily news and commentary site on jihad activity, Jihad Watch (www.jihadwatch.org) from colleagues Christine Douglass-Williams and Hugh Fitzgerald, as well as my mysterious, knowledgeable, and indefatigable tech expert Marc. If Jihad Watch is, as I hope it to be, a beacon of the truth in a field that is overrun by disinformation and misinformation, it is largely because of their efforts, and the support and help of Michael Finch of the David Horowitz Freedom Center.

I'm honored that this book is one of the initial offerings of the new Bombardier Books, and hope to work with David S. Bernstein on many future bombing missions. This book was different from my others in numerous ways, and David guided me with particular acuity through all manner of minefields. If it weren't for his sense of taste and proportion, his focus, and his vision for what this book could and should be, it simply wouldn't be worth reading. If it is, thank Bernstein, and Adam Bellow as well. One morning as I walked the beautiful streets of Charleston, South Carolina, Bellow and I had a long conversation about this; his advice and feedback was well worth heeding, and I did.

No Acknowledgments page would be complete without a nod to Jeffrey Rubin, who published my first articles way back in the 1980s, guided my first book to publication, gave me the idea and inspiration for my first bestseller, *The Politically Incorrect Guide to Islam (and the Crusades)*, and helped me in more ways than I can enumerate here. Here's to you, Jeff, as always. Like all my other books, this one, in significant measure, is for you.

PREFACE

MY JOURNEY TO ISLAMOPHOBIA

When I was very young, frequently my mother and brother and I would walk up our block to the corner, and then down the next street, unpaved and with a tree squarely in the middle of the intersection and houses only on one side of the street, to a small bungalow at the end of a dirt road. There lived my grandparents, Stamatios ("Thomas," or "Tom" to his close friends) and Maria (always "Mary") Zompakos, hardy and affable people with a touch, for me, of exotica.

Their home was an exciting and intriguing world, so very different from my American house around the block. My grandparents' house was filled with the sweet aroma of my grandfather's pipe smoke, and with Greek Orthodox icons of Jesus, Mary, and various saints. My mother and grandparents would converse in Greek, but when I asked them about Greece, I learned to my surprise that none of them had lived on the Greek mainland, or even ever actually been there. My grandparents were not from Greece but from the Ottoman Empire, from Tsesmes (now Cesme) on the Aegean Sea, right across the Cesme Strait from the island of Chios.

Tsesmes, which is about fifty-five miles from Smyrna (Izmir), and all of Western Anatolia, was a majority Greek area from time immemorial. But as World War I drew to a close and the Ottoman Empire was collapsing, both Muslims who supported the Ottoman sultan and secularists who wanted to create a Turkish national state regarded the Greeks of Asia Minor not as fellow citizens of a minority religion, but as a problem to be solved.

Muslims who wanted Sharia rule regarded the Greeks, as well as the Armenians and other Christians in what would soon become Turkey, as *kuffar harbi*, infidels at war with Islam for preferring independence (and, in the Greeks' case, union with Greece) over continuing fealty to Turkish rule. The Young Turks of Kemal Ataturk and his fellow secularists regarded Islam, albeit a depoliticized, cultural Islam, as central to the Turkish identity around which they were setting out to construct the new Turkish national state. For both groups, therefore, the non-Muslims had to go.

And they did go. They were forced to. In October 1915, Ismail Enver, the Ottoman minister of war, declared that he planned to "solve the Greek problem during the war...in the same way he believe[d] he solved the Armenian problem."[1] Rafet Bey, an Ottoman official, said in November 1916 that "we must finish off the Greeks as we did with the Armenians…today I sent squads to the interior to kill every Greek on sight."[2]

Not all the Greeks were killed. Some were exiled. My grandmother, Maria Chrissafakis, who always insisted in the United States on being known as Mary, and her family escaped from Tsesmes and made their way to Nantes, France, and sometime thereafter boarded the *S.S. Chicago* bound for the United States. And so it was that my grandmother, listed as seventeen but possibly a year or so younger, along with her parents and two brothers, arrived at Ellis Island on the *Chicago* from Bordeaux on April 10, 1918. I haven't been able to locate any records of my grandfather's arrival in the United States, but the 1930 U.S. Census lists Stamatios Zompakos as hailing from "Smyrna, Turkey" and having arrived in the U.S. in 1916. It lists his wife Mary as also hailing from Smyrna, and arriving in the U.S. in 1918.

On my office wall I have a photograph of Stamatios' father, my great-grandfather, Stylianos Zompakos, looking piercingly at the camera, elaborately mustachioed and wearing zouave pantaloons and boots. He is seated next to his wife, whose name has been lost to me; she is wearing a shawl and a long-suffering look. Two teenaged daughters stand behind them, dark-eyed, serious, staring solemnly off to the left. Between the couple is my great-uncle George, looking just as solemn and grave as his ten years on the planet would allow, clutching a toy rifle.

My grandfather is not in the picture, for reasons unknown to me. As the ages of the people in the picture indicate that it was taken around the time when he was eighteen or twenty and had left the country, he may have already gone when it was taken. I do know, however, that ultimately his three siblings followed him to the U.S., as the whole family had intended to do. But it was not an easy departure. As they loaded their possessions on a boat that was to take them to Crete and open their passageway to the New World, a Turkish soldier with a rifle slung over his soldier watched them. He did not make a move toward them, but just watched them and smoked cigarettes, expressionless, as they carried their belongings to the boat.

When they were finished and about to set out from the shore, however, my great-grandfather Stylianos Zompakos remembered something he had left in the house. I do not know what it was, and indeed, no one does now. As he made his way back to the family's old house, which would soon be inhabited by Turks and all evidence of a Greek presence in the area effaced, the soldier followed him. When they got to the house, the soldier shot and killed Stylianos. The story that went around in the family was that the soldier thought Stylianos was coming back to retrieve hidden gold.

There was no gold. Nor was there any time. Horrified and appalled at the shooting, the rest of the family managed to get away quickly. Once in the United States, it didn't take long for my grandfather, Stamatios Zompakos, to settle in New York City, where he began going by the name Thomas for the ease of the locals and to manifest his pride in the country that had welcomed him, and to marry Mary, the girl from his hometown in Asia Minor. (They didn't know each other there, I was always told, and which I always found astounding.) On February 9, 1923, my mother was born. She was christened in St. Nicholas Greek Orthodox Church in lower Manhattan, the little church that was destroyed in the World Trade Center bombings of September 11, 2001.

It took me years to piece those details together, and as all of the people involved are now dead, those I managed to obtain and a scant few others are probably all I will ever know about how my family got to the United States. I used to ask my grandparents about life where they grew up. My grandmother was as loquacious about it as my grandfather was taciturn. She told me that she had grown up in an extremely beautiful place, where the weather was always good, and the people were friendly and kind. Very early every morning, she would hear the muezzin in the minaret calling the local Muslims, a minority in the area at that time, to prayer, and she thought—as Barack Obama would famously tell Nicholas Kristof decades later—that it was a strikingly beautiful sound.

Everything she told me about life in Tsesmes was positive. It made me long to go there, to see what she saw, to feel what she felt. But when I asked her why they left, she said, "We were exiled." My grandfather would say the same thing in response to my queries: "We were exiled." I was six or seven years old; I didn't know what the word meant. I found out, and asked them why they were exiled. No answer. They couldn't, or wouldn't, tell me.

So I had to find out for myself. But it would be a few years before I came to be in a position to do that. In the meantime, I grew up as a middle-class American, with the middle-American sensibilities of the mid-twentieth century. I learned to respect and revere people such as Thomas More and Nathan Hale and Dietrich Bonhoeffer and Alexander Solzhenitsyn, who stood for their convictions even at immense personal risk, including even the loss of their very lives, and even when it seemed as if the whole world were against them. I learned to have contempt for those who, conversely, temporized and trimmed and dissembled in order to gain worldly advantage or to save their skins.

I learned a deep respect for democratic principles, for the freedom of speech, and for free inquiry, and respect, too, for those whose opinions and views differed from mine. Once in the summer of 1968, when I was six years old, I asked my father which presidential candidate was the "good guy": Richard Nixon or Hubert Humphrey (I don't believe I thought to mention George Wallace). His answer dumbfounded me, and I've never forgotten it. "They're both good men," he told me. "They both want what is best for our country. They just have different ideas of what exactly that is."

That was the kind of perspective I took into adulthood, although in college I did fall prey to the fashionable Leftism that is even more virulent and omnipresent now than it was then, and which refuses to grant the possibility that those whom it hates and fears could possibly be operating in good faith, or that their views are rooted in anything other than prejudice, which is to say, hatred and fear.

After taking a few Latin American Studies courses taught by Marxist professors, I was essentially a Marxist myself, and became even more committed to this point of view through a friendship with a Revolutionary Communist Party (RCP) activist on campus named Carolyn. I thought I was on the vanguard of working for a just society, although the extent of my revolutionary activity was a summer working at Revolution Books, the Revolutionary Communist Party's bookstore. But even then I argued with Carolyn over the raw hatred and venom directed against American politicians in *The Revolutionary Worker*, the RCP's newspaper. The idea that those who oppose us are demons who must be mocked, vilified, and destroyed repelled me, and ultimately contributed to my disenchantment with the Party, and with Marxism itself.

One sunny afternoon I asked Carolyn about the millions that Stalin, Mao, Pol Pot, and others had murdered in the name of the just society we were supposedly trying to bring about. She explained to me that those weren't true Communist leaders, and that true Communism had actually never yet been implemented anywhere. With that, as much as I liked and even admired Carolyn for her fearlessness in the face of the ridicule and contempt to which she was often subjected on campus, my disenchantment with the hard-Left was complete.

I remembered that day many years later, when I first heard a Muslim spokesman wave away the Sharia-sanctioned human rights abuses of Saudi Arabia and Iran by saying that they weren't true Sharia states, and that Sharia had not actually ever been implemented, anywhere. Propagandists for totalitarianism tend to sound the same notes.

It was in college that I took a few courses on Islam, and first read the Qur'an. I was keen to do so, as I remembered what my grandmother had said about the muezzin's call. Initially I read it in spiritual-seeker mode. I wasn't considering conversion to Islam, but I was fascinated by the various forms of spirituality around the world; not long after I finished reading the Qur'an for the first time, I read the Bhagavad Gita, rather uncomprehendingly, and unsuccessfully attempted the Zohar.

The Qur'an struck me more than the other books of its kind that I tried to read, and also seemed clearer than they did. There was something about it that fascinated me, and I kept returning to it. It needs to be said now, given the circumstances of this writing, that I had no animus toward it at all. It wasn't until I began to study the history of Greece and Turkey at the time of the dissolution of the Ottoman Empire that passages of the Qur'an began to occur to me: *when the sacred months are over, kill the idolaters wherever you find them* (9:5) and *Indeed, they who disbelieved among the People of the Book and the polytheists will be in the fire of Hell, abiding eternally therein. Those are the most vile of created beings* (98:6) and the like.

Slowly it began to dawn on me, as I leafed through the pages of the Qur'an, and began to study the mainstream Islamic interpretations of the Qur'an, as well as the Hadith and the history of Islam, that I had the key to what had happened to my family, the answer to my childhood question, *Why were you exiled?* It only made me more fascinated. I read the Qur'an again and again on my own, outside the context of any college class, along with the voluminous Hadith literature (the words and deeds of Muhammad, which when deemed authentic are normative for Islamic law, as well as commentary on the Qur'an and much more) and more Islamic history. At the beginning of these explorations, the Iranian hostage crisis was going on, and I began to see that I had the key to understanding why the Iranians took the hostages—the deep reason why, beyond their list of grievances against Jimmy Carter and the United States.

This was an intellectual realization. The Qur'an had verses exhorting believers to wage war, and Islam had doctrines of warfare against unbelievers, and it looked to me as if these were playing out in world events, past and present.

There are, in short, very good reasons to be an Islamophobe, that is, to be concerned about Islam for the devastation that it brings into the lives of human beings both Muslim and non-Muslim. It is not hatred and bigotry to be the right kind of Islamophobe, that is, as opposed to one who attacks innocent Muslims, something that is never justified.

Indeed, the only chance for the survival of free societies into the latter part of the twenty-first century may be if large numbers of people join me in becoming this kind of unrepentant Islamophobe.

CHAPTER 1

NOTORIOUS

I AM AN ISLAMOPHOBE.

It's true. I've denied it for years. But now I admit it.

Nor am I just any old Islamophobe. According to the Council on American-Islamic Relations (CAIR), I am "one of the nation's most notorious Islamophobes."[1] The Southern Poverty Law Center (SPLC) warns that I am one of the "most important propagandizing Islamophobes in the world."[2]

Kecia Ali, an associate professor of religion at Boston University, has anointed me the "grand pooh-bah of the legion of American Islamophobes."[3] Unfortunately, a hat with horns doesn't seem to go along with this title.

A lot of aggravation and abuse did go along with it, however. British Prime Minister Theresa May has boasted of having banned me from entering her country because "Islamophobia comes from the same wellspring of hatred" as anti-Semitism.[4] When I am invited to speak at universities, there are inevitably petition drives calling for me to be canceled and denouncing me in lurid terms; if the events go forward, protesters sometimes shout me down and do everything they can to make sure that my "hateful" words cannot be heard. After I spoke in Iceland recently a young Leftist slipped drugs into my drink, and no doubt went away feeling righteous.

While I am accustomed to all this now, when it first began it came as a surprise. Indeed, for years I have rejected the claim that I am an "Islamophobe," with, to my mind, very good reason: although I am (according to the SPLC) an infamous "hate group leader," I don't believe that any genuinely neutral reader will detect any hate in anything I have written.

Of course, I *would* say that, wouldn't I? Perhaps every SPLC hate group leader believes in the rightness of his cause and his innocence of the "hate" charges, although it is hard for me to understand how any actual neo-Nazi or Klansman could not think himself hateful by the very nature of his political philosophy.

When I began publishing material about Islam and terrorism, I was just an individual with political opinions within the broad mainstream of American politics, profound respect for the classical liberal intellectual tradition, and a tremendous interest in Islam stemming from my family history. I wanted to do my bit to preserve secular and pluralistic society. That was all.

Such societies seemed to be under threat, particularly after 9/11. Yet in the immediate aftermath of that attack, I was surprised that the prevailing analyses of why it had happened were wrongly focused. I was strongly exhorted by one of the people for whom I had been consulting about Islam in the 1990s to write my own book to set the record straight.

I did write that book, *Islam Unveiled: Disturbing Questions About the World's Fastest-Growing Faith*.[5] But it was not some flame-throwing polemic; indeed, I was pleased when the American Library Association's *Booklist* review called it "alarmingly cogent."[6] That was exactly what I had hoped it would be: alarming about a subject there was cause to be alarmed about, and cogent in explaining how jihadis use the texts and teachings of Islam to justify violence. I was confident it would receive thoughtful, measured responses from Muslims who rejected and abhorred what happened on 9/11.

Instead, the kind of response I was going to receive became clear on February 25, 2003, when I appeared on MSNBC TV's *Nachman* show. I was on with Ibrahim Hooper of CAIR, and when the discussion turned to support for the 9/11 attacks among Muslims in the U.S., I invoked Naqshbandi Sufi leader Muhammad Hisham Kabbani's 1999 testimony before a State Department Open Forum. Based on his personal visits to 114 mosques in the United States and his study of their literature, Kabbani stated that eighty percent of mosques in the U.S. taught the same view of Islam espoused by the Islamic jihadists.[7]

Hooper, in response, said nothing about Kabbani or mosques in the United States. He did not, as I had expected, protest that Kabbani was wrong, and that mosques in the U.S. taught the importance of Muslims living as equals in a secular society in which there was no established religion. Instead, he called me a "hatemonger."

This was my first encounter with a tactic that has come to be used with astonishing effectiveness to shut down not just mainstream consideration of the points I have raised in my books and other writings, but all serious discussion of these issues.

In the mid-2000s, the point of view I represent became almost mainstream. In 2005 and 2006 I published two books that made *The New York Times* bestseller list: *The Politically Incorrect Guide to Islam (and the Crusades)* and *The Truth About Muhammad.* I appeared so often on Fox News that I got to be friends with some of the drivers who would take me to the studio. An FBI agent invited me to give seminars to in the Bureau, on the Qur'an and Sunnah and what they disclose about the terrorist mindset. I gave similar seminars to military groups, and on one occasion to the CIA, where the agents sat solemnly around a huge oak table with nameplates that gave only their first names. In 2007, I even traveled to Berlin at the invitation of the U.S. State Department to participate in a symposium on the jihad cosponsored by the German Foreign Ministry.

All that seems inconceivable today, and it is—because of the charge of "Islamophobia."

By this time, I was used to being attacked from the Left as a hatemonger. But I was surprised when the mainstream Right, never fully comfortable with demonstrations of how Islamic texts and teachings exhorted violence after George W. Bush proclaimed that Islam was a religion of peace, began to move sharply away from allowing open discussion of the possibility that it wasn't.

I was an invited speaker at the Conservative Political Action Conference (CPAC) in 2003 and again in 2007. At CPAC 2007 I debated Dinesh D'Souza on the question of whether or not Islam was a religion of peace; later, a CPAC board member informed me that an entire planning meeting of the board before the conference had been devoted to trying to find someone who could decisively defeat me in debate.

It was flattering that they thought it so important to refute me, but it was also disquieting. Clearly I represented a perspective that mainstream Right leaders wanted to stamp out among conservatives.

Indeed, there would soon be no room in the mainstream of either party for any perspective other than that Islam was a religion of peace that had been hijacked by a tiny minority of extremists. Any hint that Islamic texts might contain exhortations to violence was hateful in itself, and Islamophobic.

The invitations to address the FBI, the Joint Terrorism Task Force, and military groups kept coming for a while. But it became increasingly common for someone to take me aside and explain how happy they were that I was speaking there, but that I really must not make my appearance public, or they would catch hell from the Council on American-Islamic Relations.

I saw why they were so cautious in August 2010, when CAIR found out that I had spoken on a military base, as well as to FBI agents, and began a national campaign, demanding that FBI director Robert Mueller apologize for having me speak and promise not to do it again. Mueller did not apologize, at least not publicly, but after that I never again invited to address any intelligence or military groups.

The following year, Farhana Khera, an attorney with an organization known as Muslim Advocates, wrote to John Brennan, then Assistant to the President on National Security for Homeland Security and Counter Terrorism and later director of the CIA, complaining that "the FBI's library at the FBI training academy in Quantico, Virginia" contained my books; that a reading list compiled by the FBI's Law Enforcement Communications Unit recommended my book *The Truth About Muhammad*; and that I had presented seminars and lectures on 'the belief system of Islamic jihadists' to the Joint Terrorism Task Force and the U.S. Attorney's Anti-Terrorism Advisory Council.[8]

Khera demanded that all this end, and it did. The idea that analysis of Islamic texts and teachings regarding warfare against unbelievers was hateful "Islamophobia" was now entrenched at the highest levels of the U.S. government, and there it has stayed.

And so my status as an international pariah is now sealed. Nor did this happen just to me, but to everyone who dared suggest a connection between Islam and terrorism. Not only are we classified by the Southern Poverty Law Center as "hate group leaders," but we figure prominently in numerous "reports" on the sinister beliefs and activities of various "Islamophobes." I am widely dismissed, often by people who have never read a line of anything I have actually written, as a bigot, a racist, a foe of all things decent and true. I am routinely characterized in the media as "anti-Muslim." I've been called the flip side of Osama bin Laden and other jihadists, as in: "I condemn bin Laden, and I also condemn his counterpart on the other side, Robert Spencer."

When I speak on college campuses, I have to hire security guards for protection against the frenzied guardians of tolerance and peace. Once several years ago, when I was invited to speak on a matter having nothing whatsoever to do with Islam, the host canceled my appearance under pressure from a self-appointed crusader against "Islamophobia."[9]

I've been banned from entering Great Britain, and from a college campus, solely for not holding the accepted view that Islam is a religion of peace.[10] If I fly American Airlines, I am subjected to time-consuming extra security checks—because I am a notorious "Islamophobe."[11]

When I meet new people, I am sometimes embarrassed to tell them who I am and what I do. And yet I can't stop. Because I know that what I am saying is true.

Islamophobia—Good and Bad

For years, I have denied the label "Islamophobe" because it is most commonly used to refer to people who have an irrational bigotry or hatred toward Muslims. I don't.

Now I will own the label. But I must add a crucial caveat: I am not an Islamophobe within the meaning of those who have affixed this label on me. In other words, I am not the "bad" kind of Islamophobe who wants any innocent people, Muslim or non-Muslim, to be victimized. Instead I am what I would call the "good" kind of Islamophobe, someone who is honest enough to call a problem a problem, even when the whole world wishes to ignore and deny its existence.

This is a key distinction that is, to my knowledge, never made. In fact, "Islamophobia" studies, whether produced by Muslim organizations of Leftist non-Muslim groups, tend to use the term without defining it clearly, conflating several quite distinct phenomena that may not really be associated with one another at all.

These studies are filled with accounts of innocent Muslims being accosted and insulted in shopping malls, drunken louts (nowadays sporting "Make America Great Again" hats) haranguing cowed hijab-wearing Muslim women as "terrorists" and telling them to "go home," and strips of bacon or even pigs' heads left at mosques.

On June 19, 2017, a non-Muslim plowed a van into a crowd outside the Finsbury Park mosque in London, killing one man and injuring nine other people. The driver was reported to have said, "I want to kill Muslims."[12] This attack was widely blamed upon "Islamophobia": anti-Muslim rhetoric supposedly moved this man to kill.[13]

There is no evidence for that in the Finsbury Park case, and I do not believe that I or any other "Islamophobe" has that kind of power or influence. If anyone dislikes Muslims today, it is much more likely that it is because of Osama bin Laden and Anwar al-Awlaki than the likes of Robert Spencer and my colleague Pamela Geller, whom the SPLC dubbed "the anti-Muslim movement's most visible and flamboyant figurehead."[14]

All such attacks on peaceful Muslims are reprehensible, and there is no excuse or justification for them whatsoever. If that's Islamophobia, then I want nothing to do with it. I have never gotten liquored up and screamed obscenities at a random passersby wearing Muslim garb, nor do I condone anyone who has done such a thing. I don't believe in harassment, or vigilantism, or vandalism, or any attacks on mosques or the people in them.

The problem with many analyses of Islamophobia, however, is that they tend to condemn under the same rubric of bias and bigotry any analysis of how jihadis use the texts and teachings of Islam to justify violence and recruit among peaceful Muslims. Thus, at the March 2008 meeting in Senegal of the umbrella group for the fifty-seven Muslim majority governments now known as the Organization of Islamic Cooperation (OIC), the assembled Muslim leaders declared that it was going to develop a "legal instrument" to combat the threat to Islam from "political cartoonists," i.e., those who dared to draw cartoons of Muhammad, the prophet of Islam, and "bigots."[15]

In short, the most important agenda at this meeting for combating Islamophobia was not combating vigilantes and vandals, but quelling criticism of Islam in the public square. And this agenda would be advanced under the banner of fighting against Islamophobia.

If the OIC really wants to fight against the "bad" Islamophobia that takes the form of vigilante attacks against innocent Muslims, it could start by addressing what it also insists is Islamophobia: examination of the Islamic texts and teachings that are used to justify violence and oppression by Muslims. If it came up with a genuine attempt to mitigate the literal force of passages such as these, and fought sincerely against jihad terror, the bad kind of Islamophobia would evanesce.

The crux of the distinction between bad and good Islamophobia is not whether one is being blinded by an irrational fear of Islam, but whether such fear is ever rational and reasonable. Bad Islamophobia—understood as harassment of or discrimination against individual Muslims—certainly exists. Such behavior is never justified, and it is not reasonable to be afraid that every ordinary Muslim everywhere around the world will suddenly go berserk and start cutting off infidels' heads. That said, there is plenty of reason to be concerned about Muslims who embrace a fanatical commitment to reestablishing the caliphate on the basis of "true" or "pure" Islam.

Since 9/11, the left and the national press have worked hand in glove to stigmatize those who would question the official U.S. government position that Islam is a religion of peace. Thus Barack Obama lamented in March 2016 that "the Republican base had been fed this notion that Islam is inherently violent."[16]

How could anyone get such an absurd, Islamophobic idea? Perhaps from the Qur'an, which in many places enjoins warfare against unbelievers. The Qur'an directs Muslims to "kill them wherever you come upon them" (2:191), "kill them wherever you find them" (4:89), "kill the idolaters wherever you find them" (9:5). It quotes Allah saying "I will cast terror into the unbelievers' hearts" (8:12) and tells Muslims to "make ready for them whatever force and strings of horses you can, to strike terror into the enemy of Allah and your enemy" (8:60). It tells Muslims to fight non-Muslims until "religion is all for Allah" (8:39).

The Qur'an tells Muslims to fight against "the People of the Book until they pay the jizya with willing submission and feel themselves subdued" (9:29). The "People of the Book" is the Qur'an's designation for Jews, Christians, and other monotheists who have a book they consider to be divine revelation. In Islamic law, the People of the Book have a special status: while polytheists, atheists, and others who are not People of the Book must ultimately be compelled to convert to Islam or die, the People of the Book have a third option: submission to Islamic hegemony and acceptance of a second-class status marked by the payment of a tax (*jizya*) and various humiliating and discriminatory regulations designed to ensure that the People of the Book "feel themselves subdued."

There is much more, including the justification for suicide bombing in the promise of Paradise to those who "kill and are killed" for Allah (9:111) and for beheading: "When you meet the unbelievers, strike their necks" (47:4).

These and other verses give the clear impression that Muslims have an obligation to wage war against unbelievers. I'm frequently charged with cherry-picking violent passages out of the Qur'an and ignoring mitigating peaceful passages, but in reality, these verses of warfare have been interpreted by Islamic authorities throughout history as being normative for all time in a way that more peaceful passages are not.

Muhammad, the prophet of Islam, participated in battles and called upon his followers to wage war against unbelievers. In another hadith (reports of Muhammad's words and deeds which, when deemed authentic, are normative for Islamic law), Muhammad says: "I have been commanded to fight against people so long as they do not declare that there is no god but Allah, and he who professed it was guaranteed the protection of his property and life on my behalf..."[17] This means that one's property and life is not guaranteed protection if one does not become Muslim: a prescription for endless warfare against unbelievers. According to Islamic tradition, Muhammad was the political leader of Medina, and claimed that even his political decrees were sanctioned by Allah—hence the Qur'an's repeated calls to obey Allah and his messenger. The Qur'an at one point even goes so far as to say: "He who obeys the Messenger has obeyed Allah" (4:80).[18]

Other Kinds of Violence

Besides all that, there is the misogyny. The Qur'an calls for the beating of women "from whom you fear disobedience": "Men are the managers of the affairs of women for that Allah has made one superior to the other, and for that they have expended of their property. Righteous women are therefore obedient, guarding the secret for Allah's guarding. And those from whom you fear disobedience, warn them, banish them to their couches, and beat them. If they then obey you, look not for any way against them; Allah is All-high, All-great." (4:34)

Muhammad adds in a hadith that women are "deficient in religion and intellect," and comprise the majority of those spending eternity in hellfire.[19] Women are essentially slaves of men; they will be curse by the angels for refusing their husbands sex: "If a husband calls his wife to his bed [i.e. to have sexual relation] and she refuses and causes him to sleep in anger, the angels will curse her till morning." (Bukhari 4.54.460)

There is much, much more, including the draconian punishments the Qur'an specifies for the vague crime of a spreading "corruption" upon the earth: "This is the recompense of those who fight against Allah and His Messenger, and strive upon the earth corruption: they shall be slaughtered, or crucified, or their hands and feet shall alternately be struck off; or they shall be banished from the land. That is a degradation for them in this world; and in the world to come awaits them a mighty chastisement." (5:33)

All this in the founding documents of a religion, and from its most revered figure, make for a culture of violence. And that culture is making its character increasingly obvious in the West.

A History of Conquest

Shortly after these texts were supposed to have been written, the conquests began.[20] Beginning in the 630s, just after Muhammad is traditionally believed to have died in 632, armies streamed out of Arabia and swiftly conquered Damascus, much of Iraq, Jerusalem, Caesarea, Armenia, Egypt, and North Africa. Nowadays the claim is common that these were easy conquests because the people of these regions were so sick of Byzantine oppression that they welcomed the invaders as liberators. In reality, however, the caliph Umar, whom Islamic tradition says ruled from 634 to 644, once asked a critic a revealing question: "Do you think that these vast countries, Syria,

Mesopotamia, Kufa, Basra, Misr [Egypt] do not have to be covered with troops who must be well paid?"[21] If the natives had welcomed the conquerors, why did their lands have to be "covered with troops?"

By 711, the Arab conquerors controlled an empire that stretched from Spain to India, and entered France, where they were repulsed in 732. Like the Islamic State (ISIS) in Iraq and Syria fourteen centuries later, the Islamic jihadis in France burned churches in Bordeaux and Poitiers before they were pushed back into Spain.[22]

None of these lands and nations had ever attacked Arabia or the Muslims (although in the ninth century Muslims fashioned accounts, of doubtful historicity, of Byzantine persecution of early Muslims); these were gratuitous imperialistic endeavors.

And they continued. India, too, felt the force of jihad. Hindu historian Sita Ram Goel notes that by 1206, the Muslim invaders had conquered "the Punjab, Sindh, Delhi, and the Doab up to Kanauj."[23] The jihad also continued elsewhere. When the Ottoman Sultan Mehmet besieged Constantinople in 1453, he offered the Byzantines a triple choice: "surrender of the city, death by the sword, or conversion to Islam."[24] This was based upon the tradition in which Muhammad told the Muslims to offer unbelievers conversion to Islam or submission to Islamic hegemony, or war if they refused both.[25]

No one made a secret of what was fueling all this. Even the great twelfth-century Muslim philosopher Averroes said it plainly: "the Muslims are agreed that the aim of warfare against the People of the Book...is twofold: either conversion to Islam, or payment of poll-tax (*jizya*)."[26] Nowadays that would get Averroes labeled an "extremist," as would be the thirteenth-century Muslim jurist Ibn Taymiyya, who defined jihad as "the punishment of recalcitrant groups, such as those that can only be brought under the sway of the Imam by a decisive fight....For whoever has heard the summons of the Messenger of God, peace be upon him, and has not responded to it, must be fought, 'until there is no persecution and the religion is God's entirely' (Koran 2:193, 8:39)."[27]

Not only was the idea that Islam was violent not hidden or consigned to "Islamophobia"; it was a point of pride. The pioneering Muslim historian and sociologist Ibn Khaldun compared Islam favorably to other religions because of jihad: "The other religious groups did not have a universal mission, and the holy war was not a religious duty to them, save only for purposes of defence. It has thus come about that the person in charge of religious affairs in (other religious groups) is not concerned with power politics at all." But Muslim leaders, by contrast, must be concerned with "power politics," because Islam is "under obligation to gain power over other nations."[28]

After the Ottoman siege of Vienna was broken on September 11, 1683, the Ottoman caliphate went into decline, and was ultimately dubbed "the sick man of Europe." Jihad became a less common feature of the European landscape, not because Islamic theology had been reformed, but because Muslims generally no longer had sufficient means to pursue it.

Not only non-Muslims, but Muslims who get out of line are threatened. Islam also mandates death for those who leave Islam. Muhammad is reported as saying: "Whoever changed his Islamic religion, then kill him."[29] His word, in this and so much else, is law.

That makes Islam, for untold numbers of people, a captor. There is no doubt that there are many people who are identified as Muslims who would leave the religion if they would not have to live in fear of being killed for doing so. When we refuse to criticize Islam, we are turning our backs on the millions of people who suffer from being forced to live under tyrannical Islamic regimes. Just as it was immoral to turn our backs on those oppressed by Communist governments during the Cold War, we betray our own values when we turn a blind eye to Muslim suffering, and instead praise their oppressors.

The Crisis of Islam in Europe

The situation in Europe today vividly illustrates the dangers of admitting tens of thousands of Muslim immigrants from mostly poor, socially backward countries into modern Western societies. If we want to understand why there is a rational basis for Islamophobia, we need to pay attention to what is happening there now. For if responsible steps are not taken, we are likely to have the same problems here in the U.S.

German Chancellor Angela Merkel, keen to alleviate the humanitarian crisis in Syria and the surrounding regions, opened Germany's doors to the refugee influx of 2015. Other Western European countries did as well. Yet while there is no doubt that some of the refugees are grateful for the hospitality they have been shown, others clearly aren't. All of the Islamic jihadis who murdered 130 people in Paris in a series of jihad attacks in November 2015 were refugees who had recently been welcomed into Europe.[30] Germany's domestic intelligence agency admitted in July 2017 that hundreds of jihadis had entered the country among the refugees, and that 24,000 jihadis were active in Germany.[31]

Muslim migrants in Europe have also been responsible for an appalling epidemic of rape, sexual assault, theft, petty crime, and looting. In the first half of 2016, migrants in Germany, who are overwhelmingly Muslim, committed 142,500 crimes, an average of 780 every day. This was a significant increase from 2015, during which migrants committed 200,000 crimes.[32]

On New Year's Eve, December 31, 2015, Muslim migrants committed as many as 2,000 mass rapes and sexual assaults in Cologne, Stockholm, and other major European cities.[33] Such assaults weren't limited to that day alone; Sweden has been called the "rape capital of the world" because of the notorious activities of Muslim migrants.[34] Muslim migrants have made Malmö, once a peaceful city, crime-ridden and hazardous.[35]

In Sweden, Muslim migrants from Afghanistan are 79 times more likely to commit rape and other sexual crimes than native Swedes. Migrants and refugees commit 92 percent of rapes in Sweden. Rapists in Sweden come from Iraq, Afghanistan, Somalia, Eritrea, Syria, Gambia, Iran, Palestine, Chile, and Kosovo, in that order;

rapists of Swedish background do not exist in sufficient numbers to make the top ten, and all the nations on that list except Chile and Eritrea are majority Muslim.[36]

Even before the migrant influx, while on a speaking tour in Germany in 2011, I was told by the sixteen-year-old daughter of one of the event organizers that she was routinely harassed on the way to school: Muslims on the commuter trains would call her a "whore" and a "slut" because her hair and arms were not covered. This happened, she said, every day.

And in the British town of Rotherham, Muslim gangs brutalized, sexually assaulted, and raped over 1,400 young British girls, while authorities remained extremely reluctant to say or do anything in response, for fear of being labeled "racist."[37]

Yet hardly anything is being said about this. In the summer of 2016, Krystyna Pawłowicz, a member of the Polish parliament, charged German authorities with attempting to "cover up the crimes of their Arab guests, or even shift the blame upon themselves."[38] There was also evidence that migrant crimes were being covered up in the Netherlands and Sweden as well.[39]

These cover-ups apparently proceeded from a fear that non-Muslims would begin to have negative views of Islam. Yet the sexual assaults *did* have to do with Islam. The Qur'an dictates that a Muslim man may have sexual relations with the "captives of the right hand," that is, captured non-Muslim women (4:3; 4:24; 23:1-6; 33:50; 70:30). The Qur'an also says that women should veil themselves so that they may not be molested (33:59), with the implication being that if they are not veiled, they may indeed be molested.

American and European liberals who are concerned about "Islamophobia" should consider the implications of that for their own daughters.

The Qur'an provides an Islamic justification for these mass rapes and assaults that has never been discussed in the establishment media, or at any governmental level in any country. Such a discussion could have important implications for how to persuade the migrants to stop behaving in this manner, and how easy it will be to do so, but this discussion cannot be had: it's Islamophobic. Feminists have been completely indifferent, even though what women face in Europe is far more serious than the plight of women in the U.S. today. Fear of being labeled an Islamophobe apparently trumps even feminism's core concerns.

The establishment media has largely ignored the Muslim migrant crime wave in Europe, with the exception of the slightly down-market British tabloids such as the *Daily Mail* and the *Express*. And even the *Daily Mail* has been devastating in its treatment of foes of jihad and Sharia supremacism, reserving particular venom for Dutch politician Geert Wilders, who makes no secret of his dislike for the elements of Islam that contravene universal principles of human rights and has called for an end to the immigrant influx.[40]

The *Daily Mail* has also been relentlessly unfair to those in England, such as Tommy Robinson and Paul Weston, who have dared to criticize Islam. For all its refreshing honesty about the magnitude of the problem, the *Daily Mail* seems to be too afraid of charges of "Islamophobia" to support those who want to do anything about it.

In some European countries, "Islamophobia" can get one fined or even imprisoned. Legendary actress Brigitte Bardot has been fined several times in France for "Islamophobic" statements.[41] Italian journalist Oriana Fallaci died before she could be tried for "Islamophobic" statements in her two post-9/11 masterworks, *The Rage and the Pride* and *The Force of Reason*.[42] Numerous European human rights activists have been tried simply for noting accurately that Europe has a massive problem on its hands due to the rapid entry of so many people who believe that European society and mores are corrupt and inferior to those of Sharia.

Because of the power of charges of Islamophobia, Europe today is more squalid, dangerous, and politically precarious than it has been since the run-up to World War II. Genuinely neo-Nazi parties are resurging, gaining members from among those who are frustrated to the breaking point by the failure of European leaders to do anything about their valid concerns beyond labeling them "Islamophobic."

The international Left decries the rise of the nationalist right wing, but it is their baby. They created it. Had it not been for their tendency to smear any opposition to their migration schemes as racist and neo-Nazi, the concerns of those who see Europe descending into chaos and civil war could have been addressed within the existing system. Instead, the European Union is now in deep crisis, Paris is burning, and the whole continent could quite conceivably erupt into another war.

All because of "Islamophobia."

No sane American could want what is happening in Europe to happen here. That's why it is high time we had a national discussion of whether these charges of "Islamophobia" are really justified or wise. For the jihad threat is real, as is the Sharia threat.

Islamophobia in the Public Square

It is already quite clear that it is not possible for "Islamophobes" to get a fair hearing in the public square. What's more, even legitimate attempts to do something effective about the problem of Islamic terrorism all too often run into the Islamophobia label as if it were a buzzsaw, cutting away the chance for any genuine discussion of actual problems.

Candidate Donald Trump found this out in December 2015, when he uttered the fateful words: "Donald J. Trump is calling for a total and complete shutdown of Muslims entering the United States until our country's representatives can figure out what the hell is going on."[43]

The ensuing firestorm was massive, and has never died down. Trump was an Islamophobe. Once he became President and signed an executive order temporarily suspending immigration from seven Muslim countries, the chorus of condemnation increased, and his earlier call for a "complete and total shutdown of Muslims entering the United States" was used against him. Judge James Robart of the

9th Circuit Court of Appeals, in his decision to strike down Trump's initial ban, noted that "the States argue that the Executive Order violates the Establishment and Equal Protection Clauses because it was intended to disfavor Muslims."[44]

Then Judge Derrick Watson of the U.S. District Court for Hawaii, in placing a Temporary Restraining Order (TRO) on Trump's second attempt to enact an immigration ban, noted that Trump had on the campaign trail called for "a total and complete shutdown of Muslims entering the United States," and declared that "any reasonable, objective observer would conclude, as does the Court for purposes of the instant Motion for TRO, that the stated secular purpose of the Executive Order is, at the very least, 'secondary to a religious objective' of temporarily suspending the entry of Muslims."[45] The 4th Circuit Court of Appeals, blocking Trump's ban again in May 2017, asserted that the Executive Order "in text speaks in vague terms of national security, but in context drips with religious intolerance, animus and discrimination."[46]

So it was confirmed by federal courts: Trump was an Islamophobe. He had malign intentions, and therefore his executive orders were motivated by racial or religious animus, and could not be allowed to stand.

For his part, President Trump insisted that his Executive Order was all about national security, and only national security. But this was brushed aside. Neither decision striking down the bans dealt in any serious way with that assertion. Robart falsely claimed that no terrorists had entered the United States from any of the countries covered by Trump's ban; the Hawaii decision asserted a "dearth of evidence indicating a national security purpose," without bothering to substantiate its claim.[47] The Trump administration released of 24 terror suspects who came to the U.S. from the ban countries.[48] The Supreme Court ultimately allowed a partial version of Trump's moratorium to take effect, but the charges remained on the Left that he was motivated not by bigotry, not by national security concerns.

This was characteristic of the establishment media's reaction to the Executive Order: the reasons why Trump had proposed it in the first place, as well as why he had called on the campaign trail for a total moratorium on Muslim immigration, were seldom, if ever, seriously discussed. Any such discussion was immediately shut down by charges of racism, bigotry, and Islamophobia.

There is, in fact, a perfectly reasonable case that can be made for Trump's immigration ban—one that has nothing whatsoever to do with some irrational hatred for Muslims. But try making that case that on CNN or in *The New York Times*. The case cannot be made in such venues: it's Islamophobia.

Many of the blanket characterizations about my work, as common as they are, are false. I do not believe, and have never stated, that all Muslims are terrorists or that Muslims who do not engage in terror activity are or must necessarily be bad Muslims. I have never believed or stated that the United States was in danger of being taken over by Muslims and transformed into a caliphate governed by Sharia. The Muslim Brotherhood articulated such a goal in a captured internal document, and several Muslim spokesmen in the U.S. (including Ibrahim Hooper) have let slip in unguarded moments that Sharia rule in the U.S. is their objective, but their chances of success are essentially nil. There are too many patriotic, determined, and well-armed Americans for that to happen. So no fair-minded person should try to paint me as an irrational alarmist.

What could happen, however, and probably will happen, is that those Muslim Brotherhood organizations will continue to undermine our counterterror efforts. And as Muslim immigration into the U.S continues, there will increasingly be the challenges to our way of life that we see in Europe: jihad massacres, assaults of women and gays, attacks on synagogues and individual Jews, the defacing of Christian statues and iconography, and more.

There are, in short, very good reasons to be an Islamophobe, that is, to be concerned about Islam for the devastation that it brings into the lives of human beings both Muslim and non-Muslim. It is not hatred and bigotry to be the right kind of Islamophobe; indeed, the only chance for the survival of free societies into the latter part of the twenty-first century may be if large numbers of people join me in becoming this kind of unrepentant Islamophobe.

And so in this book I am alerting well-meaning people all across the political spectrum to the threat that all too many refuse to see. By charging "Islamophobia" whenever anyone dares notice any connection between Islam and terrorism, the American Left and establishment conservatives are shouting down, and shutting down, a legitimate argument, and indeed, an argument that we must have sooner or later if we are going to survive as a free society.

CHAPTER 2

IS THERE A JIHAD THREAT TODAY?

The Real Threat

The jihad threat is real, and growing worldwide, as the evidence of 30,000 jihad attacks worldwide since 9/11 shows. A website called *thereligionofpeace.com* keeps a sourced and documented database of all those attacks, complete with the number of people killed and wounded in each. During each Ramadan, the site tracks the number of people killed by Islamic jihadis during the time when Muslims are supposed to redouble their efforts to please Allah, as well as the number of people killed by "Islamophobes." The latter number stayed at zero for years, until the Finsbury Park Mosque attack, while the number of jihad attacks increased daily. During Ramadan 2017, there were 161 jihad terror attacks, leaving 1,483 people dead and another 1,557 wounded.[1]

Nonetheless, "Islamophobia" has become, for all intents and purposes, a larger threat than jihad terror. Consider, for example, the aftermath of the jihad attack at an Ariana Grande concert in Manchester, England, that murdered 22 people and injured 59. For some time after that attack, the United Kingdom remained on high alert as police uncovered and hunted for the members of an entire jihadi network connected with the Manchester massacre.[2] Then there quickly followed the jihad attacks at the London Bridge and elsewhere in the city.

MI5 revealed shortly after the Manchester attack that there were as many as 23,000 jihad terrorists on the streets of Britain today.[3] British Prime Minister Theresa May announced that British troops would be deployed on the streets of the country's major cities, in order to try to head off another catastrophic jihad attack.[4]

But the British authorities had other priorities as well. The UK's Cambridge News reported on June 9, 2017: "Police are increasing patrols at two mosques in Cambridge after strips of bacon were…left on the car windscreens to insult fasting Muslims."[5]

This was what the British police were concerned about in the wake of the jihad massacres in Manchester and London: bacon. They were protecting Muslims and mosques from supposed "hate crimes."

Not that any such hate crimes, whenever they actually occur, are ever justified. But the proportions were off. Twenty-two people were dead in Manchester and seven in London at the hands of Islamic jihadists. One would have thought that in light of that, the Cambridge police would have laughed off a few strips of bacon in front of a mosque, and told the mosque leaders to direct their attention to more important matters, such as working to root out jihad terror sympathizers and plotters from their communities.

One would have thought wrong. It must be remembered that not long before the Manchester and London jihad massacres, Julia Ebner of Britain's supposedly "anti-extremism" and undoubtedly influential Quilliam Foundation claimed that "the threat from far-right groups is as severe as the jihadist threat."[6] (I was named in that same article as an "alt-right leader," with the strong—and flatly false—implication that I either am a neo-Nazi white supremacist, or, associate with them.)

That's what these bacon police patrols were all about: shoring up the sagging narrative that "the threat from far-right groups is as severe as the jihadist threat," and buttressing the claim that the racist, xenophobic "far-right" constitutes just as much of a threat to Britons as Islamic jihadis. A few strips of bacon next to twenty-nine dead is a sad exercise in moral equivalence, but that was all the British authorities had to work with, and so they were running with it.

Yet while Cambridge police devoted their manpower and resources to tracking down the perpetrators of "bacon hate crime," let's step back for a moment and consider the larger picture.

How many are dead in Britain as a result of "far-right" attacks? Arguably, two: Parliamentarian Jo Cox and the person killed in the Finsbury Park Mosque attack. That is two more than there should be, but still, the scale of "far-right" violence in Britain is far smaller than the scale of jihad activity. Are "far-right" leaders in Britain calling for the destruction of the British state and its replacement with an authoritarian system that denies equality of rights to women and others? Why, no. They aren't.

Islamic jihadis are killing people, and Muslim leaders in Britain have boasted about one day (probably not too very long from now) imposing Sharia on the Sceptered Isle, but that doesn't matter: Quilliam is peddling moral equivalence, and so is Theresa May, and so moral equivalence it is: the "far-right" is just as dangerous as the jihadis. Yes, twenty-nine dead, but...bacon at a mosque!

One wonders if mosque leaders were able to keep a straight face when they called the police to report this "bacon hate crime." Did they shed tears at the horror of it all? Did they plead for protection from porcine persecution? Did they fulminate about what an inhospitable place Britain is for Muslims, and long for the green fields of human rights bastions such as Pakistan? Did they demand the full force of law enforcement power be directed against the real threat—not jihad terror, but "Islamophobia?"

In any case, the police were duly called. But consider this: if the Muslims in Britain really wanted to make sure that no more bacon was left at mosques, they could accomplish that very easily, by working against jihadis in their own community, and doing everything they could to make sure that no more jihad attacks happen, instead of constantly whining and playing the victim, and claiming that counterterror efforts are unjustly singling them out.

If Muslims in the UK, and everywhere else in the West, stood up resolutely against jihad terror, acknowledged its roots in Islamic texts and teachings, and honestly worked to root out that understanding of Islam from its community and to cooperate energetically with police against jihadis, then no more non-Muslims would be frustrated by the Muslim community's duplicity and the government's supine reaction to terror. And then people would no longer do rude things such as leave bacon at mosques.

But in the final analysis, that was all it was: a rude act. And yet police were out in force in Cambridge. On bacon patrol.

Imagine if these police officers had been instead diverted to other duties, such as trying to stop the next jihad attack. Then, maybe no more blood would be spilled, and no more bacon would be deployed.

If the Cambridge police, and those who dismiss my colleagues and me as "Islamophobes," awakened to that simple fact, and to the nature and magnitude of the real threat, they would discover what the real threat is by direct experience, on their own soil. The establishment strategy regarding "Islamophobia" leads straight to Manchester and London.

Although "Islamophobia" is much more a matter of concern to the establishment media than jihad terror, "Islamophobes" have never left as much havoc in their wake as jihadis have—although the threat of vigilante attacks against innocent Muslims and others is indeed growing, as an unwanted, unwelcome, and disquieting backlash to the refusal of Western authorities to deal with the jihad threat realistically.

Those who have stigmatized everyone who calls attention to the jihad threat as "Islamophobic" are ultimately responsible for those attacks. And "Islamophobia" endangers us all in other ways as well.

"Islamophobia" Endangers Us All

Counterterror analyst Paul Sperry reported in April 2017 that the New York Police Department has "censored an anti-terror handbook to appease offended Muslims, even though it has accurately predicted radicalization patterns in recent 'homegrown' terror cases."[7]

So it was demonstrated yet again: the stigmatization and marginalization of realistic counterterror analysis is endangering Americans, and will continue to do so.

Here's how: Patrick Dunleavy, former deputy inspector general of the New York state prisons' criminal-intelligence division, noted that the discarded NYPD report "was extremely accurate on how the radicalization process works and what indicators to look for."[8] Former FBI agent John Guandolo explained: "The FBI has its hands full with over 1,000 open cases on ISIS terrorist suspects already in the US, and it needs the help of well-trained eyes and ears on the ground at the local and state level. The bad guys know if police don't know this stuff at the ground level, they win."[9]

And in December 2015 in San Bernardino, CA, when the Islamic jihadist couple Syed Rizwan Farook and Tashfeen Malik murdered fourteen people at a Christmas party, a friend of one of their neighbors recalled that the neighbor had told him about suspicious activity at the couple's home. "Sounds like she didn't do anything about it," the friend remembered. "She didn't want to do any kind of racial profiling. She's like, 'I didn't call it in… maybe it was just me thinking something that's not there.' "[10]

"She didn't want to do any kind of racial profiling." For years, she had been force-fed the notion that to be suspicious of Muslims was "bigotry" and "racial profiling"—"Islamophobia"—and so she didn't alert police to the strange activity at the home of Farook and Malik.

Fourteen people are dead so that politically correct niceties could be preserved, and no one incurred any charges of "racism."

This wasn't a singular incident. The fear of "Islamophobia" charges has overridden, or threatened to override, concern about jihad terrorism for years.

"Should I Call Someone or Is that Being Racist?"

One of the most notorious instances of this was the case of the Fort Dix Six. In January 2006, two Muslims asked a teenaged clerk at a Circuit City outlet in New Jersey to transfer a VHS tape to DVD. As he did the job, the young clerk grew increasingly alarmed: the video showed Muslims firing automatic weapons while screaming "Allahu akbar."[11]

The clerk was alarmed, but he had also been well educated in early twenty-first century sensibilities. He articulated his dilemma to a coworker: "Dude, I just saw some really weird shit. I don't know what to do. Should I call someone or is that being racist?"[12]

He decided to go ahead and be racist, and reported the men to authorities. Because of this action, on December 22, 2008, five Muslims were convicted of plotting to enter the U.S. Army base at Fort Dix, New Jersey, in order to kill as many American soldiers as they could before they were themselves killed.[13]

That the Circuit City clerk hesitated even for a moment before calling the police shows how successful the whole Islamophobia enterprise has been. How many other jihad massacres might have been stopped were it not for the potential information's hesitation to appear "Islamophobic?"

The Threat Remains

Yet for all their attempts to ignore or downplay it, Islam continues to pose a threat. And so "Islamophobia"—understood not as vigilante attacks or harassment of innocent Muslims, but as a sober and realistic appraisal of the nature of Islam and the ways in which it endangers free societies and free people—is not bigotry or racism, but, simply a rational assessment of a genuine danger.

I said "Islam," not "Muslims." The Islamic religion contains numerous texts and teachings that jihadis use to justify violence and to make recruits among peaceful Muslims, and to oppress women and non-Muslims. As much as people on the Left and the Right would like to deny that, it is a fact. That does not mean, however, that all Muslims are terrorists, or oppressors, or hateful or violent people. The teachings of a religion are one thing, and the way any given adherent of that religion puts those teachings into practice, or does not do so, is quite another. Every individual Muslim deserves to be treated with as much respect and courtesy as anyone else. And many Muslims are exemplary individuals whose magnanimity and generosity of spirit toward non-Muslims contrast sharply with the exhortations to violence against them in their holy book.

But the teachings of that holy book remain, and some Muslims do indeed take them literally.

Let us therefore review the ways in which Islamic jihad and Sharia pose a danger to various groups who typically consider themselves liberal, in the hope that these honest, well-meaning liberals may finally recognize that a threat to their freedom and safety does exist—and that it is not coming from "Islamophobes" like me but from Islam itself:

- *Islam is a threat to women*, because Islamic teachings allow the beating of women "from whom you fear disobedience," as well as the downgrading of a woman's testimony and inheritance rights. The Qur'an sanctions polygamy, child marriage, and even the sexual enslavement of captive non-Muslim women. These are not just teachings that "Islamophobes" have discovered in dusty corners of the Islamic holy book that no Muslim today takes seriously; women face all kinds of oppression throughout the Islamic world that the oppressors directly justify by reference to Islam. And while the West celebrates the hijab and castigates those who supposedly harass Muslim women who wear it, girls and women all over the world, including the U.S. and Canada, have been menaced, beaten, and even killed for *not* wearing it. And now other aspects of Sharia oppression of women, including female genital mutilation, are coming to the United States as well.

- *Islam is a threat to gays*, because it mandates a death penalty for homosexuals that is not, unlike the one in the Old Testament, a dead letter today. Nations that enforce the fullness of Islamic law today, including Iran and Saudi Arabia, routinely put gays to death, and as the Islamic State's short-lived caliphate in Iraq and Syria demonstrated anew, whenever Islamic hardliners determine to implement the fullness of Islamic law, this death penalty reappears.

- *Islam is a threat to Jews,* because in all too many Islamic teachings and traditions, Jews are the villains of the piece. The Qur'an depicts the Jews as inveterately evil and bent on destroying the well-being of the Muslims. They are the strongest of all people in enmity toward the Muslims (5:82); as fabricating things and falsely ascribing them to Allah (2:79; 3:75, 3:181); claiming that Allah's power is limited (5:64); loving to listen to lies (5:41); disobeying Allah and never observing his commands (5:13); disputing and quarreling (2:247); hiding the truth and misleading people (3:78); staging rebellion against the prophets and rejecting their guidance (2:55); being hypocritical (2:14, 2:44); giving preference to their own interests over the teachings of Muhammad (2:87); wishing evil for people and trying to mislead them (2:109); feeling pain when others are happy or fortunate (3:120); being arrogant about their being Allah's beloved people (5:18); devouring people's wealth by subterfuge (4:161); slandering the true religion and being cursed by Allah (4:46); killing the prophets (2:61); being merciless and heartless (2:74); never keeping their promises or fulfilling their words (2:100); being unrestrained in committing sins (5:79); being cowardly (59:13-14); being miserly (4:53); being transformed into apes and pigs for breaking the Sabbath (2:63-65; 5:59-60; 7:166); and more.

Accordingly, Jews are threatened in Europe to an extent they have not been since the days of Hitler. And it's getting worse by the day.

- *Islam is a threat to Christians*, for it mandates that they must either convert to Islam, submit to Islamic hegemony, and be killed—the same triple choice offered to the Jews. In 2005, political and literary analyst Stephen Schwartz, himself a convert to Islam, declared that the subjugation of the People of the Book under the rule of Islam was "part of the Islamic past that is best left to the past."[14]

  Unfortunately, Islamic jihadis did not cooperate. The Christian communities of the Middle East, some of which dated back to the time of Christ, were decimated, as jihad groups targeted Christians wholesale as symbols of the hated U.S. and West.

  In response to this persecution of Christians, as violent and virulent as any since Diocletian, Christian leaders in the West have begun various programs of "dialogue" with Muslims. These have, however, not saved a single Middle Eastern Christian from being murdered, or a single church from being demolished.

- *Islam is a threat to secular liberals*, although noting the fact will get one dismissed as a "far-right" "Islamophobe," because Islam really does have doctrines mandating the conquest and subjugation of non-Muslims, and the major Muslim organizations in the United States really do behave as if they would like nothing better than the weakening and ultimate downfall of the U.S. government and free society, by opposing virtually all counterterror initiatives; polarizing American society by claiming falsely that Muslims are the victims of large-scale persecution and harassment in the U.S.; and stigmatizing all those who call attention to the jihad threat and the devastation wrought in Europe by mass Muslim migration as "racists" and "hatemongers."

Islamic groups aren't going to overthrow the U.S. government. But they've already done a great deal in numerous ways to impede our resistance to jihad terror—not least of which has been making this book necessary to write, by making decent people unsure whether there really is a jihad threat at all, or just a problem with "Islamophobia."

- *Islam is a threat to secular Muslims*, because many have come to the West as a refuge from Sharia, and now the oppression they left behind in their home countries has followed them to their new homes. Islam in all its traditional and classic formulations mandates a death penalty for someone who is sane, adult, and leaves Islam voluntarily. This discourages apostasy, obviously, but it also makes for untold numbers of silent apostates who live outwardly as Muslims while dissenting inwardly. Islamic hardliners target these people, when they find them, no less than they target open apostates.

  Many came to America to be free of constant fears that they would be killed for living as their conscience dictated. They deserve better than to find that there is now no escape, anywhere.

But there may not be. Because to create or try to preserve a safe space for those who do not wish to live under the oppression that Sharia mandates is "Islamophobic." In the chapters that follow we will explore the threats to these groups in greater detail.

CHAPTER 3

THE THREAT TO WOMEN

Muhammad: History's First Feminist

The British feminist writer Laurie Penny has charged that non-Muslims only criticize Islamic law's mistreatment of Muslim women because of their bigotry and hatred: "Misogyny only matters when it isn't being done by white men."[1] Penny wrote acidly: "As a person who writes about women's issues, I am constantly being told that Islam is the greatest threat to gender equality in this or any other country—mostly by white men, who always know best."[2]

Penny complained that "the rhetoric and language of feminism has been co-opted by Islamophobes, who could not care less about women of any creed or colour."[3] She said of right-wing groups that spoke out against the status of women in Islamic law: "Some of their members tell me that since they are standing against the sexism of Muslim barbarians, as a feminist I should be on their side. When I disagree, I am invariably informed I deserve be shipped to Afghanistan and stoned to death."[4]

I don't think Laurie Penny should be shipped to Afghanistan and stoned to death. I'm just not sure she is aware that there really are issues regarding women and Islam that should concern her as a feminist.

Penny herself would likely deny that there are. The *Huffington Post* summed up the dominant view on the Left in an October 2016 article entitled "Muhammad Was a Feminist." It claimed:

> The prophet Muhammad would be appalled by how current Islamic Fundamentalists are treating women under their control. This suppression is done in the name of Islamic Law, known as Sharia. But the current suppression of women is shaped by cultural and history. It has little basis in the Quran and it is certainly not consistent with anything we know about what Muhammad taught or how he treated women. Of all the founders of the great religions—Buddhism, Christianity, Confucianism, Islam and Judaism—Muhammad was easily the most radical and empowering in his treatment of women. Arguably he was history's first feminist.[5]

CNN made similar claims in an October 2014 article entitled "I'm a feminist, and I converted to Islam." Author Theresa Corbin recounts that as she studied Islam before her conversion, "I was surprised many of the tenants [sic] resonated with me."[6] She encountered a "very patient Muslim lady" who "explained that, during a time when the Western world treated women like property, Islam taught that men and women were equal in the eyes of God. Islam made the woman's consent to marriage mandatory and gave women the opportunity to inherit, own property, run businesses and participate in government."[7] Corbin discovered that, "surprisingly, Islam turned out to be the religion that appealed to my feminist ideals."[8]

Corbin may have been learning from a Muslim leader such as imam Syed Soharwardy of Calgary, Alberta, who is the head of the Calgary-based Islamic Supreme Council of Canada and the founder of Muslims Against Terrorism. On April 2, 2017, Soharwardy gave a speech in Toronto entitled "Interfaith Dialogue—Understanding Islam and Muslims," in which he said: "In the holy Quran the relationship between husband and wife is described so beautifully that I don't think you'd find such a description in any scripture...The is no gender-based superiority in Islam. Only superiority in Islam is based on piety…If I would say that Islam is the most feminist religion it's not untrue. Yes, there are people, there are people of clergy also, they misinterpret, they definitely have different mindset, but they are very, very small minority."[9]

Hijab Chic

In keeping with these ideas, this is the age of hijab chic.

Feminist author Naomi Wolf wrote back in 2008 of the contrast between Western and Islamic mores regarding women's dress: "A woman swathed in black to her ankles, wearing a headscarf or a full chador, walks down a European or North American street, surrounded by other women in halter tops, miniskirts and short shorts. She passes under immense billboards on which other women swoon in sexual ecstasy, cavort in lingerie or simply stretch out languorously, almost fully naked."[10] She concluded this scenario not by criticizing Islam and Sharia's entrenched misogyny, but by suggesting a moral equivalence: "Could this image be any more iconic of the discomfort the West has with the social mores of Islam, and vice versa?"[11]

Wolf then ascribed Western discomfort with Islamic dress for women to Islamophobia:

> "Ideological battles are often waged with women's bodies as their emblems, and Western Islamophobia is no exception. When France banned headscarves in schools, it used the hijab as a proxy for Western values in general, including the appropriate status of women. When Americans were being prepared for the invasion of Afghanistan, the Taliban were demonised for denying cosmetics and hair colour to women; when the Taliban were overthrown, Western writers often noted that women had taken off their scarves."[12]

Wolf wondered if Western distaste for Islam's treatment of women wasn't simply a misunderstanding, and again drew a moral equivalence with the status of women in the West: "But are we in the West radically misinterpreting Muslim sexual mores, particularly the meaning to many Muslim women of being veiled or wearing the chador? And are we blind to our own markers of the oppression and control of women?"[13]

In that, Wolf unwittingly echoed Osama bin Laden. In his October 6, 2002, letter to the American people, the jihad terror leader thundered: "You are a nation that exploits women like consumer products or advertising tools calling upon customers to purchase them. You use women to serve passengers, visitors, and strangers to increase your profit margins. You then rant that you support the liberation of women.... You are a nation that practices the trade of sex in all its forms, directly and indirectly. Giant corporations and establishments are established on this, under the name of art, entertainment, tourism and freedom, and other deceptive names you attribute to it."[14]

Along the same lines, Wolf herself donned the headscarf, and found it cathartic: "Indeed, many Muslim women I spoke with did not feel at all subjugated by the chador or the headscarf. On the contrary, they felt liberated from what they experienced as the intrusive, commodifying, basely sexualising Western gaze.... I experienced it myself. I put on a shalwar kameez and a headscarf in Morocco for a trip to the bazaar. Yes, some of the warmth I encountered was probably from the novelty of seeing a Westerner so clothed; but, as I moved about the market—the curve of my breasts covered, the shape of my legs obscured, my long hair not flying about me—I felt a novel sense of calm and serenity. I felt, yes, in certain ways, free."[15]

As President, Barack Obama wanted to make sure that other women felt similarly free. On June 4, 2009, in Cairo, Obama delivered a landmark speech reaching out to the world's Muslims, declaring: "Moreover, freedom in America is indivisible from the freedom to practice one's religion. That is why there is a mosque in every state in our union, and over 1,200 mosques within our borders. That's why the United States government has gone to court to protect the right of women and girls to wear the hijab and to punish those who would deny it."[16]

In 2013, a Muslim woman in New York named Nazma Khan began World Hijab Day, which has grown into a popular annual international event featuring non-Muslim women (and sometimes also men) donning the hijab to show their solidarity with Muslim women who supposedly face discrimination, harassment, and prejudice in the West. Khan explained: "I thought If I could invite women of all faiths—Muslim and non-Muslim—to walk in my shoes just for one day, perhaps things would change."[17] In a 2014 press release, World Hijab Day organizers touted a video highlighting Khan's own suffering: "Nazma Khan tells us (TEARFULLY) about the persecution she faced due to her hijab and why she started World Hijab Day."[18]

The idea that non-Muslim women should wear the hijab in solidarity with Muslim women who are persecuted for wearing it has become commonplace worldwide. The German government, partnering with UNESCO, even produced a video featuring a beautiful blonde woman (with hair tumbling out from under her headscarf in most un-Islamic fashion) proclaiming "I also wear the hijab, it's beautiful!" and exhorting Westerners (not just Germans, as the video was in English) to "enjoy difference, start tolerance."[19]

The idea that hijab-wearing Muslim women face widespread intolerance in North America and Europe has also made organized events in which non-Muslims don the hijab for a day a popular phenomenon. In December 2016, a group of female students at Brigham Young University in Utah began a weekly show of solidarity entitled On Wednesdays We Wear Hijab. According to the UK's Express, "these activists, most of whom are majoring in Middle Eastern studies, say they want to spread diversity and fight discrimination. They insist the group's effort sends a message that Muslims are not alone." A participating student, Sondra Sasser, asserted that "a lot of Muslims are feeling uncomfortable about things. They are feeling scared about things or just misunderstood, and so any show of solidarity I think can be touching."[20]

Recently the claim that hijab-wearing women are routinely being harassed and brutalized by Trump-supporting louts has fueled hijab chic, although that claim has been somewhat tarnished by revelations that several of the most widely publicized incidences of this turned out to have been faked by the victims themselves.

On November 11, 2016, a Muslim student at the University of Michigan at Ann Arbor claimed that a man had accosted her, telling her that if she didn't take off her hijab, he would light her on fire.[21] Dawud Walid, executive director of the Michigan chapter of the Council on American-Islamic Relations (CAIR), declared that the "alleged attack is just the latest anti-Muslim incident reported since the election of Donald Trump as president. Our nation's leaders, and particularly President-elect Donald Trump, need to speak out forcefully against the wave of anti-Muslim incidents sweeping the country after Tuesday's election."[22]

However, after an investigation, the Ann Arbor Police Department issued a statement: "During the course of the investigation, numerous inconsistencies in the statements provided by the alleged victim were identified. Following a thorough investigation, detectives have determined the incident in question did not occur."[23] Officials declined to press charges against the Muslim student for filing a false report.[24]

The Tragedy of Yasmin Seweid

The same scenario played out a few weeks later in New York City, when on December 1, 2016, a Muslim teenager named Yasmin Seweid also claimed that drunken, ill-mannered, and boorish Trump supporters had harassed her. They tried to remove her hijab, but that wasn't the worst of it: "I heard them talk, but I had my headphones in, I wasn't really listening, I had a long day. And they came closer and I distinctly heard them saying, 'Donald Trump.' They were surrounding me from behind and they were like, 'Oh look, it's an [sic] fucking terrorist'. I didn't answer. They pulled my strap of the bag and it ripped, and that's when I turned around and I was really polite and I was like, 'can you please leave me alone'. Everyone was looking, no one said a thing, everyone just looked away."[25]

Yasmin lamented: "It breaks my heart that so many individuals chose to be bystanders while watching me get harassed verbally and physically by these disgusting pigs."[26] It was, she concluded, Donald Trump's fault: "The president-elect just promotes this stuff and is very anti-Muslim, very Islamophobic, and he's just condoning it."[27]

Yasmin's claims made international headlines. News outlet after news outlet reported them uncritically, despite the curious absence of even a single cellphone video corroborating her description of events. The *New York Daily News* called the incident a "harrowing encounter."[28] Slate noted ominously that the attack on Seweid was just "the latest in a growing wave of these types of incidents in New York and across the country."[29]

There was just one problem: Seweid wasn't really attacked. A NYPD spokesman said: "Nothing happened, and there was no victim."[30] Seweid was arrested for filing a false police report. The police official explained: "This isn't something we normally like to do but she had numerous opportunities to admit nothing happened and she kept sticking by her story. We dedicated a lot of resources to this—and don't get me wrong, this is what we do—but we had guys going back and forth, looking for video and witnesses. And we couldn't find anything."[31]

Yasmin Seweid, however, was no cynical hoaxer, and the real story of why she made up the incident with the drunken Trump supporters shows the hazards of liberals' uncritical ascribing of all criticism of Islamic doctrine and practice to Islamophobia. Seweid actually made up the story not primarily to smear Trump or his supporters, but to avoid the wrath of her strict Muslim father over her being out late and having a non-Muslim boyfriend.[32]

And so while the liberal intelligentsia uncritically accepted her story, and Yasmin herself cannily realized just what kind of story they would find believable, in purveying the claim that Seweid was the victim of an anti-Muslim hate crime, the media missed the real story: this young woman was in very real danger.

It quickly became clear that Yasmin Seweid had every reason to be afraid of her father, as he actually forced her to shave her head after the story broke of her hoax.[33] This was not, apparently, a punishment for the hoax, but for dallying with a Christian boyfriend.

Her shaved head—and even shaved eyebrows—in full view as she appeared in court with her clearly angry and disgusted father over the hate crime hoax ought to have awakened liberals who decried her imaginary attackers, as well as New York City authorities, to the danger she was in.

The shaving was designed to humiliate and subdue her. In this kind of thinking, the hair is the core of the woman's attractiveness—hence the hijab, which is supposed to remove the occasion of temptation for men. So shaving her head defeminized Yasmin and removed her attractiveness.

Once the truth about her fabricating the hate attack was revealed, some of the curious aspects of it fell into place. Not long after she initially complained of having been harassed by the Trump-supporting louts on the subway, just as the media was in full feeding frenzy mode, she went missing.

She may not have been prepared for the media spotlight. Yasmin Seweid was just 18 years old when all this happened. She likely didn't realize that she was giving the establishment media what it wanted most in this world: a case that reinforced their narrative. She gave them a story of an innocent, pious Muslim being victimized by Trump-loving "Islamophobes." She may have disappeared in a panic over the media attention for a story she knew was false.

But another possibility must also be considered: Yasmin may have disappeared because she was fleeing a family from whom she believed she was in genuine danger. Yasmin might have thought, and may still think, she could be killed for being too "Westernized"—a fate suffered by other Muslim women and girls in the U.S. and Canada.

In such cases, the killer believes he has cleansed the family's honor from the stain brought about by the sexual indiscretion of the victim. Honor killing enjoys so much acceptance in the Islamic world that the penal codes of several Muslim countries actually have reduced penalties for honor killings, because they are considered justified under certain circumstances in ways that other murders can never be.

But no one, after the story of her hoax broke, was considering the fact that Yasmin Seweid was clearly in serious danger from her father, because that would have involved accepting some facts about the acceptance of honor killing among Muslims that have been deemed "Islamophobic." Even if he had no intention of killing her, her father had already savagely abused her by forcing her to shave her head.

That was the real story here: when Yasmin Seweid was unmasked as a hoaxer, those who had been championing her cause as a victim of "Islamophobia" quickly turned away. They weren't in the slightest degree concerned with how much she was in danger from her father (and probably from other family members as well), because to take notice of that would have been to recognize, however tacitly, Islam's entrenched misogyny and institutionalized subjugation of girls and women, especially those who dare to step out of line.

And so Yasmin Seweid, her head shaved and her life quite possibly on the line, slipped back into obscurity, another object lesson of the corrosive effects of charges of "Islamophobia."

Yet hijab chic marched on.

Actress Kathy Najimy was appalled as the inauguration of Donald Trump as President was looming. The *Sister Act* actress called on non-Muslim women to wear hijabs or scarves on inauguration day. Wrote Najimy: "We wanted to create an action, visible and easy, to proclaim our commitment to freedom of religion and to the constitution—religion or no religion. We intend to show that we stand in solidarity with our about-to-be-disenfranchised Muslim sisters."[34]

Facebook marked International Women's Day on March 8, 2017, with an image of girl in hijab. *Forbes* magazine named Iran one of "The 10 Coolest Places to Go in 2017."[35] It noted that the founder of the travel-oriented *Indagare* magazine, Melissa Biggs Bradley, "is excited about the trip she just completed, to Tehran, Isfahan, Shiraz and Persepolis."[36] In her own article on her trip, Bradley observed blandly that "visitors to Iran understand that they must adapt to Sharia law and customs, under which alcohol is strictly forbidden and women must wear hijabs, or headscarves, outside their rooms."[37]

How cool!

The Apotheosis of Hijab Chic: The Ascent of Linda Sarsour

One of the strangest aspects of the extraordinarily strange presidential campaign of 2016 and its aftermath was the ascendancy of Linda Sarsour as a national feminist leader. The contradiction Sarsour's ascent to stardom revealed in the feminist movement was glaring enough, but even worse was how the mainstream adulation of Sarsour showed how completely triumphant the "Islamophobia" narrative has been.

The day after Donald Trump was inaugurated as President of the United States, thousands of feminists descended upon the nation's capital for the Women's March on Washington in order to counter what the marchers considered to be his baneful influence. Women's March organizers explained: "The rhetoric of the past election cycle has insulted, demonized, and threatened many of us—immigrants of all statuses, Muslims and those of diverse religious faiths, people who identify as LGBTQIA, Native people, Black and Brown people, people with disabilities, survivors of sexual assault—and our communities are hurting and scared. We are confronted with the question of how to move forward in the face of national and international concern and fear."[38]

Accordingly, the marchers intended to "send a bold message to our new government on their first day in office, and to the world that women's rights are human rights. We stand together, recognizing that defending the most marginalized among us is defending all of us."[39]

The Women's March on Washington was meant to celebrate diversity: "We support the advocacy and resistance movements that reflect our multiple and intersecting identities. We call on all defenders of human rights to join us....'It is not our differences that divide us. It is our inability to recognize, accept, and celebrate those differences.'—Audre Lorde."[40] The mission statement vowed: "We will not rest until women have parity and equity at all levels of leadership in society. We work peacefully while recognizing there is no true peace without justice and equity for all."[41]

That diversity, however, was a matter of appearance only: race, ethnicity, dress, body type, and so on. No diversity of thought was encouraged. In fact, several days before the March, the March organizers removed the pro-life group New Wave Feminists from its list of sponsors, explaining: "The Women's March platform is pro-choice and that has been our stance from day one. We want to assure all of our partners, as well as participants, that we are pro-choice as clearly stated in our Unity Principles...the anti-choice organization in question is not a partner of the Women's March on Washington. We apologize for this error."[42]

"Shariah Law Is Reasonable"

Yet in enforcing this ideological purity, the Women's March organizers had no problem with including Sarsour, the Executive Director of the Arab American Association of New York and a prominent Muslim activist, as one of its four national co-chairs. Sarsour's bio at the Women's March site identifies her as an "award-winning, Brooklyn-born Palestinian-American-Muslim racial justice and civil rights activist, community organizer, social media maverick, and mother of three."[43] It didn't mention her open support for Islamic law, which in its treatment of women is not at all compatible with the idea of women having "parity and equity at all levels of leadership in society."

On September 22, 2011, Sarsour tweeted: "shariah law is reasonable and once u read into the details it makes a lot of sense. People just know the basics."[44] Her position didn't change over time. On

May 12, 2015, she tweeted: "If you are still paying interest than Sharia Law hasn't taken over America. #justsaying."[45] And on April 10, 2016, Sarsour tweeted about Sharia again: "Sharia Law is misunderstood & has been pushed as some evil Muslim agenda."[46]

Is the problem that people have with Sharia really one of not knowing it in depth and misunderstanding it? If that is so, then paradoxically enough, all too many of those who are doing the misunderstanding are Muslims who are attempting to understand Sharia accurately and apply its principles scrupulously.

Beat Them

In reality, there was no misunderstanding. The Qur'an describes the relationship between husband and wife in slightly less beautiful terms than imam Syed Soharwardy would have us believe. "Men have authority over women," it says, "because Allah has made the one superior to the other, and because they spend their wealth to maintain them. Good women are obedient. They guard their unseen parts because Allah has guarded them. As for those from whom you fear disobedience, admonish them and send them to beds apart and beat them." (4:34)

Ahmadi Muslim spokesman Qasim Rashid is one of many Muslim spokesman who has tried to explain away this verse. In a 2012 article entitled "The Islamic Solution to Stop Domestic Violence," Rashid argues that "verse 4:34 employs the process of anger management, reformation and reconciliation," and that the word ordinarily translated as "beat" actually means "chastise."[47] This ignores the fact that it quite obviously means "beat" to millions of Muslims worldwide; the idea that a man can beat his wife is taken for granted and discussed on television.[48] Apparently these child brides need a considerable amount of discipline to keep them in line. A 2001 study found that "in Egypt 29 percent of married adolescents have been beaten by their husbands; of those, 41 percent were beaten during pregnancy. A study in Jordan indicated that 26 percent of reported cases of domestic violence were committed against wives under 18."[49] Because of the Qur'anic sanction for wife-beating, these numbers are vastly underreported.

The sanction of wife-beating is just the beginning. The Qur'an allows for marriage to pre-pubescent girls, as it stipulates that Islamic divorce procedures "shall apply to those who have not yet menstruated" (65:4). Throughout a woman's life, she is viewed as a possession of a man, to be used as he wills: "Your women are a tilth for you, so go to your tilth as you will" (2:223). Her testimony is worth only half of his: "Get two witnesses, out of your own men, and if there are not two men, then a man and two women, such as you choose, for witnesses, so that if one of them errs, the other can remind her" (2:282). It rules that a son's inheritance should be twice the size of that of a daughter: "Allah directs you as regards your children's inheritance: to the male, a portion equal to that of two females" (4:11).

The Qur'an also allows men to marry up to four wives, and even grants men permission to have sex with slave girls: "If you fear that you shall not be able to deal justly with the orphans, marry women of your choice, two or three or four; but if you fear that ye shall not be able to deal justly, then only one, or one that your right hands possess, that will be more suitable, to prevent you from doing injustice" (4:3).

Islamic law stipulates that a man's prayer is annulled if a dog or a woman passes in front of him as he is praying. A hadith has his favorite wife, Aisha, saying: "The things which annul the prayers were mentioned before me. They said, 'Prayer is annulled by a dog, a donkey and a woman (if they pass in front of the praying people).' I said, 'You have made us (i.e. women) dogs.' "[50]

In another hadith, Muhammad says charmingly that most women end up in hell: "I looked into Paradise and I saw that the majority of its people were the poor. And I looked into Hell and I saw that the majority of its people are women."[51] When asked about this, he explained that women were "ungrateful to their companions (husbands) and ungrateful for good treatment."[52] Another version of this has him explaining that women are "deficient in intelligence and religious commitment"—in intelligence because the testimony of one man is equal to that of two women, and in religious commitment because women are not to pray or fast while menstruating.[53]

Leaving the House too Much

Saudi Arabia, which bases its legal system strictly upon Sharia, frequently encounters criticism for its discrimination against women: they are not allowed to appear in public without their heads covered, they must have a male "guardian's" permission to venture outside the home, and most notoriously, are not allowed to drive. (That last provision is not based explicitly upon a Sharia provision, but upon a general concern to prevent "corruption," as one Saudi Islamic scholar detailed: "taking off hijab, loss of modesty, leaving the house too much, streets becoming overcrowded, going against and defying her husband, and depriving some of the youth from driving."[54]) The *Washington Post* reported in 2015 that, "because of these factors, international bodies consistently rank Saudi Arabia low on matters of gender equality. In 2014, the World Economics Forum ranked it 130 out of 142 countries in its annual report on gender equality."[55]

Do the Saudis not understand Sharia, or grasp only its basics? Or is the idea of women having "parity and equity at all levels of leadership in society" contradictory to Sharia principles?

Was Saudi Arabia just a hardline Sharia state, while other Muslim countries implemented an interpretation of Sharia that was kinder to women? If so, where exactly was that interpretation of Sharia?

The "Corruption" of "Gender Equality"

The world's other renowned Sharia state is the Islamic Republic of Iran. Women hardly fare better there than they do in Saudi Arabia. On March 19, 2017, Iranians celebrated the birthday of Fatima, one of the daughters of Muhammad, the prophet of Islam. Iran's Supreme Leader, Ayatollah Ali Khamenei, seized the opportunity to expatiate on the evils of how women are treated in the West. Not surprisingly, he blamed the Jews: "Making women a commodity and an object of gratification in the Western world is most likely among Zionist plots aiming to destroy the society."[56]

That Zionist plot didn't just include the objectification of women, but the very idea of the equality of men and women: "Today, Western thinkers and those who pursue issues such as gender equality regret the corruption which it has brought about."[57]

Did the Ayatollah Khamenei have a superficial understanding of Sharia, confined to the "basics?" Did he misunderstand Sharia? Khamenei is a *marja*, a source of emulation—an honorific given in Shi'ite Islam to clerics who have devoted years to intensive study of Islam, and are therefore to be emulated in their teachings and actions by their followers and students. When a cleric becomes a *marja*, he is given the title Grand Ayatollah, and is considered to be one of the foremost authorities on Shi'ite theology and law. As of this writing, there are only 64 Grand Ayatollahs worldwide for the world's two hundred million Shi'ite Muslims. Khamenei is among them.

Is it likely that this man, who has devoted his life to understanding Islam correctly and communicating it properly, would get it wrong on the crucial questions of gender equality and women's rights?

Khamenei wasn't simply expressing his private opinion, either. Human Rights Watch reported in October 2015 that "women's rights are severely restricted in Iran, to the point where women are even forbidden from watching men's sports in stadiums. That ban includes Iran's national obsession—volleyball.... Women confront serious discrimination on issues such as marriage, divorce, and child custody. Women have been sent to jail for publicly speaking out in favor of equal rights for women. Because the government wants Iran's population to grow, it's even moving to ban voluntary medical procedures women can undergo to avoid becoming pregnant. And that's just the beginning."[58]

Julie Lenarz of Britain's Human Security Center charged in December 2015 that in Iran, "women are stoned for being raped."[59] This is because of the assumption, quite widespread among Muslims, that women are responsible for making sure that men are not tempted to commit sexual sins, and likewise responsible if men do so anyway. This is the rationale behind the veil, which is mandatory for women in Iran. In March 2017, the al-Arabiya news agency reported that there had been an increase in acid attacks in Iran, with men spraying acid in the faces of women whom they deemed to be improperly veiled.[60]

Yet the dismal situation for women in Iran, and that country's dismal human rights record in general, arouses little interest in the West. Lenarz said that to notice how the Islamic Republic abuses its citizens was bad business: "In a despicable form of moral myopia, the gold rush for business, as the international sanctions regime begins to unravel, has made Western governments blind to the suffering of ordinary Iranians at the hands of the Ayatollahs."[61] That may be what inhibits people from speaking out about the situation of women in Iran—or it may be that they're afraid of being considered Islamophobic.

The Contradiction

Iran has a women's soccer team that competes internationally. However, in September 2015 the husband of its captain, Niloufar Ardalan, forbade her to participate in the Asian Football Confederation's women's championship competition in Malaysia.[62] This was in accord with Sharia. Radio Free Europe/Radio Liberty reported: "Ardalan says she will not be able to compete in an upcoming tournament in Malaysia because her husband has refused to grant her permission to travel abroad as required by Islamic laws enforced in Iran."[63]

What would Linda Sarsour have done if her husband had forbidden her to participate in the Women's March?

As absurd as it may seem, it's a real question. It's reasonable to assume that Sarsour's husband, Maher Abu Tamer, approves of her political activities, but what if he didn't? Sarsour is a Sharia-compliant Muslim. She has described her adherence to Sharia rules regarding the veiling of women as voluntary: "I CHOOSE to wear hijab. No one forced me to wear it. It does not oppress me (Do I come off as oppressed?) Hijab for me is part of my quest for liberation, it is a part of my identity, it is an every day reminder of my faith. Hijab is modesty - judge me by my character and not by my looks (I know that's hard cause so many hijabis are gorgeous lol but you get the point)."[64]

She has dismissed assertions that the hijab is a sign of oppression: "If I was oppressed by my hijab, I wouldn't be wearing it. Trust me. A piece of cloth doesn't oppress, people do. So stop oppressing me."[65] How is anyone oppressing her? By claiming that the hijab is a symbol of oppression. She has declared: "If your feminism does not include me and my hijab—then you can keep your feminism."[66]

Very well. But Sarsour's "reasonable" Sharia law also gives husbands the right to take away their wives' choice when it comes to wearing the hijab, as well as venturing out without permission and numerous other matters. According to the strictures of Islamic law, Maher Abu Tamer could have forbidden Linda Sarsour from participating in the Women's March. Evidently, he chose not to do so. But as far as Sharia is concerned, he would have been well within his rights had he chosen otherwise, and Sarsour publicly defends Sharia and the right of a husband to restrict his wife's movements is part of Sharia, it is reasonable to assume that Sarsour herself recognizes that her husband could forbid her to engage in any or all of her activism.

What would Sarsour have done if she had been forbidden to participate in the Women's March? Even more importantly, what would the non-Muslim feminists who participated in the Women's March have done?

Allah Akbar, Pussy Grabs Back

Non-Muslim feminist leaders are not prepared for that question. They have eagerly incorporated Muslims among the allegedly victimized classes with which they are standing, as the Washington March website enumerates them: "immigrants of all statuses, Muslims and those of diverse religious faiths, people who identify as LGBTQIA, Native people, Black and Brown people, people with disabilities, survivors of sexual assault." And at the Women's March in Berlin, a non-Muslim marcher, standing in front of a poster emblazoned "PUSSY GRABS BACK/END WHITE SUPREMACY" at the microphone chanted "Allah akbar" (not "*Allahu* akbar," which is the correct form, but "*Allah* akbar," which was abundant indication that the one doing the chanting was non-Muslim, albeit she did her best to imitate the vocal flourishes of the muezzin in the minaret). The assembled marchers cheered lustily.[67]

"Pussy grabs back" was also one of the marchers' favored chants. This was in reference to Donald Trump's notorious secretly recorded remarks from 2005: "You know, I'm automatically attracted to beautiful—I just start kissing them. It's like a magnet. Just kiss. I don't even wait. And when you're a star, they let you do it. You can do anything.... Grab 'em by the pussy. You can do anything."[68]

"Pussy grabs back" was thus a declaration of assertiveness: Women were not going to put up with being groped or sexually assaulted without fighting back. So to the Women's Marchers in Berlin it all made sense; they thought that by chanting "Allah akbar," they were standing in solidarity with Muslims, whom they thought were oppressed in the U.S., or were about to be oppressed by the grabby President Trump.

Yet Trump wasn't alone in his impulse to grab women's genitalia: it was shared, in a quite different way, by none other than feminist hero Linda Sarsour.

An intriguingly similar desire was expressed in 2011 by Sarsour, in the course of arguing that Islam was compatible with feminist ideals, or taught female equality: Sarsour actually equated feminism with Islam, suggesting that two prominent female critics of Islam were somehow less female, or less feminist, for speaking out against the hatred and violence that is justified in Islamic law.

Sarsour even implied that one of these female critics of Islam, Ayaan Hirsi Ali, deserved to be violently attacked. Sarsour tweeted on March 8, 2011: "Brigitte Gabriel = Ayaan Hirsi Ali. She's asking 4 an a$$ whippin'. I wish I could take their vaginas away—they don't deserve to be women."[69]

The bitter irony behind Sarsour's unhinged rhetoric was that Hirsi Ali has in reality suffered the closest thing to having her vagina taken away: she was a victim of female genital mutilation—the excision of the clitoris—as a child in her native Somalia. Female genital mutilation is a disturbingly common practice among many Muslims. The idea behind it is that this cutting reduces women's sexual pleasure, so as to render them more easily controlled. Sarsour was likely to have known that Hirsi Ali was a victim of female genital mutilation when she wrote her tweet, as Hirsi Ali's harrowing description of what happened to her gained international attention after she wrote about it in her 2007 memoir *Infidel*:

> Grandma caught hold of me and gripped my upper body… Two other women held my legs apart. The man, who was probably an itinerant traditional circumciser from the blacksmith clan, picked up a pair of scissors. With the other hand, he caught hold of the place between my legs and started tweaking it, like Grandma milking a goat...
>
> Then the scissors went down between my legs and the man cut off my inner labia and clitoris. I heard it, like a butcher snipping the fat off a piece of meat. A piercing pain shot up between my legs, indescribable, and I howled. Then came the sewing: the long, blunt needle clumsily pushed into my bleeding outer labia, my loud and anguished protests, Grandma's words of comfort and encouragement… When the sewing was finished, the man cut the thread off with his teeth. That is all I can recall of it.
>
> I must have fallen asleep, for it wasn't until much later that day that I realized that my legs had been tied together, to prevent me from moving to facilitate the formation of a scar. It was dark and my bladder was bursting, but it hurt too much to pee. The sharp pain was still there, and my legs were covered in blood. I

> was sweating and shivering. It wasn't until the next day that my Grandma could persuade me to pee even a little... When I just lay still the pain throbbed miserably, but when I urinated the flash of pain was as sharp as when I had been cut."[70]

Hirsi Ali earned Sarsour's ire with statements such as this: "The most important verse, which I still refer to, is in the Koran and it is the verse which says women should obey the male members of their families—their fathers and their husbands—and if they do not do that then the husband may beat his wife. That's also a side of Islam and I've pointed to it and I've said there are millions of people who carry out just that simple verse. Millions of Muslim women all around the world are oppressed in the name [of] Islam. And as a woman who was brought up with the tradition of Islam, I think it's not just my right but also my obligation to call these things by name."[71]

Because Hirsi Ali stood against Sharia-sanctioned oppression of women, Sarsour believed that she should be made to forfeit her very identity as a woman.

Feminists stood by Sarsour.

Criticism of Sarsour Is Islamophobic

When Sarsour tweeted her vicious call to violence against Hirsi Ali, there was no outcry, or even a murmur of protest. "Grab 'em by the pussy" became for the Women's Marchers emblematic of Donald Trump's unfitness to be President and of the culture of misogyny and discrimination against which they were protesting, but "I wish I could take their vaginas away" never got any notice from feminist leaders.

In fact, after *The Daily Caller* ran a piece on the day of the Women's March on Washington drawing attention to Sarsour's ties to the jihad terror group Hamas, and two days later *FrontPage Magazine* compiled an extensive report on her agitation in support of the Palestinian jihad and Hamas in particular, feminists rallied to her side.[72] The hashtag #IMarchWithLinda went viral on Twitter. *Elle* magazine, which usually devotes the lion's share of its attention to fashion, published an article entitled "Women's March Organizer Linda Sarsour Is Under Attack on Social Media: Less than 48 hours after the worldwide event, one of the women who helped plan it is facing Islamophobic attacks."[73]

Elle quoted some of the effusions of support Sarsour was receiving, including one from the official Women's March Twitter account: "We are proud to have @lsarsour as our co-chair. We will always have her back. #IMarchWithLinda."[74] Bernie Sanders tweeted: "Thank you @lsarsour for helping to organize the march and build a progressive movement. When we stand together, we win. #IMarchwithLinda"[75]

Linda Sarsour's Jihad Against Donald Trump

Sarsour didn't endorse just Sharia, but, jihad also. At the annual convention of the Islamic Society of North America (ISNA) over the July 4 weekend in 2017, she denounced the Trump administration, saying: "Why, sisters and brothers, why are we so unprepared? Why are we so afraid of this administration and the potential chaos that they will ensue on our community?"[76] Invoking Muhammad, she added: "A word of truth in front of a tyrant ruler or leader, that is the best form of jihad."[77]

Sarsour then said: "I hope that when we stand up to those who oppress our communities, that Allah accepts from us that as a form of jihad, that we are struggling against tyrants and rulers not only abroad in the Middle East or the other side of the world, but here in these United States of America, where you have fascists and white supremacists and Islamophobes reigning in the White House."[78] And also: "Our number one and top priority is to protect and defend our communities. It is not to assimilate and to please any other people in authority.... Our top priority, even higher than all those priorities, is to please Allah, and only Allah."[79]

Sarsour's highly charged words understandably caused a controversy. Sarsour herself claimed that the widely circulated clip of her calling for jihad against Trump was misleadingly edited: "Right wing tries to demonize my leadership. Editing videos is their favorite pasttime"—and she tweeted a link to her full speech.[80] In another Tweet, she claimed the mantle of Martin Luther King: "My work is CRYSTAL CLEAR as an activist rooted in Kingian non-violence. This is y my teams r effective cause we r powerful w/o violence."[81] And in keeping with the tried-and-tested practice of Islamic supremacists all over the West, she claimed victim status: "Stay focused and pray for the protection of those on the front lines of the movements for justice. We are under threat."[82]

Meanwhile, the media, ever ready to circle the wagons and rally around one of their own, no matter how egregious the offense committed, pulled out all the stops to defend Sarsour and heap contempt on the racist, right-wing yahoos who dared to think that her words constituted an incitement to violence against President Trump.

"Women's March Organizer Linda Sarsour Spoke of 'Jihad.' But She Wasn't Talking About Violence," Time Magazine reassured us.[83] The Wrap told us about "3 Things Conservatives Got Very Wrong About Linda Sarsour's Speech."[84] The Huffington Post gloated: "Linda Sarsour Said 'Jihad' In A Speech And Conservatives Freaked Out."[85] *ThinkProgress* laughed: "A Muslim activist referenced jihad and the right freaked out because they don't know what it means."[86]

CNN commentator Marc Lamont Hill tweeted: "The people disagreeing with @lsarsour clearly don't understand what Jihad means."[87] The *Huffington Post* likewise said that those who were concerned about Sarsour's words were ignorant fools:

> The word "jihad" has long been misused and misunderstood by both Muslim extremists and people seeking to spread hatred against Muslims. But for the majority of the world's 1.6 billion Muslims, "jihad" is a word that literally means "to struggle." It's a concept within Islam that represents a commitment to serve God, and to be good to yourself and your neighbors. It can be personal, like struggling to get through a rough workday, or overarching, like striving to seek justice for all people.

As Sarsour recounted in her speech, the Prophet Muhammad is said to have described the best form of jihad as "a word of truth in front of a tyrant, ruler or leader."[88]

Likewise, *The Wrap*:

> Many non-Muslims mistakenly believe the word "jihad" means "holy war," when in fact, it means "struggle" or "striving," according to the Islamic Supreme Council of America. "It can refer to internal as well as external efforts to be a good Muslims or believer, as well as working to inform people about the faith of Islam," the Council said. "Jihad is not a violent concept. [It] is not a declaration of war against other religions." Also, "The concept of jihad has been hijacked by many political and religious groups over the ages in a bid to justify various forms of violence… Scholars say this misuse of jihad contradicts Islam."
>
> In her speech, Sarsour quoted a passage in the Quran where the Prophet Muhammad explains that the best form of jihad or struggle is "a word of truth in front of a tyrant rule or leader…" Sarsour followed with, "I hope that when we stand up to those who oppress our communities, that Allah accepts that from us as a form of jihad, that we are struggling against tyrants and rulers…" She then cited "fascists and white supremacists and Islamophobes reigning in the White House."
>
> Though she did make a not-so-subtle reference to President Trump and his constituents, Sarsour in no way incited violence against them. In using the word "jihad," she merely encouraged her audience to stand up to discrimination.[89]

The quotation from Muhammad doesn't actually appear in the Qur'an, but it is in a hadith. But Islamic law is also quite clear that jihad involves violence. The Shafi'i legal manual (the Shafi'is are a school of Islamic jurisprudence) *'Umdat al-Salik* (*Reliance of the Traveller*), which has been certified by al-Azhar, the foremost authority in Sunni Islam, as conforming to the "practice and faith of the orthodox Sunni community," makes it quite clear: "Jihad means to war against non-Muslims, and is etymologically derived from the word 'mujahada', signifying warfare to establish the religion."[90]

What's more, if jihad is simply a word spoken against a tyrant, then why is there an entire chapter of the Qur'an entitled "Booty" or "The Spoils of War" (al-Anfal, chapter eight). What spoils ensue from a word of truth spoken in front of a tyrant ruler or leader? If jihad is simply a word of truth spoken in front of a tyrant, how is a Muslim supposed to make Jews and Christians "pay the jizya with willing submission and feel themselves subdued" (Qur'an 9:29)?

If jihad is simply a word of truth spoken in front of a tyrant, why have thousands upon thousands of Muslims worldwide joined violent jihad groups? Why are there any violent jihad groups at all? Why is this misunderstanding of jihad so widespread?

However, the centrality in Islamic law of jihad as warfare against unbelievers does not in itself mean that Sarsour was inciting violence against Trump. But Linda Sarsour isn't stupid. Nor is she unaware of what Muslims are doing in the name of jihad around the world today. When she says, "I hope that when we stand up to those who oppress our communities, that Allah accepts from us that as a form of jihad," she herself may mean a non-violent standing up, but she has to know that when other Muslims who know the real meaning of jihad in Islam hear that, they will hear it as a call to violence. She must know that when she says that "our number one and top priority is to protect and defend our communities" and that "our top priority, even higher than all those priorities, is to please Allah, and only Allah," that some Muslims will think of how pleased Allah is with the deaths of unbelievers, since he has guaranteed Paradise to those who "kill and are killed" for him (Qur'an 9:111).

All the damage control of the Leftist media, heaping contempt upon conservatives for being so stupid as to think that jihad involves violence, is simply more of the denial and willful ignorance regarding jihad that the political and media elites constantly force upon us. The truth they refuse to realize, and smear us as "Islamophobes" for realizing, is that Muslims worldwide who commit violence against unbelievers regard that violence as a form of jihad, and know that the Qur'an and Sunnah teach warfare against unbelievers.

Linda Sarsour no doubt knows this as well, and as such, knew just how incendiary her words really were. And if a Muslim decides to wage jihad, in its Qur'anic and traditional sense, against President Trump, she should be held legally responsible for this incitement.

"That's No Man's Decision to Make"—Really?

But the real problem, as always, were the Islamophobes. The liberal fascination with the hijab and determination to defend those who wear it from Trump-supporting rednecks who would rip it from their heads given half a chance overlooked the unpleasant fact that for all too many Muslim women in Iran and elsewhere, the hijab wasn't chic at all, but a very real symbol of oppression backed by a genuine threat of violence if they dared not to wear it.

Another example of the feminist West's disconnect from reality on this issue came in April 2017, in a *BuzzFeed* article entitled "After Someone Claimed This Teen's Dad Would 'Beat Her' For Taking Off Her Hijab, She Texted Her Dad."[91] The article introduced us to "17-year-old Lamyaa from Pennsylvania," whose father was living in Saudi Arabia. Lamyaa, said *BuzzFeed*, was "part of an active group chat started by one of her friends where the subject of President Trump and the tense political climate was brought up."[92]

Lamyaa explained: "I personally had very strong views [on Trump] considering the presidency did impact me because I am an Arab, Muslim woman."[93] But when she made her views known in the chat, according to *BuzzFeed*, a vicious Islamophobe responded: "Stop defending Islam Bitch shut up you couldn't take that scarf off or your dad would beat your ass."[94]

Lamyaa decided to show this racist yahoo a thing or two, so she texted her father in Saudi Arabia: "I was thinking I want to take my hijab off."[95] Her father responded: "Sweetheart that's not my decision to make / That's no man's decision to make / If it's what you feel like you want to do, go ahead. I'll support you no matter what."[96]

BuzzFeed exulted: "Lamyaa wanted to share her dad's response publicly to dispel this kind of 'mentality' people have toward all Muslim women who wear a hijab. Her texts with her dad have gone massively viral, with over 142,000 retweets currently."

Lamyaa's exchange was trumpeted as evidence that women, specifically hijab-wearing women, are not oppressed and are wearing it, as Sarsour and others insist, by their own choice. Lamyaa did receive some pushback, however, from people who pointed out that for many Muslim women, wearing the hijab is quite clearly not a choice. Lamyaa responded by defending Islam: "Women—in the Middle East specifically—face oppression but it is due to culture not religion."[97]

This is a common argument, but it is no more coherent for being common. It strains credulity beyond the breaking point to think that the Kingdom of Saudi Arabia, the Kingdom of the Two Holy Places, which prides itself on enforcing Sharia in its fullness, would allow this cultural hangover that supposedly contradicts Islam to persist.

What's more, Lamyaa's father may be a generous soul, but he is not in the slightest degree representative of the Saudi position on women's freedom to wear the hijab or not. Just last December, a Saudi woman was arrested for venturing out in public with her head uncovered; she also received numerous death threats from Saudi men who would heap contempt upon the idea that to wear or not wear the hijab is "no man's decision to make."[98] No one in Saudi Arabia piped up at the time to remind authorities that the forced hijab was "cultural" and not "religious."

And it is, in fact, religious. A hadith depicts Muhammad saying to a woman, "'O Asma, when a woman reaches the age of menstruation, it does not suit her that she displays her parts of body except this and this,' and he pointed to her face and hands."[99]

When considered authentic by Islamic scholars, Muhammad's words are normative for Islamic law.

BuzzFeed and the other establishment media outlets were thrilled that Lamyaa struck back against President Trump and the "Islamophobes." Great. And how infinitely greater it would have been if the claims that are being made on the basis of her father's statements were even remotely true.

Fashionable Victims

Yet nothing is more fashionable these days, and more in, than a hijab-wearing Muslim woman. Sawsan Morrar, a student in the University of California at Berkeley's Graduate School of Journalism, was honored as a 2017 White House Correspondents' Association Scholar. Ms. Morrar promptly took to the pages of the *Washington Post* in April 2017 to complain about this, and to reinforce her status as a victim.[100]

Morrar was undoubtedly chosen as a 2017 White House Correspondents' Association Scholar because she wears a hijab. The White House Correspondents' Association clearly wanted to use her and her hijab as symbols, to tweak President Trump about his supposed "anti-Muslim bias."

Sawsan Morrar was, for the White House Correspondents' Association, one living, breathing symbol of everything that was "Islamophobic" about Donald Trump.

There was just one problem: Sawsan Morrar didn't want to be taken as merely a symbol. Sawsan Morrar, like so many young women before her who advanced far on their figures or their smile or the way the director felt when he looked at them, wanted to be *valued as a person.*

She didn't appear to realize that the Left, for all its preening about its own tolerance and multiculturalism, couldn't have cared less about her as a person. But she did sense that something was wrong, and so fell back on that tried-and-tested response that so many Muslims in the U.S. have employed before: she claimed victimhood.

Nowadays, our society's most celebrated heroes are victims of one kind or another, and Sawsan Morrar seemed to want to make sure that her victimhood bona fides would not be questioned. Victimhood status is currency these days. If you're a victim, all manner of doors open to you that might otherwise have remained closed: doors to the adulation of the Left; doors to free passes from scrutiny (legal or otherwise) that you might otherwise have received; doors to a privileged status that elevates you above ordinary non-victim folk.

And few, if any, groups are more skilled and indefatigable at pursuing victim status than Islamic advocacy groups in the U.S. They have successfully established in the public discourse the wholesale fiction that Muslimas who wear hijab are routinely insulted, harassed, and brutalized in the United States. Her piece in the *Washington Post* was an extension of that endeavor, *sans* (as always) the insults, harassment, and brutalization.

And so this award-winning hijab-wearing journalist, who was award-winning wholly and solely because she was hijab-wearing, said: "Those who tune in to watch this year's White House Correspondents' Association dinner on Saturday will hear my name called as I take the stage to accept a journalism scholarship. They won't see my portfolio of work, and they will likely forget my name. But they're sure to notice and remember one thing about me: my headscarf."[101]

Maybe so. But wasn't that the idea? Wasn't wearing the hijab a proclamation to the world that here was a Muslim woman who is preserving her modesty and piety, in contrast to the non-Muslim women who walk around with heads uncovered? If Sawsan Morrar wanted to be remembered for something other than the hijab, there was one simple way to ensure that: don't wear it.

She also said: "And as I prepare to attend, I know some at the event may not perceive me as a fellow reporter who, like them, relishes the thought of meeting journalists I admire. Muslims don't have the luxury of being a fusion of their achievements, interests and uniqueness. Rather, in the eyes of others, we are only Muslim."[102]

On what did she base this claim? Nothing whatsoever, of course. But this was the Trump administration, and this was the *Washington Post*. This was what fighting back against "Islamophobia" looked like.

Morrar concluded: "I do hope that when I am called on stage at the dinner, I will be recognized for my achievements in journalism and not used to portray some striking juxtaposition between the Trump administration and the Muslim community."[103]

Don't kid yourself, Ms. Morrar, about your helpful Leftist comrades and allies. They will smile, they will congratulate you, they will praise your achievements, whatever they may be, and however large or small. But your being a Muslim, and a hijabi at that, was the *only* reason why you were there. To the White House Correspondents' Association, your only purpose and value was that you were a Muslim who wore a hijab, and thus constituted for that association a virtue-signaling rebuke to President Trump. If you had taken off your hijab and converted to Christianity or became an atheist, would you have been chosen as a 2017 White House Correspondents' Association Scholar? Not in a million years.

The Real Oppressed

In reality, the real oppressed group was not hijab-wearing Muslim women.

While the best and the brightest happily don hijabs in solidarity with Muslim women oppressed by Islamophobia, the real oppression is elsewhere. But where is the feminist concern for Aqsa Parvez, whose Muslim father choked her to death with her hijab after she refused to wear it?[104] Or Amina Muse Ali, a Christian woman in Somalia whom Muslims murdered because she wasn't wearing a hijab?[105]

The list goes on and on: 40 women were murdered in Iraq in 2007 for not wearing the hijab.[106] Alya Al-Safar's Muslim cousin threatened to kill her and harm her family because she stopped wearing the hijab in Britain.[107] Amira Osman Hamid faced whipping in Sudan for refusing to wear the hijab.[108] An Egyptian girl, also named Amira, committed suicide after being brutalized for her family for refusing to wear the hijab.[109] Muslim and non-Muslim teachers at the Islamic College of South Australia were told that they had to wear the hijab or be fired.[110] Police shot women in Chechnya with paintballs because they weren't wearing the hijab.[111] Men with automatic rifles threatened other women in Chechnya for not wearing the hijab.[112] Elementary school teachers in Tunisia were threatened with death for not wearing the hijab.[113]

Syrian schoolgirls were forbidden to go to school unless they wore the hijab.[114] Hamas forced the women in Gaza to wear the hijab.[115] Women in Iran protested against the regime by daring to take off their legally required hijab.[116] Muslim thugs threatened to murder women in London if they didn't wear the hijab.[117] An anonymous young Muslim woman doffed her hijab outside her home and started living a double life in fear of her parents.[118] Fifteen girls in Saudi Arabia were killed when the religious police wouldn't let them leave their burning school building because they had taken off their hijabs in their all-female environment.[119]

Who is standing in solidarity with them, or all the other women and girls who have been killed or threatened, or who live in fear for daring not to wear the hijab? Do they have any place in these celebrations of the beauty and free choice of those who wear the hijab? Is there anyone who cares about the free choice of those who do not wear the hijab?

Those who taunt or brutalize hijab-wearing women are louts and creeps, and should be prosecuted if they commit any acts of violence. At the same time, the women who don't wear hijab in Muslim countries are far more likely to be victims of violence than hijabis in the West. Who stands with them?

Freedom of Religion or Freedom from Genital Mutilation?

Likewise, who stands with the Muslim girls and women worldwide who, like Ayaan Hirsi Ali, have been forced to undergo genital mutilation?

On April 13, 2017, a Muslim doctor in Detroit named Jumana Nagarwala was charged with mutilating the genitals of two seven-year-old girls.[120] Shortly thereafter, two associates of Dr. Nagarwala, Dr. Fakhruddin Attar and his wife Farida Attar, were likewise charged.[121] All three were members of the Anjuman-e-Najmi mosque in Farmington Hills, Michigan, where Nagarwala's husband, Moiz

Nagarwala, was leader and joint treasurer of the mosque, and Dr. Attar had served in the same roles.[122]

Acting Assistant Attorney General Kenneth Blanco did not minimize the horror of the charges: "According to the complaint, despite her oath to care for her patients, Dr. Nagarwala is alleged to have performed horrifying acts of brutality on the most vulnerable victims. The Department of Justice is committed to stopping female genital mutilation in this country, and will use the full power of the law to ensure that no girls suffer such physical and emotional abuse."[123]

Faced with having to defend a man accused of those "horrifying acts of brutality," Dr. Attar's attorney Mary Chartier attempted an audacious and novel defense, saying when Nagarwala and the Attars were indicted: "I do believe that the government does not fully understand the religious practices of Dr. Attar and Dr. Attar's religion, and I think that's why we are in this courthouse today, and what we'll be fighting over for the next few months."[124]

Indeed, the government is likely clueless as to the Islamic justifications for female genital mutilation, but what was truly shocking about Chartier's statement was that she clearly intended to make religious freedom the linchpin of her case for the defense. Chartier was getting right to the heart of the matter; apparently, she intended to argue that female genital mutilation (contrary to constantly repeated establishment media myth) was justified in Islam, and that therefore Dr. Attar was just exercising his freedom of religion.

If that is really what she intends to do, this will become a test case for the spread of Sharia practices in the United States: either Muslims will be allowed to violate existing U.S. laws under the rubric of the freedom of religion, or they will be called upon to obey U.S. laws even when those laws conflict with the teachings of Islam. If the court rules for the latter, the U.S. will have a chance to continue to exist as a free society. If the court rules for the former, it will be opening the door to all manner of jihad activity and Sharia practices that violate laws regarding equality of rights and equality of access to services, and no one will be able to say a word against the spread of Sharia in the U.S.

Chartier said of the defendants: "They have a religious belief to practice their religion. And they are Muslims and they're being under attack because of it. I believe that they are being persecuted because of their religious beliefs and I do not make that allegation lightly."

In reality, they were "being under attack" for mutilating girls' genitals. But Chartier was right: female genital mutilation is indeed sanctioned in Islam.

A manual of Islamic law that the most prestigious and influential institution in Sunni Islam, Cairo's al-Azhar, certifies as conforming "to the practice and faith of the orthodox Sunni community" stipulates that "circumcision is obligatory (for every male and female) (by cutting off the piece of skin on the glans of the penis of the male, but circumcision of the female is by cutting out the bazr 'clitoris' [this is called *khufaadh* 'female circumcision'])" (parenthetical and bracketed material as in the original).[125]

Why is it obligatory? Because Muhammad is held to have said so: "Abu al-Malih ibn Usama's father relates that the Prophet said: 'Circumcision is a law for men and a preservation of honour for women.'"[126] Another hadith depicts Muhammad recommending moderation in the practice, but by no means forbidding it outright: "Narrated Umm Atiyyah al-Ansariyyah: A woman used to perform circumcision in Medina. The Prophet (peace be upon him) said to her: 'Do not cut severely as that is better for a woman and more desirable for a husband.' "[127]

It is commonly claimed to be an East African problem, and indeed, according to a May 2015 Egyptian government report, 92 percent of Egyptian women between the ages of 15 and 49 had had their genitals mutilated.[128] But female genital mutilation is also common among Muslims in many other areas of the world. 93 percent of Muslim women in Malaysia have suffered this procedure, and it is common also in Indonesia.[129] In one province in Iran, 60 percent of the women have suffered FGM.[130] These extraordinarily high rates are directly related to the encouragement that Muslim clerics give to the practice. An April 2016 *Times of India* report noted that attempts to stamp out the practice in Mumbai had been stymied by a Muslim cleric (from the same Dawoodi Bohra sect to which the Michigan doctors belonged) urging, obliquely but unmistakably, that it be done. Syedna Muffadal Saifuddin declared: "The act has to happen! If it is a man, then it is right, it can be openly done, but if it is a woman then it must be done discreetly, but then the act has to be done. Please understand what I am trying to talk about."[131]

At least some Muslim leaders in non-Muslim countries, including some in the West, agree with Saifuddin. A Muslim cleric in Russia said that "all women should be circumcised."[132] Even in the United States, a leading U.S. Muslim jurist from the Assembly of Muslim Jurists of America (AMJA) said it was an "honor" in Islam.[133]

And so it is becoming more common in the West. A marabout—a Muslim holy man—was arrested in France in 2012 for having it done on his daughters.[134] In the UK, there were 5,500 cases of FGM in 2016 alone.[135]

Imam Afroz Ali, founder and president of the Al-Ghazzali Centre for Islamic Sciences and Human Development in Sydney, Australia, declared that "Islamic law permits by definition, by prophetic statement and by practice female circumcision."[136] He denied, however, that female circumcision and female genital mutilation were the same thing: "The definition under Islamic law for female circumcision is exclusively the removal of the uppermost extra skin at the top of the clitoral glans. Female circumcision in its legitimate form is a personal and human right of a woman; genital mutilation is a horrible crime."[137]

While this may have seemed reassuring, it was a distinction without a difference, as the distinction that Ali was trying to make depended upon a subjective judgment. Everyone who performed this practice might have a different idea of what constituted the "extra skin at the top of the clitoral glans." What's more, many of those who perform this procedure go considerably farther than simply the removal of some "extra skin." In fact, the World Health Organization reports that limiting the procedure to removal of "only the prepuce (the fold of skin surrounding the clitoris)" happens only "in very rare cases."[138] Much more frequent are "the partial or total removal of the clitoris," as well as "the partial or total removal of the clitoris and the labia minora (the inner folds of the vulva), with or without excision of the labia majora (the outer folds of skin of the vulva)," and even "the narrowing of the vaginal opening through the creation of a covering seal" that is "formed by cutting and repositioning the labia minora, or labia majora, sometimes through stitching, with or without removal of the clitoris (clitoridectomy)."[139]

All this is certain, because of the rapid rate of Muslim immigration, to become increasingly common in the United States. And if Mary Chartier succeeds, it will become legal, as a matter of freedom of religion.

It is a commonplace of "Islamophobia" rhetoric to claim that those who call attention to the aspects of Sharia that are incompatible with human rights and American law are motivated by a desire, presumably borne out sheer bigotry or racism, to restrict the religious freedom of Muslims in the United States. Peter Beinart wrote in *The Atlantic* in April 2017 that an obscure Justice Department official, Eric Treene, had "become a reviled figure on the Trump-era right. His sin: defending the religious freedoms of American Muslims."[140]

Beinart demonstrated only the dimmest grasp of what actually constituted religious freedom. He wrote that "conservative Christians who remain committed to religious freedom for Muslims… have fewer and fewer supporters in the pews." How does he know this? Because "the University of North Carolina's Charles Kurzman notes that between 2001 and 2010, according to an average of nine polls taken during that period, 29 percent of Republicans expressed negative views of Muslims."[141] As far as Beinart was concerned, apparently expressing negative views of Muslims was the same as wanting to deny them religious freedom, but his leaps of logic aside, the claim was clear: wanting to deny Muslims religious freedom was a conservative vice that all good people on the Left should reject.

So will the American Left embrace female genital mutilation, as a matter of Muslim religious freedom, or would it stand up for the rights of the girls and women who have been so pitilessly victimized by this practice? Up to now they have managed to avoid this question by claiming that female genital mutilation doesn't actually have Islamic sanction. Linda Sarsour herself tweeted after the arrest of Dr. Nagarwala: "FGM has no place in Detroit or any where else in the world. FGM is barbaric & is NOT an Islamic practice."[142]

This statement was patently counterfactual; was Sarsour hoping to head off the inevitable clash between women's rights and Islamic religious freedom? Whether Sarsour was or not, by basing her defense of the Muslim doctors charged with performing or abetting this barbaric procedure on their Islamic identity and freedom of religion, Mary Chartier seemed determined to hasten that clash.

Whatever the outcome of those cases, the clash is inevitable: feminists will ultimately have to choose between women's rights and Islam. Some have tried to head off this clash by taking refuge in the language of choice that became hallowed among feminists during the abortion battles: some women choose to wear hijab, some do not, some women dye their hair green, some do not, some women are lesbians, some are straight—let a hundred flowers bloom!

Very well. But what of the girls who were forced to undergo genital mutilation as children? What about the girls and women threatened, brutalized, and even killed for refusing to wear the hijab? Do they have rights as well? Does feminism have anything to say on their behalf?

Thus far, there has been only silence.

The fear of charges of "Islamophobia" seems to be able to quiet even the voices that are otherwise the most strident.

CHAPTER 4

THE THREAT TO GAYS

A Lasting Partnership?

On June 12, 2017, the first anniversary of the jihad massacre at the Pulse nightclub in Orlando, Florida, gay activist Scott Simpson wrote in *The Advocate* that the event brought Muslims and gays together, united as victims against the forces of hatred and bigotry that Donald Trump represented.

A Muslim gunned down 49 people and wounded another 53 at a gay nightclub in the name of Allah and Islam, and a gay leader wrote in a gay magazine that the massacre has united people who hold the same beliefs as the killer with people who share the orientation of his victims—against a man who has vowed to take steps to prevent such massacres from happening again.

Simpson based this on the idea that both Muslims and gays are routinely brutalized by thuggish Trump-supporting louts: "Across the country, American Muslims girded themselves for what has become a terrifying but familiar backlash against them. When anyone with a Muslim-sounding name makes headlines for a crime or an attack, the entire Muslim community is usually blamed. Vandals opened fire on a Texas mosque and Muslim men were beaten or shot in Orlando, the Bronx, Queens, Brooklyn, and Minnesota.... Anti-Muslim violence has surged under the rhetoric of the Trump campaign, making 2016 the most brutal year for American Muslims since the backlash following 9/11."[1]

This was not the first sign of this "lasting partnership" against bigotry and "Islamophobia."

Gays Against Calling Attention to Islam's View of Gays

Back in 2013, when the American Freedom Defense Initiative (AFDI), of which I am cofounder and vice president, ran ads on buses in San Francisco highlighting the mistreatment of gays in Islamic law, gay advocates in San Francisco and elsewhere condemned not that mistreatment, but our ads.

Theresa Sparks, a transgender who was the chief of San Francisco's Human Rights Commission, declared that AFDI President Pamela Geller was "posting these ads to suggest that all Muslims hate gays. Some cultures do discriminate, and that's wrong. It all depends who you're talking to. But she's trying to generalize and cast this wide net around a diverse group of people."[2]

The ads actually consisted simply of quotes from Muslim leaders regarding Islam's death penalty for homosexuality, including Sheikh Yusuf al-Qaradawi, the most influential Sunni cleric in the world, and Mahmoud Ahmadinejad, former President of the foremost Shi'ite entity in the world, the Islamic Republic of Iran. The ads neither stated nor suggested that "all Muslims hate gays." Sparks was not reported as saying anything about the anti-gay statements of the Muslim leaders quoted in the ads.

The *San Francisco Examiner* added: "Sparks, who is transgender, said it's actually easier to get insurance for sexual transition procedures in Iran than in America."[3]

Sparks was understating the case; the Iranian government will actually foot the bill for gender reassignment surgery itself. But the Islamic Republic of Iran is hardly the bastion of enlightened attitudes toward gays and transgenders that Sparks was implying. Sparks didn't mention the fact that Iran forces gays to undergo gender reassignment surgery, whether they want to or not, as a "cure" for homosexuality.[4] An Iranian-born filmmaker, Tanaz Eshaghian, pointed out "the pressure felt by gay men and women in Iran to have sexual reassignment surgeries as a means of legitimizing their sexual orientation. As gay individuals, they are committing a crime. As transsexuals, they can exist under Iranian law."[5]

None of that seemed to register with gay activists in the U.S. One of them, Chris Stedman, an atheist who is Assistant Humanist Chaplain at Harvard, published an article in *Salon.com* entitled "Stop trying to split gays and Muslims," also attacking our ads.[6] Noting with indignation the AFDI "series of anti-Muslim advertisements in San Francisco quoting Muslim individuals making anti-LGBT statements," Stedman declared his "appreciation that the LGBT community in San Francisco is standing up against her efforts to drive a wedge between LGBT folks and Muslims."[7]

As far as Stedman was concerned, the real problem was those who called attention to the plight of gays under Islamic law, not the actual mistreatment of gays under Islamic law.

The same thing happened in April 2017, when I appeared at the University at Buffalo. I say I "appeared," because to say "I spoke" would be exaggerating a bit. Rather, I spoke a few sentences and made a couple of points in between being screamed at by Leftist and Islamic supremacist fascists who think they're opposing fascism. One young man held a sign that read "Queers Against Islamophobia."

The crowd booed energetically when I attempted to read from Islamic authorities about Islam's death penalty for homosexuality. Even to read from Islamic sources is hate, apparently, at the University at Buffalo—unless, of course, one endorses such penalties rather than oppose them.

Other gays also stand in solidarity with Muslims against Islamophobes.

Bashthefash...Me

In April 2017, the College Republicans chapter at Truman State University in Kirksville, Missouri, invited me to speak there. Eight days before the event, this invitation came to the attention of a young Kirksville resident who called herself Bella Waddle.

Waddle tweeted: "Truman's College Repubs are hosting anti-Muslim extremist Robert Spencer on the 13th. I think y'all know what to do... #bashthefash," followed by an emoji of a fist. Someone identified on Twitter only as Sarah got the point immediately and tweeted in reply: "PUNCH! HIS! FACE!"

Another individual with "BlackLivesMatter" as part of his Twitter bio voiced indignation at the Islamophobic establishment that he imagined to be running Truman State University, even though this was a private event, not sponsored by the university: "@TrumanState should be ashamed for hosting a bigoted extremist like @jihadwatchRS [my Twitter handle]. Solidarity to those defying this."

Bella Waddle herself was determined to show defiance, tweeting several days before the event: "We're organizing to make sure he knows he isn't welcome here. And apparently he's heard about it."

Yes, Bella, I did hear about it. And I can assure you that I knew from the outset that I would not be welcome at Truman State University, except by those who invited me and others who supported them.

But your opposition, Bella, and your organizing, raised a few questions that remain important long after my appearance at Truman State.

Bella Waddle identified herself on her Facebook page as "Just another queer anarchist," ending her Facebook bio with three symbols that were far more incompatible than Bella appeared to know: the hammer and sickle, the peace sign, and a heart. On Bella's Vine page, Waddle identified herself as Jordan Waddle; the page featured photographs of a male who was clearly the same person as Bella, *sans* flowing wig, lipstick, and woman's clothing, and who told us that the pronouns she prefers that people use of her are "she" and "her." In an earlier tweet, Bella explained: "When my parents tried to turn me into a heterosexual I don't think they expected me to become a heterosexual woman but here we are."[8]

So this self-described "queer anarchist" thought of me as an "anti-Muslim extremist" who ought not to have been given a platform at Truman State University or, presumably, anywhere else.

Nonetheless, despite her hostility, I regret that while I was at Truman State (where my address went off without incident, albeit with my own security team, a heavy police presence and an extremely hostile crowd, eager to show its opposition to my "Islamophobia"), I didn't get a chance to sit down for a coffee with Bella. For it was for Bella Waddle and others like her that I actually went to Truman State, and they are the ones I would most like to chat with, given the opportunity (and, given their taste for violence against those whom they hate, maybe a security guard or two).

"You cannot arrest or repress people who just don't exist in the republic"

I would have asked Bella if she was aware of some events that were in the news just before I came to Truman State. *The New York Times* reported on April 1, 2017, that "over the past week, men ranging in age from 16 to 50 have disappeared from the streets of Chechnya."[9] These weren't just random individuals: "the Chechen authorities were arresting and killing gay men," and over 100 had been done away with in this way so far.[10]

The Russian newspaper *Novaya Gazeta* confirmed that these men were targeted "in connection with their nontraditional sexual orientation, or suspicion of such."[11] Yet Alvi Karimov, a spokesman for Chechen leader Ramzan Kadyrov, dismissed this report as "absolute lies and disinformation." He did so, however, not because Chechnya presented a hospitable environment for gays, but because "you cannot arrest or repress people who just don't exist in the republic. If such people existed in Chechnya, law enforcement would not have to worry about them, as their own relatives would have sent them to where they could never return."[12]

Novaya Gazeta, however, reported that an order had indeed gone out to arrest and kill gays: "In Chechnya, the command was given for a 'prophylactic sweep' and it went as far as real murders."[13]

The same day this article appeared, Bella Waddle tweeted: "I hope y'all like drag queens and political statements because ya gurl Bella is performing at Wrongdaddys tonight @ 9pm."[14]

Would ya gurl Bella or any other transgender person living today in the U.S. be willing to take her act to the Chechen capital of Grozny, and dance in full drag in any public place there?

Now *that* would be a political statement.

Two weeks before her announcement of her dance, Bella tweeted what was apparently a response to a critic: "I've spent my entire life being excluded & vilified because of my gender expression. Don't tell ME about MY own experiences."[15]

Very well. I feel for Bella. I can only imagine the awkwardness, the anguish, the confusion, the despair. But can she imagine what would happen if she were to appear in full drag on the streets of any Muslim country?

Shortly after the arrests in Chechnya came to light, the news got even worse: the Chechen government was putting gays into a concentration camp, where they were being tortured with electric shocks, and some killed unless they promised to leave Chechnya.[16]

Chechnya was not singular. Were Bella Waddle to travel to virtually any Muslim country, she would on arrival almost certainly wish that she were back in conservative Christian Kirksville, Missouri, feeling excluded and vilified and dancing her pain away at Wrongdaddy's.

Most notorious is the Islamic State (ISIS). In March 2017 in Mosul, a young man who was accused of homosexuality was stoned to death.[17] This was a departure from ISIS's usual practice of throwing accused homosexuals off the roofs of tall buildings, which they did as recently as January 2017.[18]

LGBT advocates who decry "Islamophobia" may object that the Islamic State is "extremist," and assert that more moderate Muslim nations don't treat gays so harshly. And that's true; there are no specific penalties for homosexual activity in five Muslim-majority nations: Albania, Indonesia, Jordan, Mali, and Turkey.[19]

None of these, however, is known for strict enforcement of Islamic law. In nations where Islamic law is rigorously followed, including Afghanistan, Iran, Saudi Arabia, Somalia, Sudan, and Yemen, homosexuality is punishable by death.[20] It is also a death penalty offense in Mauritania, Nigeria, Qatar, and the United Arab Emirates.[21]

Wherever gays are persecuted in Muslim countries, the persecution is justified by Islamic law. Where gays are not persecuted, there is no benign version of Islamic law that justifies this good treatment, but just a relaxation of strictures.

Noting Islam's View of Gays Is Islamophobic

But even as Chechnya is not singular, neither is Bella Waddle: she has intellectual compatriots in the Democratic National Committee (DNC). In January 2017, Vincent Tolliver, a candidate for chairmanship of the DNC, was removed from the race for criticizing one of his rivals for the post, Rep. Keith Ellison (D-MN), a Muslim, because of Islamic teaching regarding homosexuality. Tolliver wrote of Ellison: "His being a Muslim is precisely why DNC voters should not vote for him. Muslims discriminate against gays. Islamic law is clear on the subject, and being gay is a direct violation of it. In some Muslim countries, being gay is a crime punishable by death."[22]

All this was accurate. The Qur'an contains numerous condemnations of homosexual activity, including this one: "And Lot when he said to his people, 'Do you commit such immorality as no one has preceded you with from among the worlds? Indeed, you approach men with desire, instead of women. Rather, you are a transgressing people.'… And We rained upon them a rain. Then see how was the end of the criminals." (Qur'an 7:80-84)

The online translation *Quran.com* adds "of stones" an explanatory gloss after "rain"; that understanding of the passage is one reason why the Islamic State and other Muslim groups sometimes stone gays to death.

A hadith—an account of the words and deeds of Muhammad, the prophet of Islam—specifies the punishment for homosexuality: "The Messenger of Allah (peace and blessings of Allah be upon him) said, 'Whoever you find doing the action of the people of Loot, execute the one who does it and the one to whom it is done.' "[23]

Tolliver concluded: "Clearly, Mr. Ellison is not the person to lead the DNC or any other organization committed to not discriminating based on gender identity or sexual orientation....A vote for Representative Ellison by any member of the DNC would be divisive and unconscionable, not to mention counterproductive to the immediate and necessary steps of rebuilding the Democratic Party."[24]

Upon learning of Tolliver's remarks, the DNC removed him from the list of candidates for the chairmanship.

Interim Chairwoman Donna Brazile explained: "The Democratic Party welcomes all Americans from all backgrounds. What we do not welcome is people discriminating against others based on who they are or how they worship. We expect candidates for Chair of the Party to conduct a respectful campaign based on issues. To assure that, we ask all our Chair candidates to pledge 'to uphold the interests, welfare and success of the Democratic Party of the United States,' and to participate in the process 'in good faith.' Mr. Tolliver's disgusting comments attacking the religion of a fellow candidate fall far short of that standard. Accordingly, Mr. Tolliver is no longer a candidate for DNC Chair."[25]

Brett Morrow, a spokesman for Keith Ellison, accused Tolliver of "fan[ning] the flames of intolerance" and assured the public that Ellison would "fight for the core Democratic values of tolerance and inclusion."[26]

No Democratic Party leader bothered to address the substance of Tolliver's remarks. No one attempted to disprove what he had said, and anyone who might have tried would have failed, since what he had said was true. Nor did any enterprising journalist challenge Ellison with any questions about how he reconciled Islam's teaching on homosexuality with "the core Democratic values of tolerance and inclusion." It was simply assumed on all sides that Tolliver had committed a grave offense by calling attention to Islam's view of gays, and that was that.

Saying "Kill the Gays" Is Okay—If You're Muslim

This solicitude for Muslims and Islam was not at all uncommon. In October 2016, the British government allowed an Iranian Muslim cleric, Shaykh Hamza Sodagar, to enter the country for a lecture tour. Some were alarmed at this, for Sodagar had previously been caught on video saying: "If there's homosexual men, the punishment is one of five things. One—the easiest one maybe—chop their head off, that's the easiest. Second—burn them to death. Third—throw 'em off a cliff. Fourth—tear down a wall on them so they die under that. Fifth—a combination of the above."[27]

Despite this, Sodagar had no problem entering Britain and giving his lectures. Yet the British government in the summer of 2013 banned me from entering the country for making the quite accurate and correct observation that Islam "is a religion and is a belief system that mandates warfare against unbelievers for the purpose for establishing a societal model that is absolutely incompatible with Western society."[28]

The government of The Netherlands was likewise solicitous of Muslim sensibilities regarding gays. Late in 2016, Dutch officials discovered that Muslims on online forums were calling for gays to be "burned, decapitated and slaughtered."[29] The Muslims posting such material were, however, not prosecuted. The taxpayer-funded Dutch "anti-discrimination bureau" MiND declared that although such statements would usually be criminally actionable, in this case they weren't because the people making them were Muslims. MiND "media advisors" explained: "The remarks must be seen in the context of religious beliefs in Islam, which juridically takes away the insulting character."[30] The calls for the murder of gays were made, said MiND, in "the context of a public debate about how to interpret the Quran," and "some Muslims understand from the Quran that gays should be killed....In the context of religious expression that exists in the Netherlands there is a large degree of freedom of expression. In addition, the expressions are used in the context of the public debate, which also removes the offending character."[31]

There was no indication that any Dutch government agency would be so forgiving of a non-Muslim group that had called for gays, or anyone else, to be killed.

In light of this solicitude, which is by no means limited to the Dutch, it is no surprise that violence against gays in an increasingly common feature of the European landscape. In Sweden, which up until quite recently was known throughout the world for its tolerant attitude toward homosexuality, two teenage Muslim migrants in December 2015 beat a gay man to death, then dressed the corpse in women's clothing and, for good measure, wrapped a snake around the neck of the lifeless body.

The man's offense? He offered the pair clothes and food and invited them back to his apartment. Once there, they beat him and tied him up, verbally abused him for being gay, and shot video of their torturing him.[32]

Early in 2016, a gay Syrian refugee in The Netherlands, Alaa Ammar, described what happened when a group of Muslim refugees happened upon him and some of his gay friends: "After five minutes, they started looking. After 10 minutes, they started to talk. After one hour, they came to us. After three hours, they started fighting with us."[33]

The Associated Press noted that "across Europe, gay, lesbian and transgender migrants say they suffer from verbal, physical and sexual abuse in refugee shelters, and some have been forced to move out," and reported that there were "scores of documented cases in The Netherlands, Germany, Spain, Denmark, Sweden and Finland, with the abuse usually coming from fellow refugees and sometimes security staff and translators."[34]

AP added that "in Germany, the Lesbian and Gay Federation counted 106 cases of violence against homosexual and transgender refugees in the Berlin region from August through the end of January. Most of the cases came from refugee centers, and 13 included sexual abuse."[35]

These were not inconsiderable numbers, and it was the same story all over Europe. In March 2016, two gay men left a restaurant near the Habsburg Schönbrunn Palace in Vienna and hailed a cab. A Muslim cab driver picked them up, but grew enraged when the two men began to kiss in the back seat of the cab. The driver demanded that they stop kissing, and added: "people like you should be shot dead."[36] At that point, the pair asked the driver to stop and let them out of the cab, and refused to pay for the partial trip; the driver ended up punching one of them in the face.[37]

Shortly before dawn on the morning of May 8, 2016, a 26-year-old former male model named Aaron Woods was attacked by a Muslim who began screaming anti-gay abuse at him and punched him in the face. Woods's friend Brian Markintosh said of Woods: "He's such a gentle giant"—Woods is 6 feet 6 inches. "He's the kindest person you could imagine. This geezer broke his jaw with a knuckleduster. He was filming the young gay guys. And when he was attacking him he was shouting all this Muslim stuff but no one wants to hear that."[38]

Markintosh is right. Despite this, it was a wearisome sign of the times that, according to the *Brighton & Hove News*, "Sussex Police said that it was not aware of any racial or religious element to the assault."[39]

There was plenty of incitement for this violence around Europe. On Friday, July 10, 2015, the Vice President of the Hungarian Muslim Community, Imam Ahmed Miklós Kovács, preached a sermon declaring that "these homosexuals are the filthiest of Allah's creatures. A Muslim must never accept this disease, this terrible depraved thing. He must never color his profile picture on Facebook in the colors of the rainbow, and must never applaud [homosexuals] and express solidarity with them."[40]

He warned that "these days [homosexuals] are celebrating their disease. Effeminate homosexuals are the filthiest of Allah's creatures. They are sick, and a Muslim must never accept this ugly thing. [Homosexuals] are destroying sound moral values and societies. This filthy thing is not accepted by this country's society, and is forbidden in Islam and all the monotheistic religions."[41]

Attacks on Gays In the U.S.

Meanwhile, Muslim victimization of gays was also by no means unheard of in the U.S.

In April 2017, two converts to Islam who lived in Illinois, Joseph D. Jones and Edward Schimenti, were arrested on federal terrorism charges. They had gone to Illinois Beach State Park in Zion, Illinois, with an Islamic State flag and posed for photos there while holding it, to the alarm of passersby, and turned out to be trying to aid, and even join, the Islamic State. In the course of the investigation of the two men, it came to light that Schimenti had threatened a gay man with Sharia punishments, telling him that once Islamic law came to the United States, "We are putting you (homosexuals) on top of Sears Tower (now the Willis Tower) and we drop you."[42]

Those who are certain that such a thing can't happen here need to become aware of the fact that it already has: on January 1, 2014, during the New Year's celebrations at Seattle's gay nightclub Neighbours, a Muslim named Musab Mohamed Masmari poured gasoline on a flight of stairs and then set it alight. The fact that the perpetrator was a Muslim was given only glancing notice in establishment media accounts, but the possibility that this was an early attempt at enforcement in the U.S. of the Sharia death sentence for gays could not be ruled out.[43] In any case, Masmari was unsuccessful; despite his attempt to maximize the carnage by setting his fire on the stairs, no one was hurt.

Five months later, on June 1, 2014, a Muslim in Seattle named Ali Muhammad Brown went on a gay dating app and made a date to meet two gay men, Dwone Anderson-Young and Ahmed Said, at a Seattle gay nightclub. When the pair arrived, Brown gunned them down; then he fled to New Jersey and killed again. Finally apprehended, Brown explained that his murders were revenge for American military actions in Muslim countries: "My mission is my mission between me and my Lord. That's it. My mission is vengeance, for the lives, millions of lives are lost every day. All these lives are taken every single day by America, by this government. So a life for a life."[44]

This was Qur'anic justice: "And We ordained for them therein a life for a life, an eye for an eye, a nose for a nose, an ear for an ear, a tooth for a tooth, and for wounds is legal retribution." (5:45)

A gay couple in New York City, Jonathan Snipes and Ethan York-Adams, were more fortunate than Anderson-Young and Said. In May 2015, they went to dinner at a Dallas BBQ outlet in lower Manhattan. Also there was Bayna Lekheim El-Amin, a Muslim whom Snipes said called him and his boyfriend "faggots"—whereupon Snipes hit El-Amin with his canvas bag. Enraged, El-Amin threw Snipes to the floor and began stomping on his head.[45] He then grabbed a heavy wooden chair and bashed both Snipes and York-Adams over the head with it.

As she sentenced El-Amin to nine years in prison, Manhattan Supreme Court Justice Arlene Goldberg said to him that even though he was hit first, he had no right to respond with such brutality. Goldberg told El-Amin: "That you did not cause serious physical injury to them was only by luck."[46] El-Amin insisted that he had not called the men "faggots" and that he had been an LGBT activist.[47]

The possibility that he might have been influenced by his religious texts' calls for violence against homosexuals was never discussed in court or in any of the media coverage of the incident, and perhaps Islam played no role in El-Amin's actions. Even if it had, however, the establishment media was so careful not to offend Muslim sensibilities or portray Muslims in a negative light that it may very well have not been reported.

Certainly, the Islamic motivation of the worst attack by Muslims against gays in the West—so far—was energetically covered up by both the media and law enforcement officials. That attack came in the Pulse nightclub in Orlando, Florida, on June 12, 2016. A young Muslim named Omar Mateen opened fire in the crowded club, murdering 49 people and injuring another 53. As he paused to reload, he also made several calls to the 911 emergency number.

What he said wasn't released until months later, but when it was, there could be no doubt about his intentions. "This is Mateen," he told the 911 operator. After some words in Arabic, he continued: "I want to let you know I'm in Orlando and I did the shooting."[48] Asked his name, he answered: "My name is I Pledge of Allegiance to Abu Bakr al-Baghdadi of the Islamic State."[49] On a second call, he said: "You're speaking to the person who pledged allegiance to the Islamic State."[50] He also said: "My name is Islamic soldier, okay?... Call me Mujahideen, call me the Soldier of the God."[51]

So there could be no doubt that there was a genuine threat to gays from Muslims, not only in Muslim countries but even in the U.S. Gay activists who directed their fury and scorn at those who called attention to this reality, rather than to the elements of Islamic law that validated the practices of Muslim countries that oppressed gays and even justified terror attacks against them, were, to say the least, short-sighted.

But gay activists could be forgiven for not being fully aware of the jihadist threat to gay communities; after all, that threat was covered up at the highest levels. Apparently, even to note the facts about Omar Mateen's jihad attack at the Pulse gay nightclub was in itself "Islamophobic."

Covering Up Islamic Attacks on Gays in the U.S.

None of the statements of Omar Mateen that I quoted above were known at the time. A week after the attack, Attorney General Loretta

Lynch announced that the FBI would release transcripts of the 911 calls that Mateen made during his massacre. Lynch said that the transcript would include "the killer's calls with law enforcement, from inside the club. These are the calls with the Orlando PD negotiating team, who he was, where he was."[52]

However, said Lynch, there would be one significant omission: "What we're not going to do is further proclaim this man's pledges of allegiance to terrorist groups, and further his propaganda. We are not going to hear him make his assertions of allegiance" to the Islamic State.[53]

Lynch added, apparently unaware of the irony: "We're trying to get as much information about this investigation out as possible."[54]

But not, apparently, anything that might shed light on the ideology that led him to carry out the attack in the first place.

After saying that the Islamic content of the calls would be edited out, Lynch backtracked somewhat, saying: "We will hear him talk about some of those things, but we are not going to hear him make his assertions of allegiance and that. It will not be audio, it will be a printed transcript."[55]

Lynch also mentioned another remarkable omission: the released transcripts would also not contain any statements Mateen made about gays. Not because the FBI was going to edit out those passages as well, but because Mateen didn't say anything about gays at all: "You know, he didn't get into that. So we're still exploring why he chose this particular place to attack. We're asking people who have information to come forward … We are trying to learn everything we can about this individual's motivations."[56]

Lynch and the Obama administration determined *a priori* that Mateen's Islamic statements were irrelevant. She then announced that the establishment media's favored explanation of the attack as motivated by homicidal homophobia was not supported by the killer's own statements.

So Lynch was casting about for some way to understand why he committed mass murder at the Pulse nightclub, because she couldn't prove his priority was murdering gays and refused even to allow Americans to know what he actually said about how his actions were rooted in loyalty to Islam and the Islamic State.

Lynch dismissed the explanation right in front of her face: Mateen killed gays because he was an adherent of the Islamic State, and the Islamic State has called for attacks on American civilians during this Ramadan.

If Lynch had really wanted to know why Mateen chose the Pulse for his attack (after scouting out Disney World), even though he said nothing about it during his 911 calls, she might have considered that the Islamic State as well as many Islamic governments regularly kill gays, and reflect on the fact that Islam mandates that gays be put to death.

But instead, she declared: "We're not going to…further his propaganda."[57]

The outcry was immediate. Lynch and the Justice Department were widely denounced for attempting to cover up Mateen's motives. House Speaker Paul Ryan (R-WI) said the decision to hold back parts of what Mateen said was "preposterous. We know the shooter was a radical Islamist extremist inspired by ISIS. We also know he intentionally targeted the LGBT community. The administration should release the full, un-redacted transcript so the public is clear-eyed about who did this, and why."[58]

The FBI and Justice Department quickly backtracked, explaining in a joint statement that they initially released redacted transcripts because they "did not want to provide the killer or terrorist organizations with a publicity platform for hateful propaganda."[59] However, they said that the controversy over the redactions had "caused unnecessary distraction," and so they were releasing the full transcripts.[60]

And they did. But the damage was done. The idea that revealing the full truth about a jihad murderer's statements would only "provide the killer or terrorist organizations with a publicity platform for hateful propaganda" circulated widely. It wasn't far from that idea to the claim that to speak honestly about the motives and goals of jihad killers and terrorist organizations rendered one an "anti-Muslim extremist."

"Terror from the Right"

One of the primary originators of the idea that there even were such people as "anti-Muslim extremists," the Southern Poverty Law Center (SPLC), was not just intent on concealing Omar Mateen's jihadist motivations; the SPLC even tried to portray Mateen as a "right-wing extremist."

The Daily Caller reported in December 2016 that the SPLC "considers the Orlando nightclub shooting, an ISIS-inspired attack that left 49 dead, a right-wing plot, along with the shootings of police officers by anti-white terrorists."[61]

The SPLC's list, "Terror from the Right," claims to be "a synopsis of radical-right terrorist plots, conspiracies and racist rampages," but it includes Mateen's massacre.[62]

This called to mind the persistent claim that attacks from "right-wing extremists" are more common than attacks from Islamic jihadists. What's ironic is that it was the Orlando jihad massacre itself that exploded this common lie.

That does not, however, keep it from being common. In November 2016, just before the story broke of the SPLC's misclassification of the Orlando massacre, Georgetown University professor Engy Abdelkader appeared on Tucker Carlson's Fox show and made the outlandish claim that the FBI had said that "white supremacist groups" were more of a terror threat than Islamic jihadists.[63]

The FBI made no such claim; in reality, it originated with far-Left pressure groups. Back in June 2015, the George Soros-funded New America Foundation published a study that garnered enthusiastic international publicity, as it purported to demonstrate that "right-wing extremists" and "white supremacists" were a larger threat to the U.S. than Islamic jihadis.[64]

The mainstream media was thrilled. *Mediaite* crowed: "White Americans Are Biggest Terror Threat in U.S.," although after the absurdity of the study was exposed, this headline was changed to "White Americans Are Biggest Terror Threat in U.S. Once You Exclude The Death Of 3,000 Americans."[65] *The New York Times* exulted: "Homegrown Extremists Tied to Deadlier Toll Than Jihadists in U.S. Since 9/11."[66] The *Huffington Post* cheered: "White Supremacists More Dangerous To America Than Foreign Terrorists, Study Says."[67] NPR rejoiced: "Right-Wing Extremists More Dangerous Than Islamic Terrorists In U.S."[68] *TruthDig* was also happy: "White Right-Wing Terrorists Are Biggest Threat to Americans, Study Finds."[69] And on and on.

The media delight stemmed from the fact that the study confirmed its biases and relentless endeavor to downplay and deny the jihad threat. Thus *The New York Times* and NPR and the rest were not in the least interested in the fact that the New America Foundation study was obviously skewed, as it was based on the number of those killed by jihadis and by right-wing extremists since September 12, 2001, leaving out 9/11. The study also ignored the many, many foiled jihad plots, and the fact that jihadis are part of an international movement that has killed many thousands of people, while right-wingers and white supremacists are not. It stated that right-wing extremists had killed 48 people from September 12, 2001, to June 2015, while Islamic jihadists had killed only 26 people in the U.S. in that span. If 9/11 had been added, the tally would have been 3,032 killed by Islamic jihadists and 48 by purported right-wing extremists.

But all right, let's play by the New America Foundation's rules. Counting the Orlando jihad massacre, but leaving out 9/11 as the NAF study did, the death toll now stands at 76 killed by Islamic jihadis, and 48 by purported right-wing extremists (I repeat "purported" because to get to its count of 48, the NAF counted as "right-wing" attacks killings that were perpetrated by people who were obviously deranged psychopaths devoid of any ideology).

Did *The New York Times* issue an amended report? Did NPR? *Mediaite*? *HuffPo*? Or any of the other "news" organizations that so enthusiastically propagated this false study in the summer of 2015?

No, they did not. Nor did they offer any studies of hatred for gays among Muslims, and how Islam's teachings of jihad might victimize gays again, as they did in Orlando.

Yet even many months after the Orlando jihad massacre, the SPLC inflated the numbers of "right-wing extremist" attacks by including Islamic jihad attacks among them.

No wonder the Left is so complacent about the jihad threat, while so exercised about the supposed threat from the "right-wing." They are being told by respected shapers of opinion that there is no threat from jihad, and significant threat from "right-wing extremists."

Did Catholicism Drive Omar Mateen to Kill Gays?

One Catholic bishop even suggested that it was Christianity that drove Mateen to kill.

Robert Lynch (no relation to Loretta), the Roman Catholic Bishop of St. Petersburg, Florida, blamed not Islam's death penalty for homosexuals or its jihad imperative, but his own Catholic faith for Mateen's massacre. Writing the day after the attack, Lynch claimed that "religion, including our own," was responsible for the killings, since it "targets, mostly verbally, and also often breeds contempt for gays, lesbians and transgender people." Lynch claimed that "attacks today on LGBT men and women often plant the seed of contempt, then hatred, which can ultimately lead to violence."[70] He added that unless this hatred and contempt was addressed, "we can expect more Orlandos."[71] He didn't explain why Mateen, who was not a Catholic, would be moved to kill by Catholic teaching.

Bishop Lynch did, however, show that he was aware that Mateen was a Muslim, not a Catholic, as he took the opportunity to declare that it would be "un-American" to try to keep Muslim immigrants out of the United States, and said that there were "as many good, peace loving and God fearing Muslims to be found as Catholics or Methodists or Mormons or Seventh Day Adventists."[72]

Around the same time that Bishop Lynch published this message, a personal ad appeared in the "men-seeking-men" section of the San Diego Craigslist online bulletin board. It was entitled "We need more Orlando's" [sic] and feature a photo of a gun being fired. The ad read: "Orlando was long overdue. Cleanse your community of the filth that gives decent gay men and women a bad name. Those people were walking diseases, bug chasers, and thank god for AIDS and 9-11 and now Orlando. San Diego you are next …"[73]

Craigslist quickly took this ad down, but the message was nonetheless clear. Would "Queers Against Islamophobia" be able to prevail against the people who posted that ad and others like them?

Meanwhile, Omar Mateen was much more likely to have been incited to kill gays not by the Catholic Church, but by Muslim preachers who called for the application of the Sharia death penalty for homosexuality. In April 2016, Dr. Farrokh Sekaleshfar spoke at the Husseini Islamic Center in Sanford, Florida, about a half-hour's drive from the Pulse nightclub in Orlando.

Sekaleshfar spoke at the University of Michigan in 2013 and called for homosexuals to be put to death, but emphasized that the killing must be done in a compassionate fashion, "because the sinner is Allah's creation. You could never hate Allah's creation." He claimed that the death penalty for homosexuality was an act of love, because it secured the victim a place in Paradise: "We see the physical killing as something brutal, and this is the point when human hatred toward the act has to be done out of love. You have to be happy for that person…we believe in an afterlife, we believe in an eternal life…and with this sentence, you will be forgiven and you won't be accountable in the hereafter….It's for his own betterment that he leaves. We have to have that compassion for people. With homosexuals, it's the same. Out of compassion, let's get rid of them now."[74]

This was preached not in Medina, but in Michigan.

Canada: Solicitude for Muslims Trumps Gay Rights

All over the West, those in charge appear to be much more worried about charges of "Islamophobia" than about the plight of gays in Muslim countries.

In the Canadian Parliament on February 10, 2017, Conservative MP Michelle Rempel challenged the Liberal government of Justin Trudeau on why it had ended a program to help gays in Iran escape from the persecutions they suffer in the Islamic Republic: "Why has the government ended the practice of prioritizing persecuted Iranian LGBT [people] as refugees to Canada?"[75]

Trudeau's Immigration Minister Ahmed Hussen responded: "We take seriously our refugee commitment to make sure that it is compassionate and focused on the most vulnerable people. We work very closely with the UN's refugee agency and private sponsors to continue to identify the most vulnerable; and that obviously includes members of the LGBTQ2 community."[76]

Rempel was not satisfied. "The minister did not answer the question," she said. "The minister used the talking point of 25,000 Syrian refugees. I'm talking about the practice of allowing and prioritizing Iranian LGBT refugees coming to Canada. Why are the Liberals turning their back on the most vulnerable? No talking points, please."[77]

Hussen continued to dodge the question, saying: "We will take no lessons from the previous government, when it comes to identifying and welcoming and being compassionate to those most vulnerable, as well as refugees in need of resettlement."[78]

Daily Xtra noted that the Trudeau government had indeed "effectively ended a 2010 program in which Canada resettled hundreds of Iranians from Turkey fleeing persecution on the grounds of sexual orientation and gender identity."[79]

Being compassionate to the most vulnerable evidently no longer included gays from Iran. This may be because the Trudeau government is intent upon restoring good relations with the Islamic Republic. In 2012, the Canadian government of Trudeau's predecessor, Stephen Harper, closed the Canadian embassy in Tehran and the Iranian embassy in Ottawa. Foreign Affairs Minister John Baird dubbed Iran "the most significant threat to global peace and security in the world today" and charged that "the Iranian regime has shown blatant disregard for the Vienna Convention and its guarantee of protection for diplomatic personnel."[80] Trudeau, however, has pledged to restore full diplomatic relations with Iran.[81]

A few gays hanging from cranes in Tehran can't be allowed to stand in the way of good relations between Iran and Canada, can they?

In April 2017, a Canadian organization called the Iranian Railroad for Queer Refugees (IRQR) reported that Iranian police had raided a private party in the Bahadoran district of the Esfahan province in central Iran, firing their guns as they arrested over thirty men on accusations of sodomy. According to the IRQR, "This unfortunate event has created chaos among the LGBT community in Esfahan since prisoners were forced to write down full names of all their LGBT friends and acquaintances. IRQR is deeply concerned about this situation since Iran has a well-documented history of persecuting homosexuals."[82]

German MP Volker Beck, who is gay, declared that "its persecution and policy of annihilation against homosexuals makes the Iranian regime an enemy of human rights. Such a country cannot be a partner of our community of values."[83] So would Beck, as a politician on the Left, support the prioritizing of gay refugees from Iran? He doubtless would, but his fellow liberals in the Trudeau government in Canada were moving in the opposite direction—and judging from Ahmed Hussen's testy and evasive responses to Michelle Rempel's questions, it seemed to be aware of how it was abandoning its stance on gay rights by doing so, but was hoping no one else would notice.

Even if gays from Iran or other Muslim countries were able to get to Canada, they might not have found a very hospitable welcome. In 2015, Farrah Marfatia, the Principal of Maingate Islamic Academy in Toronto, wrote a pamphlet, "To Talk To Your Muslim Child," offering advice to parents about how to deal with difficult issues with their children. Marfatia said of her guide: "I reached out to guidance counsellors and teachers in the public system, and they reviewed it and gave it their stamp of approval. And then, from a religious perspective, I consulted with three imams. One of the imams is also a certified teacher. We had a number of meetings, and they gave me their views from a religious perspective. Overall, about 20 people reviewed it… I am so proud of our community leaders because they have backed it up, and see value in it."

In "To Talk To Your Muslim Child," Marfatia wrote: "In terms of Homosexuality, it is considered to be a sin in all major monotheistic religions including Islam. The Prophet told us that homosexuals are cursed by Allah as are the men who imitate or dress up like women. This must be communicated to your child in a way that is age appropriate bearing in mind that the rights of homosexuals are protected by law just as our rights to freedom of religion are as well."[84] While Judaism and Christianity in their traditional formulations contain teachings condemning homosexual activity, Marfatia's declaration that "homosexuals are cursed by Allah" took on a more ominous tone in light of Islam's death penalty for such activity.

Marfatia, incidentally, was a signatory of an open letter to the Ontario Minister of Education, Mitzie Hunter, complaining about "growing incidents of Islamophobia within society" and asserting: "All children, staff and teachers are entitled to a safe, inclusive & accepting school environment free from fear and hate."[85]

It was certainly true that children were entitled to a safe, inclusive & accepting school environment free from fear and hate." But would not Islamic teaching about the death penalty for homosexuality be something that might also contribute to the "fear and hate" that a child might feel?

Canadian authorities during the tenure of Justin Trudeau as Prime Minister did not appear disposed to consider that possibility. Nor did much of anyone else.

Why Is This Happening?

The facts remain, however unwelcome they may be. Tarring me or anyone else who spoke out about the Sharia mistreatment of gays an "anti-Muslim extremist" or an "Islamophobe" doesn't change the content of Sharia, or the harsh reality for gays living in countries that enforce Sharia in whole or part. It only deflects attention away from the real problem.

What, then, can be made of people such as Bella Waddle, Theresa Sparks, Chris Stedman, and others like them, who apparently consider calling attention to Islam's death penalty for homosexuality to be more morally repugnant and worthy of condemnation than that death penalty itself?

I must confess that I find their position baffling, but it is likely attributable at least in part to the common human tendency to find the near enemy more urgently to be fought than the far enemy, even if the far enemy is, in the long run, more lethal. Waddle, Sparks, and Stedman, and others like them, have experienced opposition, and perhaps even distaste or open hostility, from conservatives for the choices they have made in life about aspects of their core identity. It is unlikely, however, that they have encountered Islamic jihadis or even Sharia supremacists who are willing to confront them openly. They weren't in the Pulse nightclub. They weren't contacted on a dating app by Ali Muhammad Brown. And so the Islamic disapproval of gays, and the Sharia death penalty for homosexual activity, remain abstractions for them. Conservative Christians, by contrast, are all too real.

There is a deeper reason, however, that is related to that one. Gay and transgender activists may be aware of the Sharia mistreatment of gays, but they don't say anything about it, and disapprove of those who do, because of "Islamophobia." Opposition to jihad terror and to Sharia oppression of gays and others is identified in the United States and Europe of the early twenty-first century as a conservative, "right-wing" issue. And there is that near enemy again. Should gays in the West today join conservatives, including Christian conservatives, in standing against Islamic oppression of gays and its call for violence against them? To do so would not only mean uniting with the enemy they hate the most, but it would also mean ostracism and vilification from the members of their community who refused to go along with them.

Few people are willing to take a stand that will lose them all their friends and possibly endanger their professional prospects as well. It has become socially unacceptable on the Left to speak out against the victimization of gays as it is sanctioned under Islamic law. Muslims are victims in the Leftist paradigm. To point out the devastation wrought by jihad and Sharia is "Islamophobic." And that's all there is to it.

Meanwhile, gays in Islamic countries are dying. And who is taking notice of that fact?

Not the American Left. The "Queers Against Islamophobia" position is dominant among those on the Left, as absurd as it is. In July 2015, *Foreign Policy* magazine, the flagship publication of the foreign policy establishment, even went so far as to proclaim that the Islamic State, an entity that frequently put homosexuals to death, recommended that the key to defeating this bloodthirsty terrorist organization was…gay marriage. In an article entitled "Can Gay Marriage Defeat the Islamic State? A few—admittedly sappy—thoughts on the power of #LoveWins," Rosa Brooks argued that the terrifying terror entity can indeed be overcome by the awesome power of the rainbow.

Brooks was no insignificant personage; she is a law professor at Georgetown University and was a counselor to the Obama administration's defense undersecretary for policy from 2009 to 2011, as well as a senior advisor at the State Department.

"Do you want to fight the Islamic State and the forces of Islamic extremist terrorism?" Brooks asked her readers, and then gave them the good news: "I'll tell you the best way to send a message to those masked gunmen in Iraq and Syria and to everyone else who gains power by sowing violence and fear. Just keep posting that second set of images"—that is, images of gay marriage supporters celebrating the Supreme Court's ruling legalizing gay marriage.[86] "Post them," Brooks commanded, "on Facebook and Twitter and Reddit and in comments all over the Internet. Send them to your friends and your family. Send them to your pen pal in France and your old roommate in Tunisia. Send them to strangers."[87]

How did Brooks get the idea that the mass posting of photos of gay marriage supporters would conquer the Islamic State? Because "that's the lesson of history: Brutality and fear can keep people down for only so long. The Nazis learned this; the Soviets learned it; the Ku Klux Klan learned it; Pol Pot learned it; the Rwandan génocidaires learned it. One of these days, the Islamic State and al Qaeda will learn it too."[88]

It is much, much more likely that the Islamic State would see the Supreme Court decision on gay marriage as evidence of the U.S.'s decadence and societal decay, and that will only serve to embolden and encourage them. But there was another glaring fallacy in this "analysis": if the Nazis and Soviets and KKK and Pol Pot and Rwandan génocidaires ever really learned that "brutality and fear can keep people down for only so long," they didn't learn it in the way Brooks seems to have thought they did.[89]

It was hard to tell how, exactly, she thought they learned this. By viewing photos of gay rights supporters? Or of loving couples of whatever persuasion? Did a photo of an embracing couple move Adolf Hitler to tears and induce him to call his genocidal armies back home and close the extermination camps? Did a photo of smiling people make Pol Pot realize that his stacks and shelves full of skulls were a terrible mistake, and lead him to resign and spend the rest of his life as a florist?

No. This kind of thing never happened, and by no stretch of the imagination is it the "lesson of history." If the Nazis ever learned that "#LoveAlwaysWins," they learned it in the blood and chaos and ruin of Berlin, as Soviet troops ran wild and raped every young German woman they could catch. #LoveAlwaysWins, indeed. The groups Brooks names learned that #LoveAlwaysWins, if they ever learned it, at the point of a gun, when they were forced by violence to stop what they were doing.

Yes, even the Klan was prosecuted in the "racist" United States. The only exception to this is the Soviet Union, but Mikhail Gorbachev didn't oversee the dissolution of the Soviet Union because he realized that the United States was not an enemy, but just a big gay hunk of love. The Soviet Union collapsed under the economic pressure that Ronald Reagan brought to bear upon it, and the societal/cultural pressure that Pope John Paul II and Lech Walesa brought upon it. It might still exist today if Walesa hadn't been willing to risk his life in the Gdansk Shipyard.

And that's what will defeat the Islamic State and other jihadis today: people willing to risk their lives to safeguard the dignity and freedom of every human being. But those who are willing to do that are the very ones who, in a case of suicidal short-sightedness, are generally vilified as "racists" and "bigots" by the supporters of gay marriage.

Love, apparently, doesn't always win.

CHAPTER 5

THE THREAT TO JEWS

I'M A VILLAIN NOT ONLY to many Muslims, but to many Jews as well.

The Anti-Defamation League (ADL) claims that I have an "established record of anti-Muslim activism" and push "conspiratorial views."[1] In 2011, the ADL's then-national director, Abraham Foxman, charged that I "promote a conspiratorial anti-Muslim agenda under the pretext of fighting radical Islam."[2]

When Canada's Jewish Defence League invited me to speak in Calgary in April 2016, a group of Muslims, Christians, and Jews denounced me, claiming that I represented "the forces of intolerance, racism, and Islamophobia." The coalition added: "We strongly disavow the dangerous message of Mr. Spencer and call upon Calgarians of all faiths and backgrounds to pursue the path of religious literacy and to support efforts to build bridges of respect and understanding between the diverse communities that make our city a vibrant and cooperative model of the Canadian value of multiculturalism."[3]

One of the Jewish signers of this manifesto, Rabbi Shaul Osadchey of Calgary's Beth Tzedec Congregation, told CBC News rather implausibly: "We're not trying to prohibit him from speaking." He explained: "Our concern is that this kind of speech then puts in people's minds different perceptions about the community and

I don't…I know that the Jewish community does not support his point of view in the main. There are obviously some people that find him to be credible, but by and large he's been discredited by human rights and civil rights organizations throughout North American, prominently the Anti-Defamation League and the Southern Poverty Law Centre in the States."[4]

Denounced, yes. Discredited? Only if concern about jihad terror and Sharia oppression is really "conspiratorial," and not grounded in fact.

The rise of anti-Semitic incidents in the United States, however, suggests that something more is going on than mere paranoid conspiracy theories.

For many observers, both Jewish and non-Jewish, however, these incidents are all Donald Trump's fault.

After all, who else could possibly be responsible?

Trump's Fault?

After a rash of threats against synagogues, when President Trump condemned anti-Semitism in February 2017, CNN was still skeptical of his motives: "scores of people still took issue with how long the statement took. It left many wondering just why he delayed taking a seemingly obvious moral course for a president in the face of bomb threats at 48 JCCs in 26 states in January and rising fears of widening nationwide anti-Semitism after additional incidents this month."[5]

CNN and other establishment media outlets pushed the narrative that Trump himself, by supposedly energizing the "far-Right," was ultimately responsible for this rise in anti-Semitism; neither CNN nor any of its colleagues, however, shed any significant light upon a much more likely cause of the anti-Semitism: the increasing presence of Muslims in the U.S.

Skeptics could see the correctness of this assessment simply by looking at what was happening at Europe.

The New Europe, Same as the Old Europe

What is beginning to happen in the U.S. is already in full swing in Europe, where Jews have in recent years been menaced more than at any time since World War II. The calls for this treatment not infrequently come from the mosques.

On March 31, 2017, Mundhir Abdallah, an imam in Copenhagen, was filmed preaching a Friday sermon at the al-Faruq Mosque in which he quoted a notorious statement attributed to Muhammad, the prophet of Islam, saying that the Last Day "will not come unless the Muslims fight the Jews and the Muslims kill them."[6]

Abdallah was not referring to a twisted, hijacked version of the true, peaceful Islam. The saying of Muhammad to which he referred is found in a collection of hadith, reports on Muhammad's words and deeds, that Islamic scholars consider to be authentic. It depicts Muhammad saying: "Abu Huraira reported Allah's Messenger (may peace be upon him) as saying: The last hour would not come unless the Muslims will fight against the Jews and the Muslims would kill them until the Jews would hide themselves behind a stone or a tree and a stone or a tree would say: Muslim, or the servant of Allah, there is a Jew behind me; come and kill him; but the tree Gharqad would not say, for it is the tree of the Jews."[7]

Abdallah also hailed the coming caliphate, the single unified state of the Muslims worldwide, and said that it would wage jihad in order to liberate Jerusalem "from the filth of the Zionists," and by so doing, "the words of the Prophet Muhammad will be fulfilled."[8]

Dan Rosenberg, a leader of Copenhagen's Jewish community, was understated when he said: "We are concerned weak and impressionable people may perceive this kind of preaching as a clear call to violence and terror against Jews."[9] Also boding ill for the future was the fact that Abdallah's words were not taken amiss by the worshippers at the al-Faruq Mosque. A reporter from Denmark's TV 2 went to the mosque on May 11, 2017 and spoke to worshippers there for two hours. But he wasn't able to find anyone who would denounce the genocidal anti-Semitism of Mundhir Abdallah.[10]

One Muslim at the mosque said of Abdallah, "I do not think he's hurting anything."[11] Another tried to convince the reporter that Islam forbids killing, but did not address the clear call to kill in Abdallah's words. Denmark's Immigration and Integration Minister, Inger Støjberg, noted correctly: "Had this happened in a Danish folk church, then there would have been people in the congregation who stood up and protested."[12] Of Abdallah's words, Støjberg remarked: "This is completely preposterous, undemocratic and awful."[13]

But neither Inger Støjberg nor anyone else seemed able or willing to do anything effective to prevent further "preposterous, undemocratic and awful" statements from being made, and even worse, to prevent Muslims from acting upon them. And they were. Italian journalist Giulio Meotti noted in March 2017 that "the European Union Agency for Fundamental Rights revealed that a third of the Jews of the Old Continent has stopped wearing religious symbols because of fear of attacks. The president of the Jewish Consistory of Marseille, Zvi Ammar, asked the Jews 'not to wear the yarmulke in the street so as not to be recognized as Jews.' "[14]

In one sadly typical incident, a 14-year-old Jewish student at the Friedenauer Gemeinschaftsschule in Berlin was driven out of the school by repeated threats and beatings from Muslim students. "I loved the fact that the school was multicultural...the kids and teachers were so cool," the boy recalled.[15] But after he enrolled in November 2016, things quickly went wrong: once he mentioned that he was Jewish, everything changed. "First my Turkish friend Emre said he could no longer hang out with me because I was Jewish. Then other pupils started saying stereotypical things about how Jews only want money and hate Muslims."[16]

The Muslim students began to abuse him verbally, and then to beat him. "This boy, Jassin, whose parents are Palestinian, asked me if I'm from Israel. I've never been to Israel. He said Palestine will burn Israel and his friends said Turkey will burn Israel. He kept kicking me. One day he came up to me from behind and he punched me in the back. I became dizzy...I had a bruise for a week or two. Every time something bad happened, I told myself I could manage it, but it only got worse."[17] The beatings became a daily occurrence.

The boy's family was appalled; they had chosen the school because of its large number of immigrant students, and had themselves recently hosted a Syrian refugee in their home. But their multicultural bona fides were of no avail, and they pulled their son out of the school. The Central Council of Jews in Germany called the boy's treatment at the school "anti-Semitism of the ugliest form."[18] Aaron Eckstaedt of the Moses Mendelssohn Jewish High School in Berlin, said that Jewish parents frequently contacted him to transfer their children to his school, "in reaction to anti-Semitic statements coming overwhelmingly from Arabic or Turkish classmates."[19]

The situation has deteriorated to the extent that in Paris, according to Meotti, "Jews are advised to 'walk in groups,' never alone." Accordingly, "40,000 Jews have left France in the last fifteen years, one-tenth of the whole French population. In the tolerant, liberal and democratic West, where Muslim minorities have become more and more assertive, Jews have become more and more 'invisible.' The European Jewish Congress has publicized a shocking poll: 'A third of the European Jews think of emigrating.' That is 700,000 people."[20]

European authorities, predictably, are doing what they can to keep this quiet. On April 4, 2017, a Muslim named Kobili Traore entered the apartment of one of his neighbors, a 66-year-old Jewish woman named Sarah Halimi. While screaming "Allahu akbar" and calling Halimi "Satan" and "dirty Jew," he began to torture her, and ultimately threw her out of her apartment window to her death.[21]

Two months later, eighteen prominent French citizens, including historian Georges Bensoussan and philosopher Alain Finkielkraut, joined Frédérique Ries, a member of the European Parliament from Belgium, to lodge a public protest of the fact that the Paris Prosecutor's Office did not charge Traore with a hate crime, and did not mention anti-Semitism in his indictment.

"French authorities," said Ries, "have treated her murder with icy silence. No national mobilization for Sarah, she died as the media remained quasi-indifferent."[22] She pointed out that Traore was not charged with a hate crime, and was confined to a mental institution, even though he showed no signs of mental illness. Some speculated that French authorities glossed over the uncomfortable facts of this case in order not to give ammunition to the presidential campaign of Marine Le Pen, who was calling for an end to France's open-door immigration policies.[23]

Reining in Marine Le Pen and the "far-right" was more important to French authorities than reining in the likes of Kobili Traore.

The same denial prevailed in Britain. In June 2017, a Muslim was arrested after he wandered through Stamford Hill, a predominantly Jewish area of London screaming "Allah, Allah" and "I'm going to kill you all."[24] Like Kobili Traore, he was deemed mentally ill. A police spokesman explained: "He was detained by officers under the Mental Health Act. No one was injured. This is not being treated as terror-related."[25]

Of course. If it were treated as terror-related, it might give fuel to Britain's "far-right."

Yet the situation was becoming precarious for Jews all over Europe not because of the "far right," but because of the increased Muslim presence there. Could the same thing happen in the United States? On a smaller scale, it is already happening. It isn't I who am responsible for, in the words of Rabbi Osadchey, putting "in people's minds different perceptions about the community"; if anyone has the idea that there is a problem of anti-Semitism among Muslims, it isn't because of me, but because of the many Muslims who have violently attacked Jews.

Anti-Semitic Incitement in the U.S.

The incitement is certainly there. Then-Ohio resident and Muslim Brotherhood member Sheikh Salah Sultan also referred to the notorious genocidal hadith in a 2008 sermon: "The stone which is thrown at the Jews hates these Jews, these Zionists, because Allah foretold, via His Prophet Muhammad, that Judgment Day will not come before the Jew and the Muslim fight. The Jew will hide behind stones and trees, and the stone and the tree will speak, saying: 'Oh Muslim, there is a Jew behind me, come and kill him.' The only exception will be the Gharqad tree.... The stone's self-awareness is such that it can distinguish Muslims from Jews."[26]

One of the foremost Islamic advocacy groups in the country, the Muslim American Society (MAS), has featured on the website of its Minnesota chapter anti-Semitic, pro-jihad quotations from the Islamic prophet Muhammad:

- "If you gain victory over the men of Jews, kill them."
- "The Hour will not be established until you fight with the Jews, and the stone behind which a Jew will be hiding will say, 'O Muslim! There is a Jew hiding behind me, so kill him.' "
- "May Allah destroy the Jews, because they used the graves of their prophets as places of worship."[27]

In December 2000, MAS President Esam S. Omeish was videotaped at a rally in Washington openly endorsing the bloody Palestinian jihad against Israeli civilians: "We the Muslims of the Washington Metropolitan area are here today in sub-freezing temperatures to tell our brothers and sisters in Palestine that you have learned the way, that you have known that the jihad way is the way to liberate your land... We are with you, we are supporting you and we will do everything that we can, insha'Allah [Allah willing], to help your cause.'"[28]

On February 25, 2013, Muslim writer Reza Aslan, renowned as a hip, secular Muslim, tweeted: "Let the Third Intifada commence."

The First (1987–1993) and Second (2000–2005) Intifadas (literally "shaking off," or "uprisings") were escalations of the Palestinian jihad against Israel, resulting in numerous jihad attacks against Israeli civilians. To call for an intifada is tantamount to calling for Israelis to be murdered on buses, and in pizza parlors, and while sleeping in their beds—all features of the two previous Intifadas.

At an anti-Israel rally in Boston in July 2014, an unidentified Muslim speaker wearing a keffiyah and a "Palestine" shirt noted with satisfaction that there were no supporters of Israel in the crowd: "They are not here and they will not be here, Inshallah" (Allah willing). "They'll be back to the sea and this time Moses is not going to be here to open the sea. They better learn how to swim." The crowd began to chant "Allahu akbar."[29]

Around the same time in Miami, demonstrators at an anti-Israel rally sponsored by the Council on American-Islamic Relations (CAIR) Florida, the Islamic Circle of North America (ICNA), Students for Justice in Palestine, the American Muslim Association of North America, American Muslims for Emergency & Relief, Syrian American Council of South Florida, and the American Muslims Foundation chanted "From the river to the sea, Palestine will be free," a goal that would require eliminating the Jewish state entirely and killing millions of Jews.[30]

In Arabic, the protesters chanted: "Khaybar, Khaybar, O Jews. Muhammad's army will return." This chant refers to an incident in the life of the Islamic prophet Muhammad, when he attacked and massacred the Jews living at the Arabian oasis of Khaybar. The chant is warning that another massacre will soon ensue. In English, the protesters openly screamed their support for jihad terror: "We are Hamas! We are Jihad! Hamas kicked your ass."[31]

In December 2015, a Michigan-based Palestinian Muslim activist named Lina Allan published a video telling people who opposed Palestinians stabbing Jewish civilians to "go back to watching Turkish soap operas." Allan likened criticizing the stabbing of Jews to defending animal rights "at best." Allan is no bloodthirsty crank; according to the Middle East Media Research Institute (MEMRI), "she represented the State Department's U.S.-Middle East Partnership Initiative (MEPI) in the Jameed Festival in Jordan, according to an interview she gave to the Jordanian Roya TV."[32]

Louis Farrakhan's Nation of Islam also contributed to this climate of anti-Semitism. In February 2017, the Nation held its annual meeting in Detroit, where thousands of Nation members chanted "Allahu akbar" as Farrakhan strode to the podium. Farrakhan took the occasion to bash the Jews: "I want to disabuse the Jews today of the false claim that you are the chosen of God—that Israel or Palestine belongs to you. I want to disabuse you of that. I'm going to tell you about your future. You that think you have power to frighten and dominate the peoples of the world. I'm here to announce the end of your time."

Farrakhan then appeared to conflate this Jew-hatred with the Nation's traditional hatred of white people, giving the impression that the white people who had supposedly oppressed the world's people of color were Jews. For after speaking of the Jews' supposed desire to "dominate the peoples of the world," he thundered: "For 6,000 years, the people of the earth have suffered under a mischief-making rule. Bloodshed and war, hatred and strife, all because a man with a new color—or the lack thereof—thought that he was better than all of those who inhabited the earth before he was even a thought. But I am here to announce today the end of his world and the beginning of a brand new reality that all human beings will enjoy peace, freedom justice and equality under the rule of Allah."[33]

All human beings, that is, except Jews and white people in general.

On November 18, 2016, the imam Abdul Alim Musa, director and founder of the Islamic Institute of Counter-Zionist American Psychological Warfare, preached a Friday sermon at the Al-Islam Mosque in Washington, D.C. that was rife with anti-Jewish paranoia. Recalling the 1993 World Trade Center jihad bombing, he blamed it on "Zionists":

> The Zionists began to bomb, murder, and destroy buildings. In 1993, they did the first World Trade Center [attack] and blamed it on us, and then we got all the security acts that we have now, basically. Then the Muslims began to get scared, and they set the Muslims up real good. We say they created a "Hitlerian"

> environment. A "Hitlerian" environment is an environment in America exactly like the one that existed in Germany before World War II.[34]

Not content to blame the first World Trade Center jihad attack on Jews, Musa blamed them also for the rise to power of Adolf Hitler:

It is the same as Adolf Hitler. Who brought him to power? The Zionists brought him to power so they could maintain their global power. They will bring a fool to power any time they can to do their bidding. Isn't that right? So they brought him to power.[35]

Musa then resorted to the familiar Leftist trope that Israelis were behaving like the Nazis:

> Now, here we are—the innocent Muslims. Who brought him to power? the people who know more about how he operated than anybody in the world, right? Remember the movies we saw about… in the late '40s… throughout the '50s and '60s—the old movies on TV. They all talk about how the Nazis took over towns, and group punishment, and all of that. Do you know that the Zionists treat the Palestinians—word for word, minute for minute, letter for letter—exactly like the Nazis treated the Europeans? Exactly. No miss at all… He treats Palestinians exactly [the same way]—that is the Zionist.[36]

And not just the Palestinians:

> What's the final analysis? Because the world is being threatened by Zionists… They divide the people all up, and we are going to unify all the people. We are going to invite people to Islam… It may be a little sweetie-pie Islam, but it will be fine. It's good enough. We have to rescue the poor, dumb American people….[37]

This paranoia was not singular to Musa. In December 2016, a federal grand jury in San Antonio, Texas indicted a 21-year-old convert to Islam, Gavin Friedman, on charges that he had threatened to murder Barack Obama. In January 2016, Friedman wrote to

Obama saying that he was going to kill him so that he himself could be martyred in the name of Allah. Three months later, according to the indictment, Friedman wrote again to the President, "specifically stating that he is going to assassinate Obama because Obama is a puppet for (ZOG) Zionist Organized Government."[38] The idea that Obama was a tool of Israel is a staple of Islamic jihadi polemic against the United States; it is unlikely that investigators tried to determine whether or not Friedman had heard such rhetoric in the mosque where he converted to Islam, which is a shame, as it would have been an important and fruitful line of inquiry.

Anti-Semitism on Campus

While the imam Musa likened Israel to the Nazis, Muslims on campus trafficked in Hitlerian rhetoric regarding Jews. The Canary Mission database "was created in order to document people and groups that are promoting hatred of the USA, Israel and the Jewish people." In February 2017, Canary Mission released an astonishing dossier of statements made by Muslim students at the University of Texas, Arlington (UTA), including "Jews only live once" and "stuff Jews in the oven." The dossier noted that "24 UTA students and graduates have likened Israel to Nazi Germany, called for violence against Jews and both denied and championed the Holocaust in Facebook and Twitter posts. [The] majority of the posts come from former and current students affiliated with the school's chapters of Students for Justice in Palestine (SJP) and Muslim Student Association (MSA)."

One Muslim student at UTA, Ismail Said Aboukar, who was a member of both the SJP and the MSA, denied the Holocaust, referring to it as "#LiesToldInSchool," but appeared to wish that it had actually happened, writing that the "world would be sooo much better without jews man [sic]."

Another SJP member, Nancy Salem, retweeted a joke that asked: "How many Jews died in the Holocaust?" and then answered: "Not enough, HAHAHAHA."[39]

Abdul Kareem Alkady is a registered nurse at the Erie County Medical Center in Buffalo, New York, and a former member of the Muslim Student Association at the University of Buffalo. Although he is a nurse, he really wants to kill Jews:

My life calling is to take down these Jews! And if yu become one of them then I'm sorry...yur next!!"

On October 14, 2014, Alkady tweeted: "Look at the Jewish guys face? Wallah I would just punch him right in the fuckin jaw.... The hate I have towards Zionists and people that support Israel is growing. It's consuming me wallah."

The student senate of the University of California at Davis on January 29, 2015 passed an SJP-sponsored resolution calling on the university to divest from "corporations that aid in the Israeli occupation of Palestine and illegal settlements in Palestinian territories, violating both international humanitarian law and international human rights." One of the student senators who voted for the resolution, a Muslim named Azka Fayyaz, wrote on Facebook that "Hamas & Sharia law have taken over UC Davis."[40]

Celebrating a murderous jihad terror group was bad enough, but some Muslims on campus took the intimidation even further. In April 2016, Israeli politician Tzipi Livni spoke as part of a panel discussion at Harvard University, where a leader of Harvard's Muslim student community, Harvard Law School student Husam El-Qoulaq (who had a long history of anti-Israel activism), disrupted the panel by asking: "I'm question [sic] about the odor of Tzipi Livni, very smelly, and I was just wondering."[41]

After the ensuing firestorm, El-Qoulaq felt compelled to issue an apology, in which he claimed: "I would never, ever, ever call anyone, under any circumstances, a 'smelly Jew'. Such a comment is utterly repugnant, and I am absolutely horrified that some readers have been led to believe that I would ever say such a thing. With regards to what I actually did say, I can see now, after speaking with the authors of this article and many other members of the Jewish community at HLS, how my words could have been interpreted as a reference to an anti-Semitic stereotype, one that I was entirely unaware of prior to the publication of this article."[42]

Despite El-Qoulaq's manifest rudeness and obnoxiousness, and the implausibility of his apology, Harvard did everything it could to protect his identity. *The Daily Caller* reported: "But despite the fact that the 'smelly' question was made at a very public event with numerous eyewitnesses, Harvard and others have tried very hard to suppress El-Qoulaq's identity. His name wasn't included in [Harvard Law School Dean Martha] Minow's email condemnation, it wasn't added to his apology in the Harvard Law Record (despite his invitation to have offended Harvard students reach out to him), and a video recording of the event was even censored to take out his question, thereby preventing it from aiding in his identification."[43]

Would Harvard Law School have been so quick to protect the identity of a non-Muslim student who asked a Muslim politician why he or she was so "smelly?" The answer is obvious.

El-Qoulaq was simply hateful; other Muslim students on campus have gone further.

Thuggery on Campus

Many of the Muslims openly writing this hatred of Jews on social media sites were members of Muslim campus groups. In February 2010 at the University of California, Irvine (UCI), one of these Muslim groups went beyond mere talk. The Israeli ambassador to the U.S., Michael Oren, attempted to give a speech there on relations between the United States and Israel but was ultimately unable to do so. After Muslim students heckled and interrupted him repeatedly, he left the stage.

Before Oren appeared, the UCI Muslim Student Union (MSU) chapter had issued a statement that read, in part:

> As people of conscience, we oppose Michael Oren's invitation to our campus. Propagating murder is not a responsible expression of free speech....

> We strongly condemn the university for cosponsoring, and therefore, inadvertently supporting the ambassador of a state that is condemned by more UN Human Rights Council resolutions than all other countries in the world combined....

Oren took part in a culture that has no qualms with terrorizing the innocent, killing civilians, demolishing their homes, and illegally occupying their land. Oren is an outspoken supporter of the recent war on Gaza and stands in the way of international law by refusing to cooperate with the United Nation's Goldstone Report, a fact-finding mission endorsed by the UN Human Rights Council.[44]

The statement repeated Palestinian charges against Israel, claiming that the Jewish state had "massacred" fourteen hundred people in Gaza.[45] This was an extremely dubious charge, as was the assumption that the United Nations, in its incessant condemnations of Israel, was a neutral and impartial observer.

The most important aspect of the MSU statement, however, was not its claims about Israel and Gaza, but its assumption that the university was "inadvertently supporting" Oren's views just by cosponsoring the event. This was a complete rejection of the idea of the university as a place where all ideas can be discussed and accepted or rejected on their own merits. As far as the Muslim Student Union was concerned, giving someone a platform was tantamount to endorsing his views—so only those with acceptable opinions should be given a platform.

But applying that principle would mean turning universities into one-party states in which only one point of view is allowed. Surely on a university campus, if anywhere, airing opposing views should be viewed not as an intolerable affront but as an opportunity to grow intellectually and to learn to engage opposing viewpoints in a mature and effective manner.

In September 2011, seven Muslim students from UCI and three from the University of California, Riverside, were found guilty of disrupting Oren's speech and sentenced to informal probation and community service. But that hardly put a crimp in the anti-free speech campaign on campus. Shakeel Syed of the Islamic Shura Council of Southern California called the verdict "absolutely unbelievable…I believe the heart of America has died today."[46] Defenders of the students likened them to Martin Luther King, Jr., and Rosa Parks.[47] Many on the Left, sympathetic to the Palestinian cause, doubtless agreed.

But District Attorney Tony Rackauckas was more on point when he said: "History requires us to draw a line in the sand against this sort of organized thuggery."[48]

Instead, the thuggery just became more brazen. At Temple University in August 2014, SJP members called Daniel Vessal, a Camera on Campus fellow and a member of the Jewish fraternity AEPi, "kike" and "baby killer," and punched him in the face. Vessal explained that it all happened because he was trying to initiate a genuine dialogue:

> I'm walking down Polett Walk, one of the main walkways through Temple University and I see the SJP table. I go up to them and I really just wanted to see what angle they were coming from. I went up to the table and started talking to them. I said, "listen, you shouldn't be protesting Israel—if anything protest the terrorists."
>
> At that point I walked away and after a little back and forth. I came back to the table after a little while and explained that the Palestinians have a right to a state just like anyone else but that SJP should come at the right people. I said, "when Hamas stops sending the rockets, that's when there can be peace. That's when we can start."
>
> This one girl sitting at the end of the table was just laughing and laughing at me. As she was laughing at me, people at the table were calling me a "baby killer," I said when she stops then maybe we could have a genuinely peaceful conversation.
>
> And then this kid just rocks me in the face as hard as he can. My glasses flew off. After a two-second blur I had no clue what had happened. I couldn't believe the kid actually hit me.

> When the police came over and were filing the report the kids at the table were screaming "You Zionist pig, you racist, that's what you get." If anything, I thought they would be apologetic for someone in their organization doing something like that.[49]

Police did not arrest the attacker. Vessal remarked: "I don't understand why after physical assault he just got sent home. This was not anti-Israel at all, it was completely anti-Semitic." Police also refused to shut down the SJP's information table. Witnesses confirmed that SJP called Vessal a "kike" after he was hit. One remarked: "Out of nowhere, a member of the group strikes Daniel, straight in the jaw with a closed fist. This led to Daniel going straight to the ground, losing his glasses and in immediate pain. While on the ground, the members in this group were just pointing at Daniel and were laughing at him. In addition, names including kike, stupid Jew, and Zionist, were used by the members in reference to Daniel."[50]

Vessal concluded: "Before this I just thought Students for Justice in Palestine was crazy but I didn't know it would lead to violence."[51]

According to *The Jerusalem Post*, "In 2015, more than 30 organizations, including Jewish fraternity AEPI, the Simon Wiesenthal Center and the Zionist Organization of America wrote to University of California regent Bruce D. Varner in July, requesting that substantive measures be taken to combat rising anti-Semitism on UC-affiliated campuses."[52]

No substantive measures were taken. In May 2016, Eliana Kopley, a sophomore at the University of California at Irvine (UCI), was trying to enter a screening of an Israeli documentary about the IDF called *Beneath the Helmet* when she was accosted by an angry mob screaming "Long live the Intifada!" and "Fuck Israel!"[53] The protesters prevented her from entering the building where the film was being shown, and even chased her into a nearby building, where they pounded on the doors and windows while continuing to scream their slogans. Police ultimately escorted Kopley into the screening.[54]

The UCI chapter of Students for Justice in Palestine was thrilled with this thuggery, and praised the mob.[55]

Likewise in a November 2015 rally organized by Students for Justice in Palestine (SJP) at Hunter College, a campus of the City University of New York (CUNY), protesters brandishing signs reading "Boycott Israel" and "Zionists out of CUNY" screamed at Jewish students: "Zionists go home!," "Zionists out of CUNY!," "Jews out of CUNY!," "Get out of America!," and "We should drag the Zionist down the street!"[56] In February 2016 at Brooklyn College, a group of hard-Left students burst into a Faculty Council meeting and began chanting "Zionists off campus!"[57] When a Jewish professor tried to get students to end their disruption of a Faculty Council meeting at Brooklyn College, they called him a "Zionist pig."[58]

The Muslim students' behavior toward Oren and at Hunter College was rapidly becoming the norm across U.S. campuses: it was becoming unsafe to be pro-Israel at an American university. As colleges grow more authoritarian in their Leftism, they are becoming increasingly inhospitable to students who oppose the Left's pet causes. The pro-Palestinian "Israeli Apartheid Week" has become an increasingly common feature of campus life, with students and adult speakers denouncing Israel for its supposed "ethnic cleansing" of Palestinians and "apartheid policies over the Palestinian people."[59] Israeli Apartheid Week often features a good deal of grievance theater, with pro-Palestinian students constructing mock "apartheid walls" and "Israeli checkpoints."

This is not an atmosphere conducive to open discussion and debate. Tammi Rossman-Benjamin, cofounder and director of the Israel advocacy AMCHA Initiative, explains that "Israeli Apartheid Week is a tremendous source of anti-Semitic expression and incitement of hatred for the Jewish state and Jews generally. Frequently during Israeli Apartheid Week and BDS campaigns, Jewish students are singled out, harassed, intimidated and even assaulted, regardless of their feelings on Israel. Jewish students report feeling afraid to display their Jewish Star necklaces, wear their Jewish sorority or fraternity letters, or walk to Hillel for Shabbat dinner during these heightened weeks."[60]

The Times of Israel described typical features of Israeli Apartheid Week: "As SJP's most publicized anti-Israel fest, IAW icons include the ugly gray apartheid wall, usually covered in 'facts' to demonize Israel; mock Israeli military 'check-points' set up to 'simulate' the daily lives of Palestinians, and ubiquitous calls to 'de-normalize' relations with Israel and implement BDS (Boycott, Divestment and Sanctions) against the Jewish state. (IAW is held in various countries worldwide between February and April; in the US this year, it is largely taking place between March 27 and April 3.)."[61]

Journalist Daniel Mael explained the SJP's larger agenda:

> Instead of promoting justice, SJP and/or its members spend almost all of their energy demonizing Israel, advocating for its eventual destruction, showing an unfortunate affinity for pro-terrorist figures, bullying and intimidating pro-Israel and Jewish students with vicious and sometimes anti-Semitic rhetoric, and even at times engaging in physical violence. While SJP may pay lip-service to peaceful aims, their rhetoric and actions make it hard to avoid the conclusion that a culture of hatred permeates nearly everything the group does—making the college experience increasingly uncomfortable, at times even dangerous, for Jewish or pro-Israel students. Perhaps equally disturbing is the limited response from university authorities that have an obligation to prevent such attacks and protect Jewish students.[62]

Amid all this, the U.S. Departments of Justice and Education urged educators to be vigilant and act decisively against bullying—of Muslims.[63] Bullying *by* Muslims didn't seem to concern them: as Jewish groups complained of on-campus harassment, Muslims and Leftists continued their push to shut down speech, with the Muslim Students Association (MSA) chapter at San Diego State University (SDSU) demanding that administrators implement a "zero tolerance policy explicitly for Islamophobic speech and actions."[64]

According to the College Fix, an online journal chronicling campus Leftism and authoritarianism, the SDSU MSA demanded not only restrictions on "Islamophobic speech," but "mandatory bystander training . . . more courses on Islam, and increase[d] funding for The Center for Intercultural Relations."[65] The MSA, fluently speaking the language of the politically correct Left, also demanded that "the SDSU administration address, alleviate, and eliminate systems of oppression that disproportionately target students of color, womyn, and all marginalized students on campus."[66]

But not the real marginalized students on campus: Jews and supporters of Israel.

Some professors were no better than the students. Abdullah Al-Arian, a history professor at Georgetown University and son of the convicted Palestinian Islamic Jihad leader Sami Al-Arian, took to Twitter in August 2014 to liken Israel to ISIS. Abdullah Al-Arian has previously expressed open support for the jihad terror group Hamas, saying with satisfaction at one point that its attacks on Israel were "exceeding all expectations." He blamed Israel and the U.S., rather than Hamas itself, for its bloodlust: "If we really take a very close look at the chronology of events that have led to this latest Israeli offensive against Gaza, we would find that actually Hamas has not chosen the option of a military or violent confrontation with Israel. It was Israel and to a certain extent even the United States that undermined that unity government. And it was only after Israel broke the ceasefire, and of course we know all about the reports of the different killings and bombings that Hamas then chose the second option or was confronted essentially with an attempt by Israel to destroy it and Gaza to destroy its presence there."[67]

In August 2015, Kaukab Siddique, an associate professor of English at Lincoln University in Oxford, Pennsylvania, called activist Pamela Geller and other defenders of the freedom of speech "dirty Jewish Zionist thugs" in the wake of the American Freedom Defense Initiative's Muhammad Art Exhibit and Cartoon Contest that was attacked by Islamic jihadis in Garland, Texas, on May 3, 2015.

When asked about his remark, Siddique declared: "I would say it again," explaining that by defying Sharia blasphemy law and drawing Muhammad, Geller "did the worst, other than killing us." The free speech event in Garland was, Siddique said, "cultural genocide."

In saying this, Siddique was tacitly endorsing the jihad attack against the event, which, if successful, could have resulted in the deaths of several hundred people. Shortly after the event, when the Islamic State (ISIS) issued a fatwa calling for Geller to be murdered, Siddique again sided with the jihadis, writing on Facebook:

> Very cleverly, the corporate media are trying to present the Texas situation as ISIS vs. Geller. The Prophet Muhammmad [sic], pbuh, is the [sic] leader of the ENTIRE UMMAH, not just of ISIS. Two of ISIS gave their lives for the honor of the Prophet, pbuh. We can't do that, but the law of this land gives us the right to speak out. ISNA, ICNA and CAIR think you can simply ignore blasphemy. Millions embraced Islam because of Malcolm. Imagine what America's oppressed people think of us when we don't speak even when our greatest sanctity is violated? Muslims, we are waiting for Allah's wrath to descend on us.[68]

Attacks, Thwarted Plots, and Threats of Violence

All this incendiary rhetoric was bound to incite some Muslims to act against Jews.

In May 2009, four Muslims were arrested for plotting to blow up two Bronx synagogues and bring down an airplane. The plot demonstrated anew the virulence and ugliness of Islamic anti-Semitism. Said one plotter: "If Jews were killed in this attack ... that would be all right." Plotter James "Abdul Rahman" Cromitie, a jailhouse convert to Islam, said: "I hate those motherfuckers, those fucking Jewish bitches.... I would like to get [destroy] a synagogue."[69] He thundered that "the worst brother in the whole Islamic world is better than 10 billion *Yahudi* [Jews]."[70]

Abdalah Mohamed, a Muslim teenager and immigrant from Kenya, in July 2014 walked into Ira's Deli in Portland, Oregon, and asked to buy a single cigarette. The clerk told him that they didn't sell cigarettes individually, and that he would have to buy a pack, whereupon Mohamed grew angry and demanded to see the owner of the deli, Iraj Rifai. When Rifai also told him that he would have to buy a pack, Mohamed's threats began: "I will blow up your store!...I'm going to send my guys to shoot up your store.... You Israeli ... I'll blow up your store in the name of Allah!...We take care of people like you." While police were investigating the threats, Mohamed called Ira's Deli and left an insulting message.[71]

The following month in New York City, a Jewish couple was walking in Manhattan's Upper East Side when two cars flying Palestinian flags and several motorcycles pulled up. The mob began yelling anti-Semitic statements at the couple, threw a water bottle that hit the wife, and punched the husband when he tried to defend her. Then they drove off.[72]

In October 2014, Leon Nathan Davis III, a convert to Islam in Augusta, Georgia, was arrested at the Atlanta airport, where he had hoped to board a flight to Turkey and make his way to Syria to join the Islamic State (ISIS); he had declared himself "ready for jihad." About a year before his arrest, Davis wrote: "One of my greatest desires is to kill Zionists and bring down Israel and the United States of America." In July 2015, he was sentenced to fifteen years in prison.[73]

In Miami Beach in March 2015, a Muslim named Diego Chaar entered the Orthodox Jewish Ohev Shalom Synagogue. The synagogue's head rabbi, Rabbi Pinchas Weberman, recounted: "A group of young men were outside in the front area, the front lawn, sitting on the benches, and they were approached by somebody who was screaming, 'Allahu akbar. I'm gonna cut your heads off.'"[74]

Chaar later explained: "I want to take them to paradise. I don't want them to burn in hell for the rest of eternity. I feel like that they're worshipping right now is nothing, it's fake. It don't exist, in my opinion." He said he had the "responsibility" to convert the congregants to Islam. "I don't got to force it upon them, but I could offer them my insight, I could offer them what I think is the truth, is the right path to Heaven." When asked why he had threatened to behead the congregants, he insisted, "Oh, I did not say that."[75]

Weberman, however, stuck by his story. "I never like to over-exaggerate, and I don't like to minimize, so what I do is, I report this to law enforcement agencies, those that I feel are responsible for it and those that I feel will take a professional approach to it and handle it. I like the Jewish community to be aware of these things. It's happened in certain places, which it was really a serious thing, and therefore, if they see anything suspicious, they should report it immediately."[76]

On Friday evening, April 29, 2016, FBI agents in Aventura, Florida, set up a sting operation featuring agents pretending to be jihad terrorists to stop a man from throwing a bomb into the Aventura Turnberry Jewish Center, which was crowded on the penultimate day of Passover. A news report on the incident noted obliquely the would-be bomber "may have converted to Islam."[77]

On July 1, 2016, a Phoenix-area Muslim named Mahin Khan told a man who turned out to be an FBI informant that he wanted to carry out a jihad massacre at a Jewish community center, although he eventually settled on a Motor Vehicle Department office in Mesa as his target. He told the informant that he wanted to make pressure cooker bombs, such as the one used in the Boston Marathon jihad bombing in 2013.[78]

In May 2017, a Muslim named Afshin Bahrampour was arrested and charged with arson and burglary in connection with two fires at Chabad of Southern Nevada Desert Torah Academy in Las Vegas. One of the fires was set inside the center, and the other in a car outside it. Fire Department spokesman Tim Szymanski was anxious, like virtually all law enforcement spokesmen these days, to downplay the possibility that this was a manifestation of Islamic anti-Semitism. Szymanski conceded that "at this time, it appears the car fire was intentionally set."[79] However, he continued: "The incident has been referred to as a hate crime. Only a prosecutor can determine if crimes committed can also be classified as a hate crime. That has not been determined at this time."[80]

Of course. In some politically inconvenient cases, it is never determined at all.

Harassment

Aside from large-scale plots, there is ongoing harassment of Jews by Muslims in the United States.

One example of vandalism that occurred in many places nationwide came in July 2014 in Miami Beach, when vandals attacked a private home, egging one car and smearing another with cream cheese, adding the words "Jew" and "Hamas."[81] The reference to Hamas made it likely that the perpetrators were Muslim. Later that same month in North Miami Beach, Muslims defaced a synagogue with spray paint, drawing swastikas and the word "Hamas" at the front entrance.[82] Then in September 2014 in Miami, Muslims painted a swastika along with the words "Iraq" and "Hamas" on a synagogue wall.[83]

In Brooklyn on March 7, 2015, two men, one of whom had the shaved head and long beard that is often characteristic of Muslim hardliners, tried to enter the Beth Yaakob synagogue. They examined the synagogue's surveillance cameras and took pictures of the building before a security guard asked them to leave the premises; an hour later, however, they were spotted in front of another Brooklyn synagogue.[84]

In April 2015, a Muslim named Rizek Musheisen went to the Ahavas Israel Synagogue in Passaic, New Jersey, where he lit firecrackers and screamed "Allahu Akbar."[85]

In October 2015, an Orthodox Jewish woman was pushing a baby carriage outside Bangladesh Muslim mosque in Brooklyn when two Muslim teenagers began throwing bottle caps at her from the mosque. According to JP Updates, "the woman told investigators she thinks stones were thrown out from a window at the mosque."

However, although "the NYPD's Hate Crimes Task Force was initially investigating the incident as a possible bias incident," it ultimately determined that "no bias was involved. The two told investigators that they had no intention to hit anyone. They were not charged with any hate crimes."[86] How the NYPD came to its conclusions was not announced.

On November 14, 2015, a Jewish businessman named Moshe Indig got into a cab in New York City. The driver was a Muslim. Indig recounted the next day:

> I took a cab from Manhattan to Brooklyn yesterday at 8 PM. I asked the driver to make a phone call. He refused but then relented and put the call on the speaker. When he saw that I was speaking Hebrew, he said: "I hate the people and the language you are speaking. If I had known that you were a Jew, I would not have given you the call."
>
> When he dropped me off in Brooklyn I started walking and suddenly he got out of the vehicle and ran toward me and started punching me in the head. I was immediately concerned that he might have a knife or some other weapon, so I hit him forcefully. He grabbed my kippah and my cellphone and ran away.
>
> I was lucky. If he had had a knife, there is no doubt that he would have killed me. His eyes were full of hatred. He turned from a cab driver to a terrorist.[87]

Also in New York City, on November 30, 2015, as lunch hour was ending, a Muslim walked into West Side Judaica store in Manhattan and shouted: "Fuck you Jews, I'll kill you all! I'm a Muslim!" Then he punched a man in the eye and ran out.[88]

Then in Brooklyn on Friday, April 1, 2016, a Muslim named Naquan Smith was spotted wandering the streets of Crown Heights, a neighborhood with a large Lubavitcher Hasidic Jewish population, brandishing a knife and screaming "Allahu akbar" at a Hasidic Jew who was passing by.[89] Also in New York City, in September of the same year, a Muslim named Akram Joudeh ran through rush hour crowds near Penn Station, brandishing a meat cleaver. He was spotted by an off-duty police officer, who tackled him, and whom he gave a six-inch gash on the jaw with the cleaver. Two months before that, Joudeh had come to the attention of police for, like Smith, screaming "Allahu akbar"—in Joudeh's case, outside a synagogue in Brooklyn. Police found two knives in Joudeh's car, but both the New York Police Department and the FBI decided that he was mentally ill, not a jihadi, and so he was free to attack the police officer in September.[90]

Also in September 2016, surveillance cameras caught a woman in Muslim garb as she took photos of the Yeshiva Imeri Yosef Spinka school in Brooklyn and walked all around the grounds, as if on a reconnaissance mission. The NYPD Intelligence Division & Counter-Terrorism Bureau made an attempt to locate and question her, but if they did so, what transpired was not publicized.[91]

The threat continues. Late in February 2017, the Islamic State called upon Muslims in the West to "unleash the pain of the Muslims" upon Jews in Western countries: "IF YOU'RE STILL IN THE WEST! Dress up like a Jew! Go to your nearest Jewish area! Make sure you have plenty of weapons under you coat!"[92]

Given the official indifference to this rising anti-Semitism in the U.S., it was likely that sooner or later, some Muslim would heed this call.

Many Jewish groups have tried to head this off by reaching out in friendship to Muslims. One typical instance of this took place in February 2016 at Temple Rodeph Torah in Marlboro, New Jersey, where Jews invited the local Muslim community over to bake bread and enjoy dinner. The *New Jersey Jewish News* reported happily that "local Jewish and Muslim women who have found that what unites them is greater than what divides them came together to bake hallah, chat, and enjoy traditional foods."[93] One of the Muslim guests, Zakiya Kathawala, explained: "We came here in the interest of tolerance and peace and to learn about each other's religion and culture."[94]

The *New Jersey Jewish News* account contained a telling detail: "When the Jewish women left the sanctuary to begin setting up for dinner, the Muslims stayed behind to lay out mats for their evening prayers facing the ark, which points in the direction of both Jerusalem and Mecca."[95]

How delightfully broad-minded and generous of the Jews to offer their sanctuary for Muslim prayer. But why did the Muslims only pray after the Jews left? Could the Jews have stayed for the Muslim prayers? Ordinarily non-Muslims are not allowed into mosques while Muslims are at prayer (and in this instance, the Temple Rodeph Torah sanctuary was serving as a mosque) unless they are there to hear the message of Islam or for some other purpose that Muslims would consider legitimate. The popular online fatwa site *IslamQA* explains that "if some kuffaar [unbelievers] ask to enter the mosque so that they can see how Muslims pray, so long as they have nothing with them that could make the mosque dirty, and there are no women among them who are dressed in a provocative fashion, or any other reason not to let them in, then there is nothing wrong with allowing them to enter and sit behind the Muslims so they can see how they pray."[96]

Were the Jewish women at Temple Rodeph Torah that night "dressed in a provocative fashion?" It is unlikely that they were covering everything but their face and hands, as Muhammad is depicted in a hadith as commanding. Did one of the visiting Muslims take one of the Temple leaders aside and discreetly explain that they should leave while the Muslims prayed?

And during the Muslim prayers in the Jewish sanctuary that night, were any of the Qur'an's verses depicting Jews as hateful enemies of Allah and the Muslims recited?

Anti-Semitism in the Qur'an

Most analysts ascribe the presence of anti-Semitism among Muslims to anger over Israel's supposed mistreatment of the Palestinians. They ignore, however, the fact that the Qur'an itself contains a great deal of anti-Semitic material. The Muslim holy book depicts the Jews as inveterately evil and bent on destroying the wellbeing of the Muslims. Official Palestinian Authority television in July 2013 featured two girls reciting a poem that included this stanza:

> You who murdered Allah's pious prophets
> Oh, you who were brought up on spilling blood
> You have been condemned to humiliation and hardship
> Oh Sons of Zion, oh most evil among creations
> Oh barbaric monkeys, wretched pigs.[97]

This was a specifically Qur'anic imprecation. The verses about killing the prophets and spilling blood, as well as the idea that the Jews have been condemned to humiliation, echoed Qur'an 3:112; and the monkeys and pigs came from Qur'an 2:62-65; 5:59-60, and 7:166.

Meanwhile, the Qur'an also says that not only have they disbelieved in revelations from Allah and killed the prophets, but they even dare to mock Allah himself: "And the Jews say, 'The hand of Allah is chained.' Chained are their hands, and cursed are they for what they say." They "strive throughout the land corruption, and Allah does not like corrupters." (5:64).

Allah gave food laws to the Jews because of their "wrongdoing," and for "… their averting many from the way of Allah" (4:160), and by doing so, "repaid them for their injustice" (6:146). Some Jews are "avid listeners to falsehood" who "distort words beyond their usages." These are "the ones for whom Allah does not intend to purify their hearts," and they will be punished not just in hellfire but in this life as well: "For them in this world is disgrace, and for them in the Hereafter is a great punishment" (5:41).

Jews dare to deny divine revelation, claiming that "Allah did not reveal to a human being anything," to which Muhammad is told to respond, "Who revealed the Scripture that Moses brought as light and guidance to the people? You [Jews] make it into pages, disclosing some of it and concealing much" (6:91).

In light of all this, it is understandable that Muslims should not get close to such people: "O you who have believed, do not take the Jews and the Christians as allies. They are allies of one another. And whoever is an ally to them among you - then indeed, he is of them. Indeed, Allah guides not the wrongdoing people" (5:51).

What's more, the Jews are "the most intense of the people in animosity toward the believers" (5:82). This, too, resonates in the contemporary Islamic consciousness. In the United States, the Muslim presence is not large enough as yet to require Jews to conceal outward signs of their identity, or to consider emigrating in large numbers. However, there is ample evidence that just such a situation is coming, if Muslim immigration is not reduced. Because Muslims believe that the Qur'an is the perfect guidebook for living in all times and places, it is nothing short of inconceivable that Muslims in the U.S. will give up or reform Qur'anic anti-Semitism. Not only will that fact have consequences; it already has.

So a parting question for Abe Foxman: is all this a "conspiratorial anti-Muslim agenda" or do Jews in the United States (as well as Canada and Europe) have very good reason to be concerned about the increased Muslim presence? Can concern for life and limb, and for the safety and security of one's children and children's children, really all be written off as mere "bigotry?"

Despite the confidence of Rabbi Osadchey that such concerns have been "discredited," they will persist, because some Muslims will continue to victimize Jews because of the hatred and violence taught in the Qur'an and Sunnah. No proliferation of Muslim-Jewish outreach dinners or denunciation of "Islamophobic" voices will change that.

What, then, can I say when someone reminds me that the Anti-Defamation League has me on its enemies' list? Only that perhaps the ADL has not sufficiently appreciated the problem of Islamic anti-Semitism, and I can certainly understand why not: it is one of the most politically incorrect things anyone can do nowadays.

Nonetheless, I can only point out what the ADL is enabling by pointing at me and others like me as the problem, rather than at the problem of Jew-hatred among Muslims. "Islamophobes" aren't victimizing Jews in Europe and the U.S., nor are they victimizing Muslims, for that matter. But the threat of Islamic anti-Semitism is very real. To ignore it, while defaming those who call attention to it, is not going to do anything to make it go away. That the ADL's stance may not turn out in the long run to have been the wisest or most prudent strategy should already be obvious. If it isn't, the next day's headlines will confirm yet again that Jews in Europe and North America face a far greater problem than that which is posed by "Islamophobes."

CHAPTER 6

THE THREAT TO CHRISTIANS

"ISIS Violates the Consensus of Mainstream Islam by Persecuting Christians?"

As Islamic State jihadis rampaged across Syria in the summer of 2015, Islamic apologist Qasim Rashid was quick to condemn them for terrorizing Christians:

> In central Syria, Daesh ("ISIS") recently destroyed an ancient monastery and a church. This, after abducting several Christians, in what has become the group's long scourge on humanity. While global Muslim leaders have categorically condemned Daesh, Daesh continues to insist their acts are permitted—even commanded—by Islam.
>
> But if, as Daesh claims, Islam obliges Muslims to raze monasteries, kidnap Christians and rape women, then several questions arise.
>
> For example, how then did an ancient Christian monastery survive this long? Built in 432, or roughly 180 years before Islam's advent, this monastery withstood nearly 1,500 years of Muslim rule in peace.
>
> Likewise, how did Syria's 2.3 million Christians, or 10 percent of the Syrian population, survive all these centuries? For centuries,

> Muhammad and Muslims have practiced a religion foreign to the one Daesh practices.[1]

The answer to this was very simple, and it wasn't the one that Rashid proffered, that "Muhammad and Muslims have practiced a religion foreign to the one Daesh practices."

The real answer was that Islamic law doesn't command Muslims simply to kill Christians indiscriminately, but to offer them three choices: conversion to Islam; subjugation as dhimmis, denied basic rights under the rule of Islamic authorities; or death. Syria's Christians and the monks of the monastery lived as dhimmis for centuries, until the Ottoman Empire, under Western pressure, abolished the dhimma in the 1850s.

After that, Christians in the Ottoman domains, and the former Ottoman domains after the fall of the empire, enjoyed almost equal rights with the Muslims—until the advent of the Islamic State, which attempted to reassert Islamic law over them.

Even the Islamic State didn't just murder Christians outright, but first ordered them to pay the jizya, the tax specified for the subjugated dhimmis is Qur'an 9:29, and return to dhimmi status. When the Christians refused, they were then considered to be *kuffar harbi*, infidels at war with Islam—an established category in Islamic law—and killed. In every step of this progression, the Islamic State acted in accord with Islamic law, the Qur'an, and Muhammad's example—as illustrated by the words attributed to Muhammad in this hadith: "Fight against those who disbelieve in Allah. Make a holy war... When you meet your enemies who are polytheists, invite them to three courses of action. If they respond to any one of these you also accept it and withhold yourself from doing them any harm. Invite them to (accept) Islam; if they respond to you, accept it from them and desist from fighting against them.... If they refuse to accept Islam, demand from them the Jizya. If they agree to pay, accept it from them and hold off your hands. If they refuse to pay the tax, seek Allah's help and fight them."[2] That's exactly what the Islamic State did.

But most Christians weren't aware of these aspects of Islamic history and theology, and were much more concerned about "Islamophobia" than about any historical or contemporary mistreatment of Christians by Muslims.

Pornographic Trash

The Catholic Church doesn't take kindly to "Islamophobes," and so it doesn't much like me, either.

Nowadays, it seems as if you can reject every element of the Nicene Creed and everything the Church teaches, and still the U.S. Catholic Bishops will consider you a Catholic in good standing if your political opinions are acceptable to them. But it seems that if you believe that Islam is not a religion of peace, you have no place in the U.S. Catholic Church.

To be sure, the Catholic Church is a very large institution. Over the years, I have published two books with Catholic publishing houses, and spoken at several Catholic universities, including DePaul, which has become notorious for its intolerance of dissenting views—and indeed, protesters there demonstrated their own righteousness by chanting slogans and unfurling a banner denouncing me.

But at least they let me speak. The same courtesy was not extended to me by several Roman Catholic bishops, including Robert McManus of Worcester, Massachusetts, Jaime Soto of Sacramento, and Kevin Farrell of Dallas, all of whom stepped in to cancel my appearance at Catholic events where I had been invited to speak.

The Melkite Greek Catholic Eparch of Newton, Massachusetts, Nicholas Samra, refused to grant his permission for me to speak when the hosts of several Catholic events approached him to ask for it (as he was my bishop at the time, they thought it appropriate to gain his approval).

Likewise, in August 2015, I was the keynote speaker at the annual conference of the North American Lutheran Church (NALC) in Dallas. While there, one of the Lutheran leaders told me that the U.S. Conference of Catholic Bishops (USCCB) sent a goodwill ambassador to the NALC conference every year, but when the Catholics discovered that I was the speaker, they withdrew their representative.

I pressed the man who told me this to tell me what reason the USCCB gave for its boycott, but he said they didn't say. Of course, I knew: I was an "Islamophobe."

Bishop Samra explained it to me more fully in an audience he graciously granted me in May 2015 (shortly before he began ignoring all communications from me, however courteous and respectful). As I shifted uncomfortably in his lushly appointed study, he told me a lengthy story about a priest who gave an ignorant Lebanese peasant woman a copy of the Bible; a week later she showed up in his office and threw the book on his desk, telling him he could keep that "pornographic trash." Apparently, the lady had stumbled upon this passage in the Old Testament Book of Ezekiel:

> And the Babylonians came to her into the bed of love, and they defiled her with their lust; and after she was polluted by them, she turned from them in disgust. When she carried on her harlotry so openly and flaunted her nakedness, I turned in disgust from her, as I had turned from her sister. Yet she increased her harlotry, remembering the days of her youth, when she played the harlot in the land of Egypt and doted upon her paramours there, whose members were like those of asses, and whose issue was like that of horses. Thus you longed for the lewdness of your youth, when the Egyptians handled your bosom and pressed your young breasts. (Ezekiel 23:17-21)

The poor lady, Samra told me, had no training in how to understand the Bible. She didn't know anything about allegory. She didn't know anything about metaphor. She looked at that passage and saw only smut.

As I listened to Samra's loquacious and meandering telling of this story, waiting expectantly for it finally to wander toward some conclusion, the point he was trying to make only dawned on me gradually: in Samra's view, *I* was that Lebanese peasant woman. I was, as far as he was concerned, reading the Qur'an and taking it at face value, while lacking the training to understand its deeper meanings as Muslim exegetes have explicated them.

Samra told me that he had studied with the world's foremost Catholic authority on Islam, whose name he could not recall, and that he had come to the realization that at its core, when properly understood, the Qur'an taught peace.

I had been trying to remain respectful in the presence of such an august personage. But at that point, I could not suppress a chuckle.

Then, to explain my unbearable effrontery, I began explaining to him that I didn't offer Qur'an interpretations of my own, but had read and studied the principal mainstream Islamic commentaries on the Qur'an (*tafasir*), as well as all six of the canonical hadith collections, the reports of Muhammad's words and deeds, which, when deemed authentic, are considered normative for Islamic law.

I was, I explained, only trying to illuminate how jihad terrorists justified their actions by pointing to Islamic texts and teachings, and to show that their interpretation of Islam was not a fringe misapprehension of what was at its core a peaceful faith, but a mainstream tradition—a fact that had to be recognized if there was ever to be genuine Islamic reform, as well as coherent and informed counterterror efforts.

To that, Samra had no response, but, as he made clear as he battered me with more windy analogies, he was unmoved.

I was, in his view as he related it to others but did not say to my face, "spreading hate."

It was certainly the fashionable view to espouse, both inside and outside the Catholic Church, but that didn't make it any easier me to accept: I was baffled as I sat on Samra's overstuffed upholstery and gazed at his lavish furnishings while he talked on and on, and remain baffled even now, as to how relating certain incontrovertible, readily demonstrable but unpopular facts constituted "spreading hate."

Nothing Personal, Just Business

The Catholic hierarchy's distaste for me wasn't personal. Nor was it unique to me. American Catholic bishops have treated anyone who spoke the truth about the jihad, including priests, in the same way. In February 2017, Fr. Peter West of St. John's Catholic Church in Orange, New Jersey, aroused controversy by, among other things, observing that moderate Islam (a concept distinct from that of moderate Muslims) was "a myth."

Jim Goodness, an Orwellian-named spokesman for the Archdiocese of Newark, commented ominously: "Certainly, a priest doesn't give up his civil liberties when he is ordained, and he maintains the same right to freedom of expression as anyone else in the United States. That said, we are concerned about Father West's comments and actions, and will be addressing them according to the protocols of the Church."[3]

What could happen to Fr. West was illustrated by the fate of another Catholic priest, Fr. Jonas Romea. Several weeks after Fr. West's remarks hit the headlines, Fr. Romea was celebrating a children's mass at St. Mary's Catholic School in Belen, New Mexico. An adult in attendance, Paulette Tafoya, later recounted: "He told them, you know, you need to be very proud with your Christian faith and don't listen to the liberals because the Muslims will chop your heads off."[4]

Despite the international publicity that the Islamic State's beheadings of Christians and other hostages had received, this was not a message Tafoya was prepared to hear. Romea was an "Islamophobe," and she swung into righteous action. "My dad and I, and my mom we were just sitting there, like, shocked." She and others complained about Romea to the diocese of Santa Fe, which, according to Albuquerque's KRQE News, promptly "sent out a letter to parents, saying the homily didn't fully embrace the message of Jesus Christ."[5]

Interesting. Was the message of Jesus Christ that Christians should not be proud of their faith? Or that one should listen to liberals? Or that Muslims wouldn't chop anyone's head off? Alas, the diocese did not explain. Of course, most likely the diocese was disturbed by Tafoya's charge that Fr. Romea had said that all Muslims wanted her dead: "I said not all Muslims are bad, they're not all trying to kill us, and he told me, if given a chance, every single Muslim would kill me."[6]

In an interview with David Carl of Albuquerque's KOAT TV, however, Romea denied this, reaching for an analogy: "Are all people burglars?"[7] When Carl responded, "No, not all people are burglars," Romea continued: "But my next question to you is this: Do you lock your doors at night?"[8]

Striving indefatigably to miss the point, Carl shot back: "I do. I do. So are you lumping in Muslims as burglars? Are you making an equivalency there?" In response to this, Romea doggedly tried to get back to the point, explaining: "I was just quoting one of the tenets in that religion that I mentioned…The news pieces that we get in the news from [the Middle East] tell us that actually, Christians are being slaughtered."[9]

Still determined to avoid reality, Carl asked him: "You don't think saying that Muslims will chop your head off is Islamophobic?"[10] Romea responded: "That is a label, and I reject that label."[11]

He wasn't going to be let off that easily. A little over a month after the controversy began, Romea issued a statement:

> After prayerful thought and reflection on the statement I made on Wednesday, the 8th of March, 2017 during the school Mass at Our Lady of Belen Church, I offer my sincere apology to all who were present during the Mass: the students, teachers, parents, grandparents, all parishioners and visitors, whom I have offended. I also offer my sincere apology to all our brothers and sisters in the Islamic Faith.
>
> I have come to realize that the Islamic Faith is not to be equated with terrorism and vice-versa. As a Catholic Christian, I look upon our brothers and sisters in the Islamic Faith with compassion and love as the Lord Jesus Christ taught us.

> I admit that I made a terrible mistake with my statement and I was wrong. I again wish to apologize to our brothers and sisters in the Islamic Faith for the recent remarks I made that do not live up to our Catholic Tradition. I ask for your prayers as I assure you of mine as we celebrate the Resurrection of our Savior.[12]

This groveling and repetitive *mea culpa* resembled nothing more closely than the coerced confessions that Stalin wrung out of his victims during the 1930s show trials of those who had dared cross him.

But it wasn't enough. On May 1, 2017, KRQE reported that "Fr. Jonas Romea, the priest at Our Lady of Belen Catholic Church who made controversial comments about Muslims wanting to behead everyone, has now been removed from the Archdiocese of Santa Fe. Many people are asking why, but neither the church or the Archdiocese is talking."[13] KRQE's introduction of Romea as the priest who had made controversial remarks about Islam underscored the likelihood that those remarks were why he was so abruptly removed. Another account published two days later reported allegations that Fr. Romea was guilty of sexual harassment, but even if that were so, the timing, as well as the haste with which he was dispatched, was questionable in the extreme.[14]

The question lingered: Was Fr. Romea removed from his position at Our Lady of Belen Church because his remarks about Islam went against current Catholic Church policy? Were priests and other Catholics facing disciplinary action for dissenting from this new superdogma, that Islam was a religion of peace?

Lost amid all the controversy over Fr. Romea's remarks was the question of whether or not what he said was actually true. Was beheading unbelievers really, as he had said, "one of the tenets in that religion that I mentioned?" The Qur'an says: "So when you meet those who disbelieve, strike necks until, when you have inflicted slaughter upon them, then secure their bonds, and either favor afterwards or ransom until the war lays down its burdens" (47:4). And: "When your Lord inspired to the angels, 'I am with you, so strengthen those who have believed. I will cast terror into the hearts of those who disbelieved, so strike upon the necks and strike from them every fingertip.'" (8:12)

"Strike necks." "Strike upon the necks." Fr. Romea got in hot water for saying, "The Muslims will chop your heads off." Will *all* Muslims chop your heads off? Obviously not; nor will all Christians love their enemies and turn the other cheek. But the Qur'anic imperative does exist. Fr. David Carl had asked Romea: "You don't think saying that Muslims will chop your head off is Islamophobic?"

Only if the truth is "Islamophobic." And apparently nowadays it is. Shedding light on unwelcome truths is "Islamophobic." Of all the Catholic leaders who canceled me from events or otherwise registered their disapproval of what I was doing, only Bishop McManus of Worcester had the courtesy to explain why publicly, and his explanation was extraordinary: "My decision to ask Mr. Spencer not to speak at the Men's Conference," he said, "resulted from a concern voiced by members of the Islamic community in Massachusetts, a concern that I came to share. That concern was that Mr. Spencer's talk about extreme, militant Islamists and the atrocities that they have perpetrated globally might undercut the positive achievements that we Catholics have attained in our inter-religious dialogue with devout Muslims and possibly generate suspicion and even fear of people who practice piously the religion of Islam."[15]

To discuss unpleasant matters such as the Muslim persecution of Christians would harm the Muslim-Christian dialogue, you see. Ignoring unwelcome realities and reaching out to Muslims in friendship would, presumably, ultimately make those negative facts go away altogether.

Outreach at the Expense of Identity?

That seemed to be the thinking of not a few Christian leaders. And so it was no great surprise when, on January 6, 2017 at St. Mary's Cathedral, the Scottish Episcopal Church's cathedral in Glasgow, an invited Muslim guest read out a passage of the Qur'an denying that Jesus is the Son of God.[16]

The incident was emblematic of how the contemporary West has lost a sense of itself, and is so "open" to "the other" that it is ripe for invasion and conquest—which is exactly what the particular "other" that was allowed to proclaim its faith at St. Mary's Cathedral has in mind.

The Qur'an reading at the cathedral was apparently part or all of the account of the birth of Jesus from chapter 19 of the Qur'an; the account follows the Biblical one closely, with some important differences, and ends with this: "That is Jesus, the son of Mary—the word of truth about which they are in dispute. It is not for Allah to take a son; exalted is He! When He decrees an affair, He only says to it, 'Be,' and it is." (Qur'an 19:35)

The passage "It is not for Allah to take a son," is in direct contradiction to what the Anglican Church is supposed to believe: "And the angel said to her, 'The Holy Spirit will come upon you, and the power of the Most High will overshadow you; therefore the child to be born will be called holy, the Son of God." (Luke 1:35)

The idea that Jesus is the Son of God is a central, foundational tenet of Christianity, held by all Christian sects, Orthodox, Catholic, and Protestant. What kind of madness had overtaken the Anglicans in Glasgow, that they would allow what is ostensibly a central belief of their faith to be denied in the place that was supposed to be the site of the purest and most vibrant expression of that faith?

Why, the madness of fear of "Islamophobia." The madness of being so avid to avoid charges of "racism" and "bigotry" that they lost their own identity in the process. Yet after an international furor, Scottish Episcopal Church officials did not apologize; on the contrary, they doubled down. In response to the outcry, the cathedral's provost, Fr. Kelvin Holdsworth, wrote:

> Those who came heard a confident Christian community proclaim their faith in Christ in no uncertain terms. We say the Nicene

> Creed at St Mary's and we believe it. Indeed, I sometimes have to tell people that I say it without my fingers crossed. Our proclamation of the divinity of Christ is at the centre of every Eucharist that takes place every Sunday. And so is the greeting of peace which we offer to one another. Peace be with you. Shalom. Salaam....
>
> Frankly, we think it is a good thing that Muslims are coming to church and hearing us proclaim the Gospel of Christ....
>
> The truth is, people confident in their faith can often learn most from one another. We are confident in our Christian faith and enjoy sharing it.
>
> The most perceptive comment this week came from someone who knows me well. "This is just absurd—St Mary's doesn't do syncretism it does hospitality."
>
> That's it in a nutshell. We don't do syncretism, we do hospitality.[17]

"We don't do syncretism, we do hospitality." Very well. But Fr. Kelvin Holdsworth failed to explain why "hospitality" required that a Qur'an verse that denied a central tenet of Christianity be read out. Nor did he note that no mosque in Scotland or anywhere else was likely to reciprocate and feature a New Testament reading proclaiming the divinity of Christ: the "hospitality" went only one way, and no one on the Christian side of this "dialogue" seemed to notice or care.

In saying that "our proclamation of the divinity of Christ is at the centre of every Eucharist that takes place every Sunday," Holdsworth was apparently defending the Qur'an reading in the cathedral by asserting that the St. Mary's often proclaimed the divinity of Christ, so one denial of it wasn't bad. That was like saying "I have met thousands of people in my life and only murdered one of them, so I uphold the sanctity of life."

But Holdsworth had more important things on his mind than maintaining the integrity of what was ostensibly his church's message: Islamophobia. He said that he could not "believe that moderate churches in the West should follow a policy of appeasement towards those who are Islamophobic." Appeasement of Islamic supremacists? That was apparently fine. But "appeasement of those who are Islamophobic?" That was over the line.

Note also his sly moral equivalence in referring to "moderate churches," as if there were "extremist" and "moderate" Christians just as there are "extremist" and "moderate" Muslims—a central, albeit wholly fictional, talking point of the contemporary Left.

Lord, what fools these Anglicans be. Of course, they had a perfect right to read from the Qur'an denying core aspects of Christianity during Christian worship. And free people have a perfect right to hold them in contempt as dhimmi appeasers giving away their own identity, culture and religion for the sake of "deepening friendships" with people who will never really consider them as friends, for they are forbidden to do so by that same Qur'an (5:51).

Clearly the religion of those at the Glasgow Anglican cathedral is not Christianity in any form, but Leftist multiculturalism. What they will ultimately find, to their shock and horror, is that their Muslim partners in this multicultural endeavor have no intention of reciprocating their generosity and hospitality, but will ultimately only subjugate them under the hegemony of Islamic law. They're already halfway there.

"I'm Christian and I LOVE the Qur'an"

But to take any notice of that fact would expose them to the risk of being accused of "Islamophobia." It is now much more fashionable in many Christian circles to profess one's love for all things Islamic. In December 2015 at a demonstration in Washington, D.C., a young woman named Jordan Denari, who later began going by the name Jordan Denari Duffner, held aloft a sign that summed up the current mainstream mindset regarding the view Christians should have of Islam. Denari's sign read: "I'm Christian and I LOVE the Qur'an."

Jordan Denari Duffner works at the anti-"Islamophobia" Bridge Initiative at Georgetown University's Saudi-funded Alwaleed bin Talal Center for Muslim-Christian Understanding.

One wonders if Ms. Duffner's attempt at Muslim-Christian understanding includes some comprehensive understanding of these verses in the book she professes to love:

Jesus is not the Son of God, and belief in the Trinity is "excess": "O People of the Book, do not commit excess in your religion or say about Allah except the truth. The Messiah, Jesus, the son of Mary, was but a messenger of Allah and His word which He directed to Mary and a soul from Him. So believe in Allah and His messengers. And do not say, 'Three'; desist—it is better for you. Indeed, Allah is but one God. Exalted is He above having a son. To Him belongs whatever is in the heavens and whatever is on the earth. And sufficient is Allah as Disposer of affairs." (4:171)

And: "It is not for Allah to take a son; exalted is He! When He decrees an affair, He only says to it, 'Be,' and it is." (19:35)

Jesus was not crucified: "And their saying, 'Indeed, we have killed the Messiah, Jesus, the son of Mary, the messenger of Allah.' And they did not kill him, nor did they crucify him; but another was made to resemble him to them. And indeed, those who differ over it are in doubt about it. They have no knowledge of it except the following of assumption. And they did not kill him, for certain." (4:157)

Those who believe in the divinity of Christ are unbelievers: "They have certainly disbelieved who say that Allah is Christ, the son of Mary. Say, 'Then who could prevent Allah at all if He had intended to destroy Christ, the son of Mary, or his mother or everyone on the earth?' And to Allah belongs the dominion of the heavens and the earth and whatever is between them. He creates what He wills, and Allah is over all things competent." (5:17)

Christians have forgotten part of the divine revelations they received: "And from those who say, 'We are Christians' We took their covenant; but they forgot a portion of that of which they were reminded. So We caused among them animosity and hatred until the Day of Resurrection. And Allah is going to inform them about what they used to do." (5:14)

Those who believe that Jesus is God's Son are accursed: "The Jews say, 'Ezra is the son of Allah'; and the Christians say, 'The Messiah is the son of Allah.' That is their statement from their mouths; they imitate the saying of those who disbelieved. May Allah destroy them; how are they deluded?" (9:30)

Christians who do not accepted Muhammad and the Qur'an are the most vile of created beings: "Indeed, they who disbelieved among the People of the Book and the polytheists will be in the fire of Hell, abiding eternally therein. Those are the most vile of created beings." (98:6)

Muslims must fight against and subjugate Christians: "Fight those who believe not in Allah nor the Last Day, nor hold that forbidden which hath been forbidden by Allah and His Messenger, nor acknowledge the religion of Truth, even if they are of the People of the Book, until they pay the Jizya with willing submission, and feel themselves subdued." (9:29)

"I'm a Christian and I LOVE Muslims?" Absolutely. Love for Muslims is one thing, however, and love for the Qur'an is another. One doesn't have to be a Christian to see that Denari's stand is anomalous. It is strange for someone who professes to be a Christian, who presumably believes that Jesus is the Son of God, the Second Person of the Trinity, who was crucified and rose from the dead for the salvation of the human race, to profess love for a book that denies all that and says that those who believe it are accursed, vile beings who should be waged war against until they submit to the hegemony of a group that believes differently.

What's more, although very few Christians would dare say so publicly nowadays, to be a Christian at all assumes a denial that Muhammad is a prophet and the Qur'an a holy book, for they both affirm as matters of faith beliefs that Christians do not hold, and, as we have seen, deny many that Christians do hold.

It was unlikely, of course, that Duffner, as she held her sign, had thought any of this through. She was just trying to be multicultural and diverse. And she was unlikely ever to stop and ponder the implications of the fact that no Muslim has been carrying around a sign saying, "I'm Muslim and I LOVE the Bible."

But that question deserved to be pondered.

"Not Consistent with the Teachings of the Catholic Church"

Meanwhile, some Christians are also working assiduously, in the same spirit of dialogue and outreach, to erase even any historical memory of the fact that there was once conflict between Christians and Muslims. The *Huffington Post* reported indignantly in April 2017 that "the Catholic diocese of Orlando, Florida, says it has reprimanded a teacher at a Catholic school in the state for giving his sixth-grade religion class an anti-Muslim reading assignment."[18] Mark Smythe of Blessed Trinity Catholic School in Ocala, Florida gave students a handout that called Muhammad's teaching "ridiculous, immoral and corrupting."[19]

Clearly Smythe was getting material from "Islamophobic" websites, no? No: his handout came from a Catholic saint, St. John Bosco.

Nevertheless, Jacquelyn Flanigan, an associate superintendent at the Diocese of Orlando's Catholic school system, said that "the information provided in the sixth grade class is not consistent with the teachings of the Catholic Church."[20]

She didn't explain the anomalous fact that the author of this supposedly un-Catholic material was a saint in the Catholic Church. So did a saint spread ideas that were "not consistent with the teachings of the Catholic Church?" How, then, did he become a saint? Why didn't his apparently heterodox, disrespectful, hateful teaching on Islam prevent his canonization?

Or is it the "teachings of the Catholic Church" that had changed? Since it is Catholic teaching that only divinely revealed dogmas are immutable, if the Church's teaching on Islam has changed, it must not be divinely revealed dogma, but mere human opinion, from which there could be respectful disagreement—couldn't there?

Flanigan "pointed to Nostra Aetate, an official Vatican document Pope Paul VI released on Oct. 28, 1965. It stated that the

Catholic Church regards Muslims 'with esteem' and urged Catholics to work with Muslims for peace and social justice."[21]

Does the necessity to regard Muslims with esteem require that Catholics must not speak about the elements of Islam that jihadis use to justify violence, including the rampant global persecution of Christians?

About John Bosco's document, the *Huffington Post* reported: "Elsewhere in the text, Muhammad is described as a 'charlatan,' 'villain,' 'ignoramus,' 'imposter' and 'false prophet' who 'couldn't even write' and 'propagated his religion, not through miracles or persuasive words, but by military force.' The Quran, the holy book of Islam, is also called 'a series of errors, the most enormous ones being against morality and the worship of the true God.' "[22]

This was strong and pejorative language. Where did Bosco get these ideas, that were inconsistent with Catholic teaching in the minds of the leaders of the diocese of Orlando that the teacher who spread this material deserved a reprimand? The *Huffington Post*, of course, took it for granted that it is false to claim these things, but there is actually a case to be made that Islam spread through force and that Islamic morality is decisively different from Christian morality. Can there be any discussion of this at all? Or is all dissent from the charge that John Bosco's claims are false to be punished and silenced?

The *Huffington Post* went on to report that "Jordan Denari Duffner, a Catholic research fellow at Georgetown University's Bridge Initiative who studies Islamophobia, said it's not uncommon for people on some conservative websites to selectively cite centuries-old anti-Muslim texts written by Catholic scholars and saints."[23]

The *Huffington Post* article presented the Bridge Initiative as if it were a neutral arbiter of what constituted "Islamophobia" and what did not. It did not offer any opposing views, such as that of the Counter Jihad Report, which noted that the Bridge Initiative portrayed "as islamophobic those who raise national security issues about the Muslim Brotherhood and its subversive efforts to support terrorism and wage 'civilizational jihad.'"[24] Nor did it mention the

Bridge Initiative's partnerships with groups linked to the Muslim Brotherhood, Hamas, and al-Qaeda.[25]

But are not such associations relevant in order to establish the perspective from which Duffner was commenting upon the controversy at Blessed Trinity Catholic School, and upon "Islamophobia" in general?

In any case, the actions of the Catholic diocese of Orlando in reprimanding a teacher for quoting a saint whose views of Islam were out of favor were a sign of the times. The primary focus of the Catholic Church was not on resisting jihad terrorism or educating its people about its nature and provenance, but rather on "Islamophobia."

Christian Persecution in the West

There were disquieting indications, however, that this focus was misplaced.

Eight of the ten worst countries for Christians to live in are majority-Muslim: Somalia, Afghanistan, Pakistan, Sudan, Syria, Iraq, Iran, and Yemen. A ninth, Eritrea, is about evenly divided between Christians and Muslims, yet Christians still face virulent persecution there.[26] Trump's travel ban included six of these countries: Somalia, Sudan, Syria, Iraq, Iran, and Yemen, plus Libya.

Trump also initially announced that Syrian Christians and other religious minorities who were facing persecution would be given preference for refugee status. At that, however, the USCCB strenuously objected. "We believe in assisting all, regardless of their religious beliefs," said Bishop Joe S. Vásquez, the chairman of the USCCB's committee on migration.[27]

Very well. Unfortunately, however, some of those refugees were not so broad-minded. In April 2017 in Sydney, Australia, a 30-year-old man who was identified in news reports only as Mike was riding the train with his girlfriend, minding his own business and talking on his cellphone. Mike, an observant Greek Orthodox Christian, was wearing a large cross. As the train passed through predominantly Muslim areas of Sydney, four young men "of Middle

Eastern appearance" accosted him and punched him repeatedly while shouting about "Allah" and screaming "Fuck Jesus"; they ripped the cross from his neck.[28]

Mike remarked: "I was born in Australia of Greek heritage. I've always worn my cross. For him to rip it off and step on it has to be a religious crime... It's not on to feel unsafe in your own country."[29] Even worse, five Transport Officers looked on during the attack, but did nothing to intervene or apprehend the attackers.

A local Orthodox priest, Fr. George Capsis, said that Mike's experience was "not an isolated incident. There are gangs of these young fellows of Muslim background who have been harassing people they identify as Christian… You don't hear about it because no one's reporting it."[30] Capsis said that three other Christians had recently been attacked, also as they rode on public transportation through Muslim areas: "It's like their territory; they don't want Christians or other types of infidels there." He said he advised Christians not to make any visible displays of their faith: "People like Greek Orthodox carry a big cross. I tell them to be practical and if they're in those areas and wearing a big cross and a group of young guys comes, hide it in your shirt. Why provoke it? If this keeps up, someone will be hurt. It's got to be nipped in the bud."[31]

Christianity Under Attack in Europe

It isn't being nipped in the bud, in Australia or elsewhere, even in Europe, Christianity's historical center. On Saturday morning, September 10, 2016, Muslims went to the Orthodox cathedral in Pristina, Kosovo, set fire to it, and after it had burned to the ground, used the ruins as a toilet. This was just one of hundreds of churches in Kosovo to have received the same treatment.[32] Three months later, Muslims in the village of Lagolio in Crete went to the Greek Orthodox Church of the Archangel Michael, a center for local pilgrimages, scrawled "Allahu akbar" on the wall, and set fire to the building, burning numerous icons and a portion of the church near the altar.[33] The same story played out in so many places.

In the Muslim-dominated Swedish city of Malmö in June 2016, a Muslim screaming "Allahu akbar" broke into St. Paul's Church, broke numerous windows, and battled police when they arrived on the scene.[34]

The situation was little different in Western Europe. Between 2008 and 2016, rates of racially motivated attacks, as well as attacks on Muslims and Jews, fell dramatically in France. However, in that same span, attacks on French churches increased by 245 percent. The French government ascribed fourteen cases to a "satanic motivation" and twenty-five cases to "anarchist" motives, but said that most of the attacks, which numbered 949, had "no religious motive."[35]

Yet this strained credulity, given Islam's notable hostility to representational art and to the cross and other Christian symbols in particular, as well as the French government's general reluctance, which it shared with all European authorities, to record the crimes of Muslim migrants. A French member of the European Parliament, Jean-Luc Schaffhausser, declared in April 2016 that "the media don't tell the truth and French people are right not to trust media, politician, parties. There is a security problem with all those migrants but government says there are no problems with them. The French authorities are not capable of managing the situation."[36]

Some Incidents Are Unmistakable, Whatever the Coverage

On July 26, 2016, Muslims entered a church in the Normandy town of Saint-Etienne-du Rouvray, where an 84-year-old priest, Fr. Jacques Hamel, was celebrating mass. Screaming "Daesh," the Arabic acronym for the Islamic State, they took several nuns hostage, and then forced Fr. Hamel to kneel and slit his throat; the UK's *The Daily Telegraph* reported that "the men's motives are still unknown."[37] An Irish monk, Fr. Mark Ephrem Nolan, who knew Fr. Hamel, recalled that the martyred priest "led a pure, simple life, with an emphasis on building friendships."[38]

This included friendships with Muslims: "Church authorities," said Nolan, "facilitated the giving of land beside his church to local

Muslims to build a mosque, and they were given use of the parish hall and other facilities during Ramadan."[39] He added of Saint-Etienne-du Rouvray that "there is a large Muslim population there, and relations are normally very good between the communities. Efforts have been made by the Christian community to be welcoming to Muslims. The Sisters even give reading lessons to Muslim kids in tower blocks."[40]

These gestures of goodwill didn't spare Fr. Hamel's life, nor did Muslims always reciprocate. Shortly after Fr. Hamel was murdered, St. George church in the tiny French town of Vivonne (Vienne) held a mass for the slain priest, during which the priest who was officiating told the congregation that the tabernacle lamp had recently been stolen, and a photo of Mohamed Lahouaiej Bouhlel, who drove a truck into a crowd in Nice in July 2016, murdering 86 people and injuring 434, placed on the altar.[41]

The German media, like that of France, has been accused of covering up Muslim migrant crime.[42] In January 2017, Muslims entered a parish center in the town of Brühl in the Rhein-Neckar district of Baden-Württemberg, where they scrawled Islamic slogans on walls and left the place, according to police, a "picture of devastation." However, in a sign of the general reluctance to admit the grim reality of migrant crime, the police also declared that they did not "assume" that the Islamic slogans were any key to the motive behind the attack.[43]

Meanwhile, after Germany's massive influx of Muslim migrants, German media noted that "not a day goes by" without an attack on Christian religious symbols.[44] Muslim migrants in Germany were even harassing and persecuting the small number of Christians among them, threatening them and pressuring them to abandon Christianity and embrace Islam. In May 2016, minority rights groups held a press conference in Berlin to call attention to this problem, and stated that 88 percent of the Christian refugees they interviewed had reported being threatened, harassed, or pressured to convert by Muslim refugees. One refugee said: "I really didn't know that after coming to Germany I would be harassed because of my faith in the very same way as back in Iran."[45]

Converts from Islam to Christianity fared the worst. The Archdiocese of Vienna noted that 83 percent of adult baptisms in 2015 were of Muslims.[46] Some Muslims elsewhere in Europe were converting to Christianity as well. But these converts often faced pushback from their former coreligionists. According to a survey of migrants reported in *Breitbart News*, "The most prevalent form of abuse was verbal insults with 96 people saying that had received abuse or threats. Eighty-six said they had been physically assaulted and 73 said they had been subjected to death threats against themselves and family members. Three quarters of the migrants also said they had been victims of multiple attacks. The perpetrators of most of the attacks were fellow migrants who look down on converts and believe them to be apostates."[47]

Paulus Kurt of the Central Council of Oriental Christians in Germany noted: "These are not isolated cases. I don't know of any refugee shelter from Garmisch to Hamburg where we have not found such cases."[48] Indeed. In Hamburg, an Afghan Muslim migrant attacked an Iranian migrant with a baton, knocking him out cold and giving him serious head injuries while shouting "I will kill you." The Iranian's offense? Converting to Christianity, which the Afghan declared was a "sin."[49] One Muslim migrant who converted to Christianity in Austria said that his conversion "could be my death sentence."[50]

It was the same story in Leipzig, where a Catholic priest, Andreas Knapp, reported that Muslim migrant children were "disrespectful" to the children of Christian migrants and even "hated them," and bullied them on a regular basis. One 13-year-old Christian boy told Knapp: "There were a lot of children who were all Muslims, and I was the only Christian. When I would go to them and say, 'Let's play football', they said, 'No, you're a Christian!' Then they insulted me because I eat pork."[51]

In August 2016, an Iranian-born pastor and convert from Islam to Christianity in Germany, Mahin Mousapour, noted the widespread

Muslim abuse of Christians in refugee centers and declared that Germany was showing Islam "too much respect."[52] Such a charge may grate on multiculturalist ears, but Mousapour was choosing her words carefully. Muslim refugees, she said, were telling their Christian counterparts that they were "impure as a dog" and that converts should be put to death for leaving Islam.[53] Mousapour recounted: "Toys of Christian children are being destroyed, Christian asylum seekers are told not only to wash their dishes after eating but also that they must clean the entire kitchen as it would otherwise be 'unclean.' Many Muslim asylum seekers call all Christians unclean. Church services are held in secret, Bibles and crucifixes have to be hidden."[54]

Mousapour herself was threatened by a knife-wielding Muslim on a German street. Of the Muslim migrant harassment, she said: "If we do nothing about it we will lose our foundations in this country."[55] Indeed.

Open Doors, a group that tracks the persecution of Christians, determined that throughout 2016, Muslim migrants in Germany attacked at least 743 Christian in refugee camps. The Open Doors report noted: "The documented cases confirm that the situation of Christian refugees in German refugee shelters is still unbearable. As a minority they are discriminated against, beaten up by and receive death threats from Muslim refugees and partly by the Muslim staff (securities, interpreters, volunteers) on grounds of their religion."[56]

Fear of "Islamophobia" charges inhibited prosecution: "We believe that the trivialization, concealment or misuse of this injustice, be it for political or other motives, will give encouragement to the perpetrators and increase the suffering of the victims."[57]

France and Germany were not alone; Muslims are registering their distaste for Christianity and Christians all over Western Europe. In Spain in September 2016, a judge barred a Muslim migrant from entering Catholic churches after he attacked and burned several images of Mary in a church in the town of Fontellas.[58] And in the Italian town of Foggia in December 2016, a young Muslim went to the Madonna del Rosario church, where he destroyed a statue of Mary and set fire to a Nativity scene; he explained to police that he did it all because he was a Muslim, and "wanted to destroy Christian symbols."[59]

Even more ominously, in September 2016, a young Muslim was arrested after a video was posted on YouTube showing him walking down the street in the Belgian city of Verviers, calling as he walked for the murder of Christians. The young man turned out to be the son of an imam, Shayh Alami, who was one of the Muslim leaders responsible for giving Verviers the reputation of being, according to the Belgian media, "one of the most important breeding grounds for Islamists in Belgium."[60] After he was arrested, he admitted to police that he was involved in an Islamic State plot to attack non-Muslims with chainsaws in a Belgian shopping center.

Amid this rising tide of violence by Muslims against Christians in Europe, Prince Charles seized the opportunity three days before Christmas 2016 to warn against not jihad terror, but the "rise of populism" that heralded a return to the "dark days of the 1930s," with Muslims in the role of the Jews.[61]

The idea that Muslims are the new Jews is an increasingly common tool Leftists use to dismiss examinations of how jihadists use Islamic texts and teachings to justify violence and make recruits among peaceful Muslims, but it also has opponents on the Left. In 2014, as part of his ongoing awakening to the nature and reality of the jihad threat, Bill Maher noted: "Jews weren't oppressing anybody. There weren't 5,000 militant Jewish groups. They didn't do a study of treatment of women around the world and find that Jews were at the bottom of it. There weren't 10 Jewish countries in the world that were putting gay people to death just for being gay."[62]

Indeed. Further, no one is calling for or justifying genocide of Muslims. No individual or group opposed to Islam is remotely comparable to the National Socialists. Not that facts have ever gotten in the way of "Islamophobia" hysteria.

Maher wasn't alone on the Left in having pointed out the absurdity of likening opposition to jihad to the lead-up to the Holocaust. The late Christopher Hitchens also refuted this idea when writing a few years ago about the notorious Ground Zero Mosque proposal:" 'Some of what people are saying in this mosque controversy is very similar to what German media was saying about Jews in the 1920s and 1930s,' Imam Abdullah Antepli, Muslim chaplain at Duke University, told *The New York Times*. Yes, we all recall the Jewish suicide bombers of that period, as we recall the Jewish yells for holy war, the Jewish demands for the veiling of women and the stoning of homosexuals, and the Jewish burning of newspapers that published cartoons they did not like."[63]

Speaking six years after Hitchens' remarks, Prince Charles showed no sign that this common sense had gotten through to him. He said of refugees that their "suffering doesn't end when they arrive seeking refuge in a foreign land," for "we are now seeing the rise of many populist groups across the world that are increasingly aggressive to those who adhere to a minority faith."[64] Of the Muslim persecution of Christians in Europe, he was silent. For Charles, only Muslims were the victims, and he even went so far as to attempt an *argumentum ad Hitlerum*: "All of this has deeply disturbing echoes of the dark days of the 1930s. My parents' generation fought and died in a battle against intolerance, monstrous extremism and inhuman attempts to exterminate the Jewish population of Europe."[65] It being the Christmas season, he asked his audience to remember "how the story of the Nativity unfolds with the fleeing of the holy family to escape violent persecution."[66] Charles seemed unaware of or indifferent to the actual source of the violent persecution that is going on today.

It Can't Happen Here? It's Already Happening Here.

Contrary to Prince Charles's lurid fantasies of neo-Nazis terrorizing poor, innocent refugees, Muslims are not facing widespread persecution in the West, and while he didn't make any mention of it, Muslim harassment and persecution of Christians is rising in the United States as well as in Europe. Much more, and more serious, is to come.

In 2014, vandals scrawled the word "Infidels!" along with a verse of the Qur'an on Saint Bartholomew's Catholic Church in Columbus, Indiana, and that same night also targeted Columbus' Lakeview Church of Christ and East Columbus Christian Church.[67] In September 2015, a Muslim wearing combat gear entered Corinth Missionary Baptist Church in Bullard, Texas, and announced that Allah had ordered him to kill Christians and "other infidels."[68] In January 2016, Valley Baptist Church in Bakersfield, California received a threat; it was written in Arabic.[69] The following month, a young Muslim in Dearborn Heights, Michigan, told a man who turned out to be an undercover FBI agent that he was planning to "shoot up" a local church for the Islamic State.[70]

A year earlier, police were called to Saint Bartholomew's Catholic Church in Columbus, Indiana, after the house of worship was vandalized with the word "Infidels!" along with a Koranic verse sanctioning death for nonbelievers. Similar graffiti was found that same night at nearby Lakeview Church of Christ and East Columbus Christian Church.

Synagogues have faced increasing threats in recent years, too. Earlier this year, the FBI disrupted a plot by a Muslim convert to blow up the Aventura Turnberry Jewish Center, in Aventura, Florida. A 2014 audit by the Anti-Defamation League (ADL) found that anti-Semitic incidents rose 21 percent across the country that year.[71]

One Sunday morning in the spring of 2016, Muslims in a green Honda Civic drove up to St. Andrew Orthodox Church in Riverside, California, during the celebration of the Divine Liturgy. The man in the front passenger seat took out a bullhorn and screamed "Allahu akbar" several times.[72]

Several of the parishioners told police that the men many also have taken some photographs of the church. The church's pastor, Fr. Josiah Trenham, observed that while several members of the congregation heard the screams of "Allahu akbar," they were not noted in the police report. "It is a deep sorrow," said Fr. Trenham, "to live this way in the 'new America.'"[73]

That is true. And the sorrow is likely to deepen further. Late in 2016, a Greek Orthodox priest told me that two Muslims had recently been attending services and then, at coffee hour, attempting to convert parishioners to Islam. Then they disappeared as abruptly as they had come, and he learned later that they had been deported for terror activity.

They didn't have to show up in person. On April 22, 2016, a fifteen-year-old member of Lamont Christian Reformed Church in Lamont, Michigan, went to the church's website to find its phone number. Instead, she found that the website had been hacked by a group calling itself the United Cyber Caliophate, which had replaced the church's information with a video featuring Islamic State spokesman Abu Muhammad al-Adnani al-Shami, who intoned menacingly: "We will conquer your Rome, break your crosses and enslave your women by the permission of Allah, the Exalted. This is His promise to us, He is glorified and He does not fail in His promise."[74] The following Sunday, only six people showed up at Lamont Christian Reformed Church.[75]

The Ghost of Christmases to Come

In December 2016, an Islamic State jihadi calling himself Abu Marya al-Iraqi published a huge list of thousands of churches in the United States, complete with their addresses. The jihadi exhorted Muslims to use the list to ensure "bloody celebrations in the Christian New Year" and to "turn the Christian New Year into a bloody horror movie."[76] In a second message, another Islamic State jihadi called upon "the sons of Islam" to carry out jihad massacres at "churches, well-known hotels, crowded coffee shops, streets, markets and public places" in the U.S., Canada, and Western Europe.[77]

Christmas came and went that year without any major jihad attack in any of the thousands of American churches on the Islamic State list. But could it never happen here? Was there no chance at all that the conditions Christians must endure in Somalia, Afghanistan,

Pakistan, Sudan, Syria, Iraq, Iran, and Yemen could ever appear in the comfortable and prosperous West?

Christmas 2016 took place amid heightened security all over Europe and North America. And that year's tense and nervous Christmas was just the beginning. There was no indication anywhere in the West that any future Christmas would be any different, for the foreseeable future.

The *Mailonline* reported that "the West has been put on increased terror alert over the festive period following the Berlin lorry tragedy. Security has been ramped up in major cities including, London, New York, Paris, Vienna and Dusseldorf, as fears grow of another 'ISIS' attack on the West. Tanks were seen in the streets of Budapest, Hungary, and soldiers were pictured at the Christmas markets in Antwerp, Belgium. The Metropolitan Police has said it is to review its plans for protecting public events over Christmas and New Year following the 'awful incidents' in Berlin and Ankara."[78]

The extra security was justified; not only did jihadis target the Christmas market in Berlin, but there were six other terror plots and attacks in the run-up to this Christmas day.[79]

Why was this happening? Why were tanks in the streets of major cities, guarding Christmas markets? Why was the entire Western world on edge?

Because European and North American authorities admitted large numbers of Muslim migrants into their countries, among whom were unknowable numbers of jihad terrorists, and allowed Sharia enclaves to grow in which hatred of unbelievers and the necessity to wage war against and subjugate them was taught.

Christmas was under siege because there are large numbers of jihad-inclined Muslims in the West. The responsibility lies with those who admitted them without regard for Islam's doctrines of religious warfare and supremacism.

In August 2014, Amel Shimoun Nona, the Chaldean Catholic Archbishop of Mosul, predicted that all this would happen. After Islamic jihadists decimated the Christian population of his area,

Nona prophesied: "Our sufferings today," he said, "are the prelude of those you, Europeans and Western Christians, will also suffer in the near future."[80]

As the few remaining Christians in the Middle East celebrate Christmas and other feast days while hoping that Muslims won't murder them for doing so, that future is now.

Nona continued: "I lost my diocese. The physical setting of my apostolate has been occupied by Islamic radicals who want us converted or dead."[81] He explained that the West was making a grave error by assuming that Islam was a religion of peace that taught the equal dignity of all human beings:

> Please, try to understand us. Your liberal and democratic principles are worth nothing here. You must consider again our reality in the Middle East, because you are welcoming in your countries an ever growing number of Muslims. Also you are in danger. You must take strong and courageous decisions, even at the cost of contradicting your principles. You think all men are equal, but that is not true: Islam does not say that all men are equal. Your values are not their values. If you do not understand this soon enough, you will become the victims of the enemy you have welcomed in your home.[82]

You will become victims of the enemy you have welcomed in your home.

And now here we are. What will future Christmases in Europe look like, unless current policies regarding Muslim migration are reversed? They will look like Christmases in Islamic lands, where Christians gather with the constant awareness that this could be the day that Islamic jihadis decide to punish them for the crime of being infidels. Muslims threw a grenade at a church in Mindanao, a Muslim-majority area of the Philippines, during Christmas Eve mass in December 2016, injuring sixteen people.[83]

No. That list may not be acted upon this year, but the more Muslims enter the U.S., the more jihadis will be among them, and the more Christians will be under threat.

These are harsh words, unwelcome to Christians and non-Christians alike, but they are nonetheless undeniable to anyone who is willing to face reality.

The conditions that will make Christian worship a precarious and dangerous exercise to engage in are already beginning to appear here, and will continue to do so with increasing frequency. And no amount of dialogue with Muslims, or outreach to them, or hosting of Muslim spokesmen in cathedrals, or curtailment of any criticism of jihad terror or Sharia, will stop the jihad from advancing.

German legislator Hans Peter Stauch sounded a rare note of common sense in late 2016 when he remarked that "the refugees that have come to us are certainly not per se to be marked as bad or criminal. But it would be and is naïve, if not outright careless, to declare that through such uncontrolled immigration 'only' the peaceful and good people have come here. It is equally naïve and careless to believe that especially the young men, who have been socialized in an archaic value system from the Middle Ages, will be magically transformed into enlightened, socially acceptable democrats after they cross our borders."[84]

Western liberals would do well to heed his words.

CHAPTER 7

THE THREAT TO SECULAR LIBERALS

A Genuine Threat?

What will happen to America's pluralistic society as a consequence of the admission into the country of large numbers of people who believe that their god has given them a law that is superior to all other laws, and that they have a responsibility to impose that law even upon the unwilling?

Liberals have generally dismissed this concern as hysterical fear-mongering, assuming that none, or only a tiny minority, of the Muslims in the U.S. or anywhere else in the West, have any such ideas. Muslims in the U.S. have no intention of bringing Sharia here, and anyone who thinks otherwise is simply a racist, bigoted Islamophobe.

These assumptions played out yet again in the media furor early in the Trump presidency over his adviser Steven K. Bannon. On February 3, 2017, the *Washington Post* published an article about Bannon's précis for a ten-year-old unproduced film project discussing the jihad threat.[1]

The *Post*'s Matea Gold described the film in lurid terms:

> The flag fluttering above the U.S. Capitol is emblazoned with a crescent and star. Chants of "Allahu Akbar" rise from inside the building.
>
> That's the provocative opening scene of a documentary-style movie outlined 10 years ago by Stephen K. Bannon that envisioned radical Muslims taking over the country and remaking it into the "Islamic States of America," according to a document describing the project obtained by The Washington Post.[2]

The tone of the Post article was clear: Bannon's abandoned film project was an absurd, preposterous exercise in hatred and fearmongering.

Matea Gold included in her article the words of Omar Ahmad, the co-founder and longtime Board chairman of the Council on American-Islamic Relations (CAIR), who once said: "Islam isn't in America to be equal to any other faith, but to become dominant. The Koran, the Muslim book of scripture, should be the highest authority in America, and Islam the only accepted religion on Earth."[3]

When confronted about these words, Ahmad vehemently denied saying them; however, the original reporter, Lisa Gardiner of the *Fremont Argus*, hardly a hardline "Islamophobe" with an axe to grind, stood by her story.[4]

What's more, CAIR spokesman Ibrahim Hooper once said: "I wouldn't want to create the impression that I wouldn't like the government of the United States to be Islamic sometime in the future."[5]

Meanwhile, according to a captured internal document, the Muslim Brotherhood (to which all the major Muslim groups in the US are linked) is dedicated in its own words to "eliminating and destroying Western civilization from within, and sabotaging its miserable house….so that it falls, and Allah's religion is victorious over other religions."[6]

Then there was Washington, DC, imam Abdul Alim Musa, who declared in 2007 that he wanted to "establish an Islamic State of America by 2050."[7]

Gold mentioned none of this, but she did add: “The proposal names two dozen conservative writers and terrorism experts who could serve as potential on-screen guests, including Robert Spencer, director of the Jihad Watch website, who is labeled by the Southern Poverty Law Center as an anti-Muslim ‘propagandist.’”[8]

Of course. Yet there are once again reasons for legitimate concern. Even if the statements of Ahmad, Hooper, and Musa were just wishful thinking given voice in unguarded moments, there was more.

“I have complete faith that Islam will invade Europe and America, because Islam has logic and a mission.” Muhammad Mahdi Othman Akef made that statement in 2004 when he took over leadership of the Muslim Brotherhood. But he didn’t mean an invasion of armies, or even of bomb-wielding terrorists: “The Europeans and the Americans,” he explained, “will come into the bosom of Islam out of conviction.”[9]

Forming that conviction in the minds of European and American non-Muslims would take a concerted effort spanning years and comprising many fronts. But the ultimate goal of the stealth jihad is clear: the elimination of Western civilization. A top Brotherhood operative in this country, Mohamed Akram, explained that the Muslim Brotherhood “must understand that their work in America is a kind of grand Jihad in eliminating and destroying the Western civilization from within and ‘sabotaging’ its miserable house by their hands and the hands of the believers so that it is eliminated and Allah’s religion is made victorious over all other religions.”[10]

Akram’s directive came in a Muslim Brotherhood memorandum from May 22, 1991 entitled “An Explanatory Memorandum on the General Strategic Goal for the Group in North America.” The document came to light during the 2007 trial of what had been the largest Islamic charity in the United States, the Holy Land Foundation for Relief and Development, which was accused of funneling charitable donations to the jihad terror group Hamas.

In the memorandum, Akram lays out a plan to do nothing less than conquer and Islamize the United States. The Brotherhood’s success in America would ultimately further the even larger goal of establishing "the global Islamic state."[11]

Akram seems to be aware of how fantastical his goal might sound—even to his fellow Muslim Brothers. He claims his plans are not "abundant extravagance, imaginations or hallucinations which passed in the mind of one of your brothers, but they are rather hopes, ambitions and challenges that I hope that you share some or most of which with me."

Arguing that those hopes and ambitions can become reality, Akram says that he perceives a "glimpse of hope" that "we have embarked on a new stage of Islamic activism stages [sic] in this continent." A new stage, yes, but not a new plan: the plan he is elucidating, he explains, is "not strange or a new submission without a root, but rather an attempt to interpret and explain some of what came in the long-term plan which we approved and adopted in our council and our conference in the year (1987)."

Over the years after the memorandum was released to the public during the Holy Land Foundation trial in 2007—the trial of what was then the nation's largest Islamic charity for funneling charitable contributions to the jihad terror group Hamas—the document's central claim that the Brotherhood's mission in the United States was "eliminating and destroying Western civilization from within and sabotaging its miserable house" became a staple of counter-jihad rhetoric: those who were trying to call attention to the insidious activity of Muslim Brotherhood-linked individuals and groups in the United States would frequently cite and quote the memorandum in order to try to impress upon Americans the gravity of the threat and the foolhardiness of the federal, as well as state and local, governments in cooperating and collaborating with Muslim Brotherhood-linked groups.

No, Not a Real Threat, Says the Left

The pushback from those groups was inevitable, albeit oddly tardy. The first direct challenge to the authenticity and importance of the document came in *The New Yorker* in May 2015, eight years after the memorandum came to light and began to be cited by foes of jihad terror. In a lengthy attack on foes of jihad terror entitled "Pamela Geller and the Anti-Islam Movement," far-Left journalist David K. Shipler wrote derisively of the document's "illusion of importance," and claimed that it was "never subjected to an adversarial test of its authenticity or significance. Examined closely, it does not stand up as an authoritative prescription for action. Rather, it appears to have been written as a plea to the Muslim Brotherhood leadership for action, by an author we know little about, Mohamed Akram. He is listed elsewhere as a secretary in the Brotherhood, but he writes in the tone of an underling. Islam watchers do not quote his appeal that the recipients 'not rush to throw these papers away due to your many occupations and worries. All that I'm asking of you is to read them and to comment on them.' These lines reveal the memo as a mere proposal, now twenty-four years old. No other copies have come to light."[12]

Unfortunately for Shipler, the Justice Department took Akram's memorandum quite seriously, and as much more than a "plea" from an "underling." Federal prosecutors during the Holy Land Foundation trial stated that it "established that ISNA [the Islamic Society of North America] and NAIT [the North American Islamic Trust] were among those organizations created by the U.S.-Muslim Brotherhood," and that it was written not by a little-known underling, but by "U.S.-Muslim Brotherhood Shura Council member Mohamed Akram Adlouni." The Shura Council is the Muslim Brotherhood's governing body. In a 1992 Muslim Brotherhood directory, Akram is listed as a member of the Brotherhood's Board of Directors and Executive Office. He was also identified as "Office Secretary," which didn't mean a clerk, but a leading officer of the organization: Secretary-General would be a more precise translation of the Arabic term used in the directory.[13]

The memorandum described, the federal prosecutors wrote, "the Brotherhood's strategic goal as a kind of 'grand *Jihad*.'"[14] Not, in other words, one man's wishful thinking.

Investigative journalist Patrick Poole also noted that a "federal court agreed in a published opinion with the Justice Department's analysis of the document when Judge Jorge Solis ruled on motions from three separate organizations named as unindicted co-conspirators in the trial—ISNA, NAIT, and the Council on American-Islamic Relations (CAIR)—asking to be removed from the Justice Department's co-conspirator list. The judge's ruling against removing the groups from the unindicted co-conspirator list was unsealed in 2010."[15] Solis refused to remove the groups from the list because of their inclusion in Akram's memorandum, which Solis quoted extensively.[16]

Shipler quibbled on this point, claiming that Solis "accepted the government's assertions by citing the seized Elbarasse documents, including the Explanatory Memorandum, without testing their accuracy in an adversarial proceeding." Yet Shipler himself admitted that Akram's memorandum was one of the documents that the Holy Land Foundation defense team had challenged. Poole points out that "by Shipler's own admission, the Elbarasse documents, including the Explanatory Memorandum, were subject to challenges on both the trial court and appellate levels. Both sides briefed the court, and judge and the appeals court panel ruled on the merits of their arguments. These are what are generally known as 'adversarial proceedings,' much as Shipler claims never occurred."[17]

Shipler likewise claimed that Solis "did not distinguish between the memo's list of 'our organizations' and 'the organizations of our friends.'" In this, wrote Poole, Shipler "leaves the false impression that Solis ignored a distinction between two separate lists, erroneously lumping them in all together." In reality, however, "the document itself made no such division between 'our organizations' and 'the organizations of our friends.' They are all included together."

Amplifying this dismissal was the Bridge Initiative, a program of the Saudi-funded Alwaleed bin Talal Center for Muslim-Christian Understanding at Georgetown University, which published a piece entitled "Civilization Jihad:" Debunking the Conspiracy Theory," on February 26, 2016.

The Bridge "debunking" centers upon the claim that the memorandum "was not a formal plan accepted by the Brotherhood, and it didn't have influence in other Muslim circles," and that claims to the contrary "unsurprisingly appeal to Americans who are already suspicious of Muslims."

Bridge attempted to support these claims with the further assertion that "according to a 2009 opinion by the presiding judge, the memo was not considered 'supporting evidence' for that alleged money laundering scheme, *nor* any other conspiracy"—including, presumably, one aimed at "eliminating and destroying Western civilization from within." Akram's language, Bridge claimed, was "wishful, and does not reflect the Muslim Brotherhood's agenda as outlined in documents obtained by the FBI. Asking that his memo be added 'to the Council agenda in its coming meeting' in 1991, Akram frames it as a 'letter' that contains his 'hopes, ambitions and challenges.' In listing a number of American Muslim organizations in the appendix, he even says: 'Imagine if they all march according to one plan!!! [sic].'"

Akram's "wish," according to Bridge, "wasn't taken up in an official way by the Brotherhood Council meeting of 1991. A report of the 'most important issues' addressed in the 1991 conference—the logical place for Akram's memo to be mentioned if it were ever considered by the group—does not reference it. And importantly, nowhere else in the public collection of Muslim Brotherhood documents from the trial is it mentioned. It would seem that Akram's pleas to the group to 'not rush to throw these papers away,' and to 'read [the pages of his letter] and to comment on them' went unheeded. There is no evidence that those whom he addressed ever took the time to 'study' or 'comment' on it. Akram may have been correct, then, to fear that his letter would be seen as 'strange' or a 'new submission without an antecedent' or 'root.'"

What's more, noted Bridge, "Akram's arguments and phrasing in Arabic are rarely found on the web and not found in Islamic doctrine or literature.... *Akram's language doesn't come up in mainstream Islamic literature, either before or after he penned the letter.*" (Italics in the original.) The memorandum was, in short, one man's "fantasy."[18]

No fantasy at all, however, was the fact that the Bridge Initiative was itself tied to the Muslim Brotherhood. Bridge's Project Director, John Esposito, has called Muslim Brotherhood Sheikh Yusuf al-Qaradawi, who advocates jihad-martyrdom suicide bombings, a champion of a "reformist interpretation of Islam and its relationship to democracy, pluralism and human rights."[19] Esposito has praised the Council on American-Islamic Relations (CAIR), which has ties to Hamas and the Muslim Brotherhood, as a "phenomenal organization."[20] He has spoken at CAIR fundraisers in order, he explained, to "show solidarity not only with the Holy Land Fund, but also with CAIR."[21]

Esposito was referring to the Holy Land Foundation, an Islamic charity that was shut down and prosecuted for funneling money to the jihad terror group Hamas. Esposito himself also refuses to condemn Hamas, as the Investigative Project notes: "In a 2000 interview in The United Association for Studies and Research's (UASR) *Middle East Affairs Journal*, Esposito refused to condemn Hamas, which at the time was already designated a Foreign Terrorist Organization (FTO) by the U.S. State Department."[22] Esposito has also co-edited a book, *Islam and Secularism in the Middle East*, with Azzam Tamimi. Palestinian political scientist Muhammad Muslih calls Tamimi "a Hamas member." Tamimi has said: "I admire the Taliban; they are courageous," and "I support Hamas."[23] In its Charter, Hamas styles itself the Muslim Brotherhood for Palestine.

In light of those and other ties to the Muslim Brotherhood, it is understandable that the Bridge Initiative would be anxious to discredit Akram's memorandum and portray it as insignificant. Bridge's case, however, founders on the facts. The Center for Security Policy (CSP) noted that "the Bridge Initiative treats the Explanatory Memorandum as the aspirations of a single man, but ignores the fact that events described in the memorandum actually happened. Most notably, the merger of the Islamic Circle of North America (ICNA) with the Muslim Brotherhood. Akram makes reference in the Explanatory Memorandum to the discussed merger of the Group with the 'Islamic Circle' (meaning the Islamic Circle of North America.)...It can in fact be shown that ICNA began to publicly identify with the Muslim American Society (MAS), which federal prosecutors have referred to as the "overt arm of the Muslim Brotherhood" by holding joint MAS-ICNA conventions beginning in 2001."[24]

The Center for Security Policy adds that "far from one man's 'fantasy' Akram describes in the Memorandum proposals for events which do in fact take place....Akram's explanatory memorandum fits into a historical context of what the Brotherhood had done in the past, was proposing to do, and what it in fact can later be shown to have accomplished."[25]

As for Bridge's claim that "Akram's arguments and phrasing in Arabic are rarely found on the web and not found in Islamic doctrine or literature," the CSP points out that "Akram's memorandum was never intended to be read by the public at large at all, but only by high level members of his own organization"—thus there is no reason for anyone to be surprised that Akram's "ideas are not widespread online."[26]

What's more, counterterror experts took Akram's memorandum quite seriously. The former U.S. deputy chief for Counterterrorism at the Department of Justice, Jeff Breinholt, remarked: "For the first time that was almost direct proof of what we had long suspected about their true political goals in the United States.... Something like the explanatory memo is a bonanza for the art of intelligence because it actually is the target or the subject speaking in their own words about what they intend. You don't have to read too much into that."[27]

Nathan Garret, a former FBI Agent and federal prosecutor, noted: "The organizations that were on that list represented a huge segment of the Islamic voice in North America at the time. The Memorandum not only named names, it candidly revealed just how the Brotherhood viewed the United States—as a target of conquest."[28]

Not a tiny minority, but a "huge segment of the Islamic voice in North America" saw the United States as a "target of conquest." Is this inconceivable (or Islamophobic)?

Is it beyond the realm of possibility that at least some of the believers in the prophethood of the man who said "I have been commanded to fight against people so long as they do not declare that there is no god but Allah," and whose holy book says "fight them until religion is all for Allah" (Qur'an 8:39) would endeavor to conquer non-Muslim lands and impose Islamic law upon them?[29]

This is not to say that the United States is in imminent danger of being conquered and turned into an Islamic state. But if the teachings of conquest are part of Islam, and they manifestly are, then they will be preached in the U.S., and civil strife is likely to result.

What Is Being Taught in the Mosques?

Consider an analogous incident in Canada. A controversy there revealed the perils of assuming, as nearly everyone does, that mosques in the West teach peace and tolerance, and that the overwhelming majority of Muslims are moderate and loyal members of secular societies. The Dar Al-Arqam Mosque in Montreal came under fire in early 2017 for hosting a Jordanian Muslim cleric, Sheikh Muhammad bin Musa Al Nasr, who preached: "O Muslim, O servant of Allah, O Muslim, O servant of Allah, there is a Jew behind me, come and kill him."[30]

A police complaint was filed, which unintentionally revealed the dilemma that Canadian authorities, and officials in all non-Muslim countries, are facing and will increasingly face, although none of them admit it. Al Nasr was simply repeating a statement that is attributed to Muhammad. Are the Canadian police going to stop imams from quoting Muhammad? Once Canada passed its "anti-Islamophobia" motion M-103, it became unlikely that they would do anything at all: only non-Muslim foes of jihad terror can commit "hate speech."

Nonetheless, the incident revealed a significant problem for secular liberalism, and secular liberals, in the West who are anxious that Islam and Muslims be fully part of their gorgeous mosaic of diverse cultures and peoples. If they take the texts of their sacred book at face value, imams in Canada (and elsewhere) could call for murder (Qur'an 2:191, 4:89, 9:5), kidnapping (Qur'an 47:4) and rape (Qur'an 4:3, 4:24, 23:1-6, 33:50, 70:30), all by quoting the Qur'an and Muhammad. If they did so, would they be engaging in incitement to violence or simply the free exercise of their religion?

Right now this question is not being considered because the possibility that those practices could have Islamic sanction is indignantly rejected. Imam Ziad Asali of the Association of Islamic Charitable Projects expressed outrage that Al Nasr had spoken at all: "I do not understand how this person was invited to come and give a sermon and spread this hatred in Montreal against any community.... To use the themes of the Prophet to spread hatred is actually something that is disrespectful towards the Prophet himself."[31]

That was music to multiculturalist ears, but Asali tried to paper over the real problem by implying that the anti-Semitic and genocidal statement attributed to Muhammad was not authentic: "The hadith is one of more than 100,000 that are written in many books, some of which are considered authentic, while others are not, said Asali."[32]

Asali's reply was misleading, although it was noteworthy that he didn't simply say straightforwardly that the hadith was inauthentic. He couldn't say that truthfully, because it meets the standards Muslim scholars have for authenticity. There are hadiths that Muslim scholars consider inauthentic, but this one appears, with minor variations, in the two hadith collections that Muslims consider most reliable: Bukhari and Muslim. What's more, it appears more than once in both, which is an indication that it was attested by multiple sources. This kind of attestation is what makes Islamic scholars consider hadiths authentic. Here is the fullest version of the statement:

> "Abu Huraira reported Allah's Messenger (may peace be upon him) as saying: The last hour would not come unless the Muslims

> will fight against the Jews and the Muslims would kill them until the Jews would hide themselves behind a stone or a tree and a stone or a tree would say: Muslim, or the servant of Allah, there is a Jew behind me; come and kill him; but the tree Gharqad would not say, for it is the tree of the Jews."[33]

So what are Canadian authorities going to do when imams keep on quoting Muhammad? What are Western authorities going to do when imams preach to their people that Muslims are commanded to fight against people (note that there is no exception, they have to fight against all people) until they confess that there is no god but Allah and Muhammad is his messenger?

What, indeed? In October 2016, Muslims outside the Dar-ul-Uloom Qadria Jilania mosque in Walthamstow, East London, distributed leaflets calling for the murder of those who violated Islam's blasphemy laws. The leaflets praised the Pakistani Muslim Mumtaz Qadri, who in 2011 murdered Salman Taseer, the governor of Punjab, for the crime of opposing Pakistan's blasphemy laws, which have been used to bring untold misery into the lives of numerous Muslims and Christians in Pakistan. "All Muslims," the East London leaflet declared, should stand with Qadri, as those who leave Islam "deserve to be assassinated."[34]

Also, what are Western authorities going to do when Muslims who are determined to subdue and Islamize Western societies emerge from among the refugees they have welcomed into their lands?

The New Europe

This has already begun. In April 2017, the German government of Angela Merkel, which had been so welcoming of Muslim migrants, agreed to outlaw child marriage after the Central Register of Foreign Nationals revealed that 1,500 non-German minors were married; this included 361 girls who were under 14. 664 of these child brides came from Syria, with many others coming from Afghanistan and Iraq.[35] Other Muslims showed a similar reluctance to assimilate: on

June 1, 2017, a group of Muslim migrants in Oldenburg, Germany stabbed another Muslim migrant to death for smoking a cigarette and declining to fast during Ramadan.[36]

Meanwhile, Muslim migrants in Europe were creating an atmosphere of increasing lawlessness, at least in areas where they predominated. In 2016, German police were hunting for 174,000 criminal suspects who were migrants, a 50 percent increase over 2015. Interior Minister Thomas de Maiziere noted that the number of crimes that refugees to Germany had committed had "increased disproportionately."[37]

In July 2016, Jaber al-Bakr, a Muslim migrant to Germany from Syria, was arrested; police found a "bomb-making lab" in his apartment in Chemnitz; he was apparently planning a jihad massacre at a Berlin airport or at a location in the German state of Saxony.[38]

That same month, Riaz Khan Ahmadzai, a 17-year-old Muslim migrant from Pakistan who was claiming to be a refugee from Afghanistan, carried an axe onto a train in the German city of Wurzburg; he began hacking at passengers and injured five people.[39] Just four days later, Ali Sonboly, a German-Iranian teenager, murdered nine people at a shopping center.[40]

There were many similar young men among the Muslim migrants in Germany. In May 2017, police arrested yet another, a 17-year-old from Syria who was suspected of plotting a jihad suicide bombing in Berlin.[41]

In a sadly typical incident, Danish police chased a speeding car into the Muslim-majority area of Bispehaven in Aarhus, only to be stoned and abused by 150 young Muslims. One tried to strangle a police officer.[42] In Italy, migrants attacked a female television reporter live on the air; her colleagues back at the studio called out her name in alarm as the video feed was lost and her screaming came through on the audio.[43]

Meanwhile, in the small French town of Alfortville, in April 2017, 200 illegal Muslim migrants stormed the town hall and occupied it for an hour, demanding the relaxation of requirements for their status in France to be legalized. They refused to leave the building; as the protest grew violent, fourteen people were injured, and police had to use tear gas to clear the building. Alfortville Mayor Luc Carvounas stated: "This illegal occupation prevented Alfortvillians from accessing public services throughout the morning, and caused anxiety among town hall staff and families who were already present in the building. Although staff received the men, and listened to their demands, the members of the collective did not wish to enter into any dialogue, instead contenting themselves with denouncing government policy." He said that the protest was simply an "exploitation of human misery for political purposes."[44]

Also in France, life was looking up in early 2017 for a Muslim migrant from Afghanistan, Mohammad Khan Wazir. Authorities removed his name from the terror watch list, and his three-year-old son Djihad (French for "jihad") returned with the boy's French mother from Islamic State territory to join him in the beautiful French Riviera town of Fréjus. But as sweet as life was in Fréjus, Mohammad Khan Wazir was unhappy. Visiting the childcare center where young Djihad was staying after his return from the Islamic State, Mohammad told center employees that Djihad's French passport still hadn't come through, and he was tired of waiting. He was "sick of all the red tape," he told them, and declared: "I'm going to go to court and shoot them all dead with a Kalashnikov."[45]

What kind of French citizen will Mohammad Khan Wazir, or young Djihad, become? What kind of a future will they and others like them make for France, and for Europe?

The same question could be asked of the parents of a 14-year-old Moroccan Muslim girl in Milan, whose parents and brother whipped her for dressing and acting in a manner they deemed "too Western."[46] Prosecutor Ciro Cascone commented: "It's an unfortunately ordinary story, like many we see, where there is a cultural factor, and a conflict between a girl born in Italy who wants to live like her friends and a traditionalist family that tries to impose her upbringing with physical and above all moral violence."[47] Milan Mayor Giuseppe Sala said ominously: "Unfortunately, it's not the first or last case of this kind, among girls who want to Westernise themselves."[48]

Yet again, this question regarding prospects for assimilation could also be asked of a 36-year-old Muslim migrant from Kosovo, who went on a rampage with an axe at a train station in Düsseldorf, Germany, injuring seven people, including two police officers. Authorities announced that he was "mentally ill."[49]

Of course. Likewise mentally disturbed was a 31-year-old Muslim migrant from Afghanistan who, early on the morning of March 24, 2017, just days after the Düsseldorf attack, spotted a 59-year-old man riding his bicycle to Bergedorf, a district of Hamburg. The migrant stopped the cyclist, had a brief verbal exchange with him, and then hit his head with a hammer. Bleeding profusely, the dazed victim managed nevertheless to get away and alert police; his attacker was arrested shortly thereafter, still wearing his blood-drenched clothes. A German police official announced: "The suspect may have a mental illness."[50]

The Rape Epidemic

Then there was the rape epidemic. On New Year's Eve in 2015, 2,000 Muslims, around half of them recent migrants, sexually assaulted 1,200 women and girls in cities across Germany. Six hundred of these assaults took place in Cologne and 400 in Hamburg. [51]

This massive rape outbreak was directly related to some core Qur'anic assumptions. The Qur'an teaches that infidel women can be lawfully taken for sexual use (cf. its allowance for a man to take "captives of the right hand," 4:3, 4:24, 23:1-6, 33:50, 70:30). The Qur'an says: "O Prophet, tell your wives and your daughters and the women of the believers to bring down over themselves of their outer garments. That is more suitable that they will be known and not be abused. And ever is Allah Forgiving and Merciful." (33:59) The implication there is that if women do not cover themselves adequately with their outer garments, they may be abused, and that such abuse would be justified.

Three young Muslims in Uppsala, Sweden, two of whom were citizens of Afghanistan, were charged in March 2017 with gang-raping a woman, and worse: as the young men attacked their victim, their friend stood by, according to prosecutors; he "laughed and in close proximity filmed the incident with his mobile phone, and posted it live or very shortly after the rape on Facebook."[52]

In Germany, five Muslim migrants committed a "serious sexual assault" against a seven-year-old girl at the Central Initial Reception Center (ZEA) for refugees in Hamburg. Said public prosecutor Nana Frombach: "We have initiated a case against five persons. There had been no urgent need for action."[53] Why not?

In a similar vein, in October 2016, an 18-year-old Muslim asylum seeker from Somalia broke into the Haus am Bürgerpark home for the disabled in the German city of Neuenhaus. Once inside, he raped a paralyzed 59-year-old man and was in the process of raping another patient of the facility when his victim's 87-year-old wife surprised him; he promptly attacked her with "great force" and murdered her.[54]

In June 2017 in Sweden, toward the beginning of Ramadan, a 60-year-old Muslim driving instructor was charged with sexually assaulting six of his female driving students. He grabbed the thighs and breasts of one, and took another's hand and put it down his pants, asking, "Why don't you put it in your mouth?"[55] He then forced her to do so. To another one of his victims he displayed the full force of his charm, saying: "If it wasn't Ramadan, I would have fucked the shit out of you."[56]

"They Want Germany to Be Islamised"

Have the Muslim migrants enriched Europe even in the midst of the crime wave that has followed in the wake of their arrival? There were reasons to restrain one's enthusiasm for the gorgeous multicultural mosaic that was being created on the Old Continent. In Switzerland, the Federal Intelligence Service (FIS) in 2016 identified 497 Muslims who were suspected of spreading jihad propaganda on the Internet.[57]

And in 2016, German states spent over $22 billion on refugee resettlement and integration, far more than had been expected.[58]

What was Germany buying? In November 2016, an Arabic-speaking translator who worked with refugees for five years in refugee centers all over Germany told the harrowing story of what she heard Muslim migrants say when they were speaking Arabic to one another and didn't think anyone who wasn't sympathetic to them was listening. The Muslim migrants, she said, had a "pure hatred" of Christians, and Muslim parents told their children not to play with children who were Christians.[59]

The migrants even told her that she was committing a sin by aiding the Christian refugees as well as the Muslim ones. She said: "They want Germany to be Islamised. They despise our country and our values," but added that they only displayed their "true colors" when no non-Muslims were nearby.[60]

Her revelations received remarkably little media attention. This was a pity, because it might have been fruitful for German authorities to explain how they thought welcoming such people into their country could possibly have a good outcome.

Amid all the chaos that Muslim migrants had unleashed in Europe, Pope Francis likened refugee camps in Europe to concentration camps, "because many of them are concentration ... because there is a great number of people left there inside them."[61]

He did not mention the fact that if the European refugee centers were indeed concentration camps, they were the first concentration camps in history that people were clamoring to get into rather than out of.

"Islamophobic" to Report Migrant Crime

European authorities have been notably slow to prosecute, and sometimes even to report, Muslim migrant crime. In April 2016, the German newspaper *Express*, which is based in Cologne, revealed that German authorities knew about the mass sexual assaults there on the previous New Year's Eve, and did not reveal them to the public. North

Rhine-Westphalia Interior Minister Rolf Jäger sent a memo to police in early January informing them that there had been "Rape, sexual offenses, thefts, robberies committed by larger foreign Group," and that "the women were in this case surrounded by the group of people and groped above their clothing, jewellery stolen and was snatched. In one case, a 19-year-old German victim had fingers inserted into her body openings [vagina and anus]. The criminal group was consistently described by the victims as North Africans, between 17-28 years of age. Investigations are continuing."[62] Despite this, however, Jäger gave no information about the sexual assaults to the public.

Even worse, the *Express* revealed an "internal police memo" that relayed "a request from the ministry," ordering police to "cancel" the word "rape" in their reports on the assaults.[63] This came after it came to light that Jäger had turned down a request for backup from Cologne's police chief on that fateful night, and then fired the chief for not acting with sufficient dispatch to stop the mass assaults.[64] After all that, it was no surprise that seven months after the assaults, police had identified only 120 of the perpetrators.[65]

It was the same story in The Netherlands. In April 2017, The Netherlands' largest newspaper, *De Telegraaf*, revealed that the country's national police force asked them to drop a freedom of information request about the number of asylum seekers involved in criminal activity, in exchange for juicy leads and other journalistic perks. "Initially," *De Telegraaf* stated, "the police had denied to this newspaper that they even collected data on crime among foreigners seeking asylum," but then admitted that it tended to "keep the figures under the hat" because the subject of migrant crime was "taboo."[66]

Caught out, police chief executive Erik Akerboom denied any intention to cover up crimes by migrants: "Unfortunately, this approach makes it look like police seek to ignore facts that are socially sensitive. Nothing is less true."[67] Why, then, did the police ask De Telegraaf to drop its request for information on criminal activity by asylum seekers? Because, said Akerboom, such data could be "misleading."[68]

Misleading? How? Akerboom didn't explain. Perhaps it could mislead people into thinking that the Muslim migrant influx into Europe wasn't such a great idea after all?

Sweden was already there. The Swedish government on September 15, 2015, issued a memo ordering police not to disclose the race or nationality of criminal suspects. This memo emphasized that this rule applied to all kinds of crimes, "from minor traffic accidents to serious crimes like muggings, beatings and murder."[69] This new rule was instituted explicitly to avoid accusations of racism: "The police are sometimes criticised for reporting on peoples' skin colour. We are perceived as racist. As the police are not racist, nor should be perceived as such, from now on, please apply these instructions."[70]

The Swedish government didn't even want private citizens complaining about migrant crime. In May 2017, authorities charged a 70-year-old Swedish woman with "incitement to racial hatred" for a Facebook post in which she said that migrants "set fire to cars, and urinate and defecate on the streets." This wasn't hearsay; she said she saw them doing it, but prosecutors charged her anyway. Sweden's Justice Minister Morgan Johansson explained in Orwellian fashion that while Sweden protected the freedom of speech, some speech was freer than others: "We have freedom of speech in Sweden. This means people have the right to hold repulsive opinions here. But there are always limits…For example when it comes to hate speech."[71] Johansson did not explain by what criteria Swedish authorities proposed to determine what constituted "hate speech."

With this chill on speaking freely about migrant crime, it was not surprising that in Sweden, even in the midst of a rape epidemic, only 13 percent of Muslim migrants are deported after having been found guilty of raping children.[72] When five Muslim migrant teens from Afghanistan were found guilty of gang-raping a boy, they weren't deported because Afghanistan was "too dangerous" and the attackers would have been "hit very hard" by the news that they had to go back there.[73]

Also in Sweden on October 4, 2016, a Muslim migrant from Iraq enticed a 14-year-old Swedish girl to his apartment in Gothenburg, where he showed her pornographic films and then raped her. He decided to film the proceedings, and in the video the girl is seen repeatedly saying "no," but he did not stop.

The attacker was initially fined and sentenced to ten months in a youth facility, but his sentence was reduced, and the rape charge expunged, on appeal. In April 2017, the Supreme Court of Western Sweden declared that the poor attacker had "ADHD problems" that gave him "difficulties in interpreting and interacting with other people as well as recognizing the standards he is expected to live up to."[74]

What of the video? The court said that it depicted the girl being anally raped, and that she was saying "no" not to sex in general, but only to anal intercourse.[75] The rapist was not deported.

Neither was Anis Amri. On December 19, 2016, Amri, a Muslim asylum seeker in Berlin, stole a truck and plowed it into a crowd at the city's famous Christmas market, murdering twelve people and wounding dozens. It later came to light that the State Criminal Office in the German state of North Rhine-Westphalia warned the ministry of the interior of the state parliament in Düsseldorf about Amri in a March 2016 letter: "Amri presents a threat in the form of a suicide attack. The commission of a terrorist attack by Amri is expected." Amri, said the letter, should be deported.

Nothing was done. Regional Interior Minister Ralf Jäger said it was not "legally possible" to deport Amri, as his native Tunisia denied that he was a Tunisian citizen.[76]

Thus, twelve people were dead due to European bureaucratic niceties.

Likewise, in Stockholm in April 2017, when a Muslim migrant from Uzbekistan drove a truck into a department store, it was soon revealed that authorities knew he had "extremist sympathies" and had been planning to deport him. Immigration officials were looking for him at the time of the attack.[77]

Noting the reluctance of authorities to act decisively against criminal Muslim migrants, some Germans began arming themselves, in contravention of German law. A website called Migrant Fright offered black market weapons to Germans, enabling buyers to avoid "annoying bureaucratic hurdles or annoying paperwork."[78] German authorities shut the website down.[79]

The Mainstreaming of Support for Jihad

Some would argue that little or nothing can be done because the migrants are exercising their freedom of religion. Did religious freedom grant to Muslims or to anyone else the license or the right to break other laws, or to work at "eliminating and destroying Western civilization from within and sabotaging its miserable house," simply because they were doing so in accord with religious precepts?

The question may seem absurd, but it isn't. Muslims with ties to Muslim Brotherhood organizations have risen to positions of immense influence in American society, and it is "Islamophobic" to question them.

One chief example of this phenomenon is Rep. Keith Ellison (D-MN). Ellison began his political activity as a defender of the incendiary anti-Semitic Nation of Islam leader Louis Farrakhan. He has called his previous defense of Farrakhan "the mistake in my past," but he never disavowed the Muslim American Society (MAS) or the Islamic Circle of North America (ICNA) after an outcry arose over his plan to give the keynote speech at their annual convention while he was running for Chair of the Democratic National Committee.[80] Ellison quietly dropped out of the event, but never uttered a critical word about MAS or ICNA, despite their numerous questionable associations.

The Investigative Project's John Rossomando noted that "the MAS convention Ellison will address will hear from radical speakers such as Ali Qaradaghi (alternately spelled Al-Qurra Daghi in the MAS-ICNA program), the secretary general of the pro-Hamas International Union of Muslim Scholars (IUMS), which is one of the world's most influential groups for Sunni Islamist clerics. It counts former Hamas Prime Minister Ismail Haniyeh as a member."[81]

Yet Ellison has longstanding ties to MAS; in 2008, he accepted $13,350 from MAS to go on a pilgrimage to Mecca.[82] It wasn't surprising that he would have had no trouble, if there had been no public notice and protest, sharing the MAS stage with Hamas supporters, in light of the fact that he said while speaking at a fund-raiser for his 2010 Congressional reelection campaign that a vote for him was a vote against Israel's supposed control of U.S. foreign policy: "The message I want to send to you by donating to this campaign," he declared, "is positioning me and positioning Muslims in general to help steer the ship of state in America.... The United States foreign policy in the Middle East is governed by what is good or bad through a country of seven million people. A region of 350 million all turns on a country of seven million. Does that make sense? Is that logic? Right?"[83]

Ellison also boasted that "there is a growing awareness in the US Congress and in the executive branch that everything anyone does, including Israel, is not fine. And there are real questions being asked."[84] He revealed that in meetings with his Jewish constituents, he challenged them to stand with Barack Obama against Israel: "Do you stand with the President on stopping settlements in east Jerusalem, because that is the policy of my president and I want to know if you're with the President. Are you with the President?"[85]

Ellison proposed that U.S. aid to Israel be tied to the Israeli building projects in East Jerusalem: "Why are we sending $2.8 billion a year over there when they won't even honor our request to stop building in East Jerusalem? Where is the future Palestinian state going to be if it's colonized before it even gets up off the ground?"[86]

He offered an alternative aiding Israel: "We should be building the bilateral business relationships between the United States and the Muslim world.... Morocco, we gotta build it up. Saudi Arabia, we gotta build it up. The Gulf countries, we gotta build them. Pakistan, we gotta build them."[87] (Saudi Arabia?)

This would be done so that ultimately Muslims in the U.S. would be able to make demands upon the government: "We need to have so much goods and services going back and forth between this country and the Muslim world that if we say we need this right here, then everyone is saying, OK. Understand my point? You've got to be strategic.... These business relationships can be leveraged to say that we need a new deal politically."[88]

MAS has links not just to Hamas, but to the Muslim Brotherhood. The *Chicago Tribune* reported in 2004 that "in recent years, the U.S. Brotherhood operated under the name Muslim American Society, according to documents and interviews. One of the nation's major Islamic groups, it was incorporated in Illinois in 1993 after a contentious debate among Brotherhood members."[89] In a validation of the accuracy of this report, it is now carried on the Muslim Brotherhood's English-language website, *Ikhwanweb*.[90])

The links between MAS and Hamas and the Muslim Brotherhood are not simply the conjectures of "Islamophobes." A Muslim scholar, al-Husein Madhany, wrote in a 2010 email to fellow Muslim and Leftist activists: "When I said that I believe MAS halaqas [religious meetings] to be a national security threat, it was only part in jest. My caution comes from what I have personally heard said at MAS halaqas during my time in graduate school and based on what I know about their ideological (but financial) ties to the Muslim Brotherhood and Hamas."[91]

It doesn't end with MAS, either; there is abundant evidence of Ellison's links to other anti-Semitic groups as well. Ellison has spoken at a convention of the Islamic Society of North America (ISNA).[92] Yet ISNA has actually admitted its ties to Hamas, which styles itself the Palestinian arm of the Muslim Brotherhood.[93] The Justice Department actually classified ISNA among entities "who are and/or were members of the US Muslim Brotherhood."[94]

Also, the Council on American-Islamic Relations (CAIR) raised large amounts of for Ellison's first campaign, and he has spoken at numerous CAIR events.[95] Yet CAIR is an unindicted co-conspirator in a Hamas terror funding case—so named by the Justice Department.[96] CAIR officials have repeatedly refused to denounce Hamas and Hizballah as terrorist groups.[97]

Yet even with all this evidence of Ellison's anti-Semitism and dalliances with Hamas-linked groups, he remained a viable candidate for DNC Chair right up to the end; the eventual victor, Tom Perez, named him Deputy Chair.

The mainstreaming of Ellison shows the priorities and perspective of the political and media establishments today: ties to pro-jihad groups are just fine, but those who are perceived to be "Islamophobes," by contrast, are to be vilified and shunned.

Shutting Down Criticism of What Is Happening—in the U.S.

In May 2017, a man named Jeremy Joseph Christian was riding a crowded commuter train in Portland, Oregon, when he began yelling at two young women, one of whom was reportedly Muslim. "You don't like it? You got a problem with what I'm saying? Fuck all you Christians and Muslims and fucking Jews, fucking die. Burn you at the stake… fucking die."[98] He added: "I'm about to stab some motherfuckers."[99]

And he did, murdering two men who came to the defense of the women he was threatening.

Despite Christian's denunciation of Jews and Christians as well as Muslims, his attack was widely reported as stemming from "Islamophobic" motives. *The New York Times*' initial story on the murders was headlined, "Two Killed in Portland While Trying to Stop Anti-Muslim Rant, Police Say."[100] The *Washington Post* published an article about his victims entitled, "'Final act of bravery': Men who were fatally stabbed trying to stop anti-Muslim rants identified."[101] After Christian continued ranting during his first appearance in court, *The Daily Telegraph* ran a story with the headline, "'I call it patriotism': Man accused of murdering two people during anti-Muslim rant defiant in court."[102]

Ted Wheeler, the mayor of Portland, went even further. In the aftermath of the attack, he asked federal authorities, who had jurisdiction over such matters, to bar two rallies from being held in Portland: a "Trump Free Speech Rally" and a "March Against Sharia."[103]

Wheeler explained: "Our city is in mourning, our community's anger is real, and the timing and subject of these events can only exacerbate an already difficult situation."[104] Referring to the organizers of the two rallies, which he called "alt-right demonstrations," he said: "I urge them to ask their supporters to stay away from Portland. There is never a place for bigotry or hatred in our community, and especially not now."[105]

Joey Gibson, the organizer of the "Trump Free Speech Rally," cried foul, saying: "There's going to be more intensity, there's going to be more threats. They're using the deaths of these two people and Jeremy Christian—they're using it to get Portland all rowdy about our June 4 rally and it's absolutely disgusting."[106]

Gibson was also involved in staging the "March Against Sharia," which he said was necessary because Islamic law "is incompatible with our Constitution and American values"; the March Against Sharia's Facebook page called upon rallygoers to "stand for human rights."[107]

Sharia is actually incompatible with the Constitution and American values in numerous particulars, including its institutionalized discrimination against women and non-Muslims, its curtailment of the freedom of speech, and its denial of the freedom of conscience. But to Ted Wheeler, to stand against such laws constituted "bigotry" and "hatred," and that was that.

His stance was too much even for the American Civil Liberties Union of Oregon, despite its frequent collaborations with groups such as the Council on American-Islamic Relations (CAIR). The Oregon ACLU commented: "It may be tempting to shut down speech we disagree with, but once we allow the government to decide what we can say, see, or hear, or who we can gather with, history shows us that the most marginalized will be disproportionately censored and punished for unpopular speech. If we allow the government to shut down speech for some, we all will pay the price down the line."[108]

Indeed. And the Portland mayor was calling for such government intervention in order to shut down criticism of Islamic law after an "Islamophobic" attack that was actually nothing of the kind.

Is this the kind of society secular liberals really want?

Maybe it is. After all, they have certainly made sure that there has been a good deal of shutting down of criticism of Islamic law.

Early in 2017, the feminist author Phyllis Chesler was set to speak via Skype at a symposium on honor violence at the University of Arkansas—until, that is, some faculty members who opposed her appearance, Joel Gordon, Mohja Kohf and Ted Swedenburg, began digging into her background and found that in 2007, she had associated with a thought criminal. They called upon UA's King Fahd Center for Middle East Studies to withdraw its support for Chesler's appearance, which led directly to her being cancelled.

Arkansas Online reported: "In expressing concerns with Chesler, faculty cited her writings on 'the ultra-right Breitbart forum' and her role as co-author of a pamphlet, The Violent Oppression of Women in Islam, with Robert Spencer, 'considered by the Southern Poverty Law Center to be 'one of America's most prolific and vociferous anti-Muslim propagandists,' the email stated."[109]

University of Arkansas professor Tom Paradise, who was responsible for getting Chesler canceled, wrote to colleagues after the deed had been done to proclaim that he was "delighted" that she had been cancelled.[110] Paradise was then suspended from his professorial duties, an unusual move in light of the likelihood that the overwhelming majority of his colleagues shared his delight.

The stigmatization and silencing of dissenting voices on campuses nationwide is inconsistent with the very idea of a university, which is supposed to be a place where ideas are accepted or dismissed on their merits alone. Chesler was canceled because, among other things, she co-wrote a pamphlet with me ten years before her scheduled appearance at the University of Arkansas.

That was an extremely remote association, and was akin to the Nazi Brownshirts getting professors fired because it was discovered that they had a Jewish great-grandmother.

Apparently now everyone who has ever said a kind word to me or stood in a room with me is to be deprived of all professional opportunities and stigmatized as a "bigot" and an "Islamophobe." This is reminiscent of the Stalinist purges, and was all the more shameful for taking place at a university.

Meanwhile, did Gordon, Kohf, and Swedenburg present any evidence that what Chesler and I wrote in that long-forgotten pamphlet was false? No. Apparently, all they said about it was this: "The pamphlet was published by David Horowitz' Freedom Center, which frequently targets students and scholars for speaking out about justice for Palestinians."[111]

More guilt by association. Now Chesler was being tarred not only with my supposed enormities, but with those of David Horowitz as well.

The professors went on: "The pamphlet is a catalogue of horrors inflicted on women that are said to be the outcome of Islam's essential nature. 'Islamic gender apartheid,' Chesler and Spencer write, 'is not caused by western imperialism, colonialism, or racism. It is indigenous to Islam both theologically and historically.'"[112]

Did they present any evidence to show this is false? Apparently not: after the increasingly common practice of Leftist academics and spokesmen everywhere, they presented their perspective as if its truth were self-evident. They apparently didn't believe that it was incumbent upon them to refute dissenting views; they just have to show that such views were *right-wing*.

What's more, did they present any evidence that the Southern Poverty Law Center was a neutral and impartial arbiter of what constitutes "hate" and what did not? Of course not.

This is not free inquiry. This is not the open and mutually respectful exchange of ideas. This certainly isn't "I may disagree with what you say, but I will defend to the death your right to say it." All these were out the window, in the service of protecting the image of Islam and stigmatizing its critics.

Have secular liberals who have turned a blind eye to such developments, or even approved of them, considered where this is all tending? Are they not aware that they could end up someday holding an unapproved opinion, and be subjected to the same forcible silencing for which they eagerly set the precedent?

Is that *really* the kind of society they want?

The Worst Form of Government, Except for All the Others

Winston Churchill said it in 1947, "Many forms of Government have been tried, and will be tried in this world of sin and woe. No one pretends that democracy is perfect or all-wise. Indeed it has been said that democracy is the worst form of Government except for all those other forms that have been tried from time to time."[113]

All these years of daily practice of Islamophobia have renewed and deepened my appreciation for the American form of government (which is, of course, not precisely a democracy), for all its manifest flaws. Government of the people, by the people and for the people is susceptible to mob rule and an assortment of other ills, but they are no worse than the afflictions that attend all other forms of government, and every American should be thankful that the Founding Fathers were not all of one religious group or sect. For that fact gave us the First Amendment, with its direction that "Congress shall make no law respecting an establishment of religion, or prohibiting the free exercise thereof."

In a world where long-distance travel is ever easier, mass migration ever more common, and differences on core principles ever more intractable, those words are the key to the establishment and maintenance of a harmonious society. Human beings are never going to agree on the questions of who we are, why we are on this earth, and what the fundamental good is. We are never all going to worship the same god, or all agree to set religion aside.

Accordingly, the only hope we have to live in relatively peaceful societies is a general agreement that we will put up with one another, without one group attempting to gain hegemony over the others and impose its vision of society upon them.

There is no doubt that such a genuinely pluralistic society is full of minefields. The relationship between religion and the precepts of morality and hence of law has been and is hotly debated by far greater minds than mine, with no definitive results. The fractures in American society today can be largely attributed to vastly differing views of what constitutes the nature and parameters of individual rights, and what practices should therefore be legal or illegal. Even those fractures, however, testify to the Founding Fathers' wisdom in placing competing religions on an equal plane, without any one of them being supported by the government and thereby forced upon the people.

In November 2011, I debated the Muslim leader Anjem Choudary, who is now in prison in Britain for jihad terror plotting, on the question "Democracy or Theocracy?"[114] Choudary argued that divine law, coming from the supreme being himself, was incomparably superior to any manmade law, and hence ought to be the guiding principle of any rightly ordered society. His case was predicated upon the assumption that Allah existed, and had bestowed upon human beings his will and the proper code by which they should live in the Qur'an and Sunnah, and the Sharia that was derived from them. I countered by pointing out this this assumption was, at best, unproven, and that those who believed that Sharia was just as manmade as the U.S. Constitution should not be forced to suffer under its precepts, and further that the same U.S. Constitution provided, with its principle of non-establishment of religion, the key whereby people of vastly differing views could live together in peace.

Secular liberals should take note. They have denounced as "Islamophobia" any concerns about the increased population of Muslims in the United States, and in the West in general. They have denounced those of us who are less sanguine about this influx as xenophobic and bigoted, and at odds not only with the American tradition of welcoming the refugee, but with the very idea of pluralism itself.

But many of those they are embracing while denouncing us as Islamophobes are somewhat less pluralistic than they think.

CHAPTER 8

THE THREAT TO SECULAR MUSLIMS

Benazir Bhutto Calls Me Out from the Grave

One night back in October 2009, a reporter called me to ask me for comment about what the late Pakistani politician Benazir Bhutto had said about me in her posthumously published book, which had just come out, *Reconciliation: Islam, Democracy, and the West.*

I was surprised. I hadn't read the book, and hadn't heard of any such attack, but I went out to a bookstore and found one, and sure enough, there it was on page 245:

> Robert Spencer is the author of the well-known Web site Jihad Watch. He uses the Internet to spread misinformation and hatred of Islam, while claiming he is merely putting forward the truth. But as in much extremist advocacy, he presents a skewed, one-sided, and inflammatory story that only helps sow the seeds of civilizational conflict. For example, he takes apparently violent verses of the Quran out of context and then does not provide any peaceful verses as a balance.

Unlike many of the more mainstream authors presented, Spencer does not understand the true Muslim faith or differentiate between moderate Muslims and violent Islamists, and so lumps them all in one boat:

> Islam is a totalitarian ideology that aims to control the religious, social and political life of mankind in all its aspects, the life of its followers without qualification, and the life of those who follow the so-called tolerated religions to a degree that prevents their activities from getting in the way of Islam in any way. And I mean Islam: I do not accept some spurious distinction between Islam and "Islamic Fundamentalism" or "Islamic terrorism." The terrorists who planted the bombs in Madrid, and those responsible for the death of more than 2,000 people on September 11, 2001 in New York and the Ayatollahs of Iran were and are all acting canonically; their actions reflect the teachings of Islam, whether found in the Koran, in the acts and sayings of the Prophet, or Islamic law based on them.[1]

I was sorry that someone so respected and renowned as Benazir Bhutto had decided I was spreading "misinformation and hatred of Islam," but my surprise and sorrow were mixed with a certain pride: the excerpt she quoted from me was elegantly written, and I was pleased with my own craftsmanship.

As it turned out, both Bhutto and I were giving me too much credit: the italicized passage in her book wasn't written by me at all. It was written by the great ex-Muslim scholar Ibn Warraq, in an essay that I had included in a collection of essays I edited in 2004, *The Myth of Islamic Tolerance*.[2]

So *that's* why it was so lucid and eloquent.

There was a certain irony to the fact that while she was excoriating me for allegedly quoting the Qur'an out of context, Benazir Bhutto attributed to me words that had actually been written by someone else. Adding to the irony was the fact that their actual author was, like Bhutto, a Pakistani who was raised a Muslim.

But that was all really beside the point. Benazir Bhutto was an international hero, a martyr to the idea of moderate Islam, as well as for women's rights and secular rule in Muslim-majority countries. That Islamic jihadis assassinated her only underscored all this. So when Benazir Bhutto denounces you, you stay denounced. It must have been really true. I was just stoking the civilizational conflict she was trying to heal, right?

Yet Bhutto herself was a casualty of that civilizational conflict. To note that it was raging was not the same thing as stoking it. And it may have been an uncomfortable or unwelcome fact, but it was a fact nonetheless: if Benazir Bhutto had been a politician in Britain or France or Germany or the United States or Canada instead of Pakistan, she may very well have not been assassinated.

Numerous Western politicians have been assassinated. The point is not that Western countries are uniquely safe for politicians in a way that Pakistan isn't. The point is that the West is accustomed to female politicians with a secular platform; Pakistan isn't. Benazir Bhutto was able to hold office there for a time, but she was never able to hold it without clamorous calls for her blood based on the unacceptability of a women ruling a Muslim nation.

There would have been no such calls in the West. As a secular Muslim, Benazir Bhutto would have been able to live comfortably in the West, and did when she attended Harvard and Oxford, in a way that she was never able to in Pakistan.

Muslims Against Sharia

They don't get much attention, but the fact is undeniable: there are many Muslims in the U.S., Canada, and Western Europe because they *don't* want to live under Sharia.

A few months before 9/11, a Muslim named Khaled Kloub moved his family from the Middle East to Vancouver, Washington. He started calling himself Kyle, and his son Mohammed became Mike. Khaled Kloub explained his mixed feelings about the move: "We knew we would be depriving our kids of a lot of their culture, but it was a matter of give and take. Education here was going to be better, you can speak your mind much more—that stuff partially makes up [for] the sacrifices."[3]

"You can speak your mind much more." That was certainly true, although it becomes less true all the time. Yet as he grew older, young Mohammed Kloub, no longer "Mike," found that even though he and his family were not practicing Muslims, his schoolmates and acquaintances frequently lumped him in with Muslims, and particularly with jihadists: "As much as I wanted to distance myself from being Arab and Muslim in that time," he recalled, "I was also aware of a difference between my identity and the white American classmates I was trying so hard to emulate. For some reason it was acceptable for them to be non-practicing Christians. They'd never be lumped into the same category as Christian fundamentalists, or Jehovah's Witnesses, or any other practicing Christians. They just got to be 'normal' Americans. But I couldn't even find a proper term for a non-practicing Muslim until I was much older and learned what 'secular' meant. As far as anyone was concerned, my name was Mohammed, which made me the same kind of Muslim as the jihadi plotting a terror attack on TV."[4]

That was unfortunate. Another secular Muslim in Washington, Ashraf Hasham, had a similar complaint: "Saying you're Muslim makes people uncomfortable. It's not like I care about making them uncomfortable, but you choose your battles. It's a safety issue." Yet Hasham didn't want to get involved in the Muslim community, with its web of religious observances and social activities, either: "My elementary school was probably the most diverse school I went to. That was the beginning of my not-so-devout, not-really-included, but also not-wanting-to-be-included attitude."[5]

Being "not-so-devout," Hasham wasn't much involved in the Muslim community, but he also apparently meant that he wasn't really included, and didn't really want to be included, in the non-Muslim community. Still, he was also not a practicing Muslim, much as non-Muslims may have identified him as one. That meant that as the Muslim population of the U.S. increases, Kloub's "white American classmates" and the non-Muslims who became uncomfortable in Hasham's presence could end up being the least of their worries.

For all the "racism" and prejudice that Hasham and Kloub experienced as people identified as Muslims in the U.S., at least here they had the choice not to practice their religion.

This would not have been so easily or uncomplicatedly true had he been living in a Muslim country. Eyed Sarraj, a Palestinian Muslim, acknowledged this obliquely when expressing his admiration for Christianity: "Christianity's message of nonviolence is very important, and it is not there in Islam, and I believe it is not there in Judaism. I would honestly say that if I could choose a religion, I would choose Christianity and its ideal of universal acceptance, love, and forgiveness. It is all so beautiful."[6]

"If I could choose a religion." Why didn't he think he had a choice? Because Islamic law mandates death for apostasy, based on Muhammad's dictum, "Whoever changed his Islamic religion, then kill him."[7] Cairo's Al-Azhar University, the most prestigious and influential institution in the Islamic world, an Islamic manual certified as a reliable guide to Sunni Muslim orthodoxy, states: "When a person who has reached puberty and is sane voluntarily apostatizes from Islam, he deserves to be killed."[8]

The website *IslamOnline*, which is operated by a group of Islam scholars under the direction of the renowned Sheikh Yusuf al-Qaradawi, stipulates: "If a sane person who has reached puberty voluntarily apostatizes from Islam, he deserves to be punished. In such a case, it is obligatory for the caliph (or his representative) to ask him to repent and return to Islam. If he does, it is accepted from him, but if he refuses, he is immediately killed." And if a Muslim grows impatient in the absence of the caliph and takes the law into his hands, there is "no blood money for killing an apostate (or any expiation)"—other words, no punishment for the killer.[9]

Hardline Muslims often view non-observant Muslims as apostates, and thus as people deserving death. That is why the only place where such nominal Muslims can live freely and peacefully in the way they choose is in the non-Muslim world. Mohammad Kloub and Ashraf Hasham may have grown impatient with non-Muslims' incomprehension of who they were and tendency to lump them in with terrorists, but in Sharia-observant countries, they would have faced far greater pressures, including the possibility of imprisonment and even execution.

In April 2017, a Saudi citizen named Ahmad Al Shamri was sentenced to be executed for leaving Islam. His crime was to upload several videos to his social media accounts, explaining why he had left Islam, and criticizing Muhammad. He was initially sentenced to death on charges of apostasy and blasphemy in February 2015. In mounting an appeal, his defense team, aware of what it was up against, even tried an insanity plea: they understood that in the minds of the Saudi judiciary, no sane person could or would want to renounce Islam, so therefore Shamri must be insane. They also claimed that he was an alcoholic and addicted to drugs.[10]

None of this self-degradation worked. Shamri gained nothing by allowing himself to be portrayed as drunk, drug-addicted, and insane simply because he had left Islam. He lost one appeal, and then another. He is on death row.

Mohammed Kloub or Ashraf Hasham, had they been in Saudi Arabia and openly expressed negative views of Islam, could have been in the same position. But not in Washington state.

A Muslim Reformer...In the U.S.

On many days when the clamor from charges of "Islamophobia" and "hatred" and "bigotry" is especially noisy, I think fondly of my old friend Tashbih Sayyed.

Tashbih Sayyed was a Muslim native of India who grew up in Pakistan; in the United States, he was the publisher of *Muslim World Today*. In 2005, he and I were part of a group that went to Israel for a week. Tahbih and his wife were either traveling on Pakistani passports or their Pakistani background itself aroused considerable suspicion among Israeli security officials; they were questioned for more than an hour before clearing them to travel to Israel.

Tashbih wasn't angry or resentful. A good-humored and affable fellow, he cheerfully avowed that he well understood the need for air security, and repeatedly avowed that he was pleased that the Israelis were so careful and thorough. And so we proceeded to Israel, where he and I enjoyed more than a few good beers as we discussed the possibilities of and prospects for Islamic reform. Tashbih enjoyed life, with no regrets and a guiltless disregard for Sharia restrictions.

Discussions of the possibilities for genuine reform in Islam are usually overloaded with cant and sloganeering, but that was never so with Tashbih. He was a man of profound insight and the courage to stand and enunciate truths that most preferred to keep concealed. Tashbih Sayyed said forthrightly what other Muslim reformers, both genuine and self-proclaimed, have hesitated to say: that there are elements of Islam that need to be critically reevaluated. He told me, "My whole life is devoted to one end: to make the Muslims understand that their theology needs to be reformed and reinterpreted. Anybody who thinks that there's nothing wrong with their theology is either a blind person or an apologist. There are many things in Muslim Scripture that need to be reshaped and reframed and reinterpreted, so that they cannot be used by terrorists to justify homicide bombings and honor killings."

An extraordinary statement: reshaping, reframing and reinterpreting Muslim scripture is not the same action as the reinterpretation and reevaluation of Jewish and Christian scripture. In the Qur'an, Allah tells Muslims: "This day I have perfected for you your religion and completed my favor upon you and have approved for you Islam as religion" (5:3). What is perfected need not be reformed, and indeed, should not be reformed. In Islam, because it is perfect, *bid'a*, innovation, is a grave sin: the religion is set in its perfect form, and the individual Muslim need only implement its dictates in his own life.

And so in saying that "anybody who thinks that there's nothing wrong with their theology is either a blind person or an apologist," Tashbih was going up against a core tenet of Islam. He was able to do so because he didn't live in Pakistan or Saudi Arabia or Iran, but in California. Tashbih Sayyed didn't live to see it, but he would not have been surprised when, in 2014, back in the Pakistan from which he came to the United States, the Pakistani Taliban (Tehrik-e-Taliban Pakistan, or TTP) murdered three employees of the *Express Tribune*, which up to then had reported forthrightly about jihad violence and even about Sharia oppression of women.

After the murders, *Express Tribune* editor Kamal Siddiqi told his staff to report "nothing against any militant organisationand [sic] its allies like the Jamaat-e-Islami, religious parties and the Tehrik-e-Insaf," all Islamic movements inside Pakistan. Express Tribune writers should touch on "nothing on condemning any terrorist attack" or "against TTP or its statements," and the paper should not carry any "opinion piece/cartoon on terrorism, militancy, the military, military operations, terror attacks."[11]

Siddiqi explained: "We do have exclusives, but we don't run them. It's very frustrating at a personal level for all journalists. But we have decided that we won't do anything at least for the foreseeable future that will come back to haunt us. The fact is three people have been killed and no one out there is protecting us. We are on our own. We have to look out for our own people."[12]

But in the United States at the time when he was writing, Tashbih Sayyed was not under such a cloud. The West's traditions of free inquiry and open discourse, and—it is not inaccurate to say—its relatively small number of Muslims that enabled Tashbih to feel free to speak his mind in a way he never would have been able to do in the country of his birth or that of his youth.

The (Safely in) St. Petersburg Declaration

In April 2007, a group of "secular Muslims, and secular persons of Muslim societies," including "believers, doubters, and unbelievers," gathered in St. Petersburg, Florida, where they issued "The St. Petersburg Declaration." The signatories included the ex-Muslims Ayaan Hirsi Ali, Magdi Allam, Ibn Warraq, Wafa Sultan, and Nonie Darwish, the Islamic reformer Tawfik Hamid, and the renowned journalist Amir Taheri. Among the affirmations of the St. Petersburg Declaration were many that violated the tenets of the Qur'an and Sunnah, including:

> We affirm the inviolable freedom of the individual conscience. We believe in the equality of all human persons.
>
> We insist upon the separation of religion from state and the observance of universal human rights....
>
> We see no colonialism, racism, or so-called "Islamaphobia" in submitting Islamic practices to criticism or condemnation when they violate human reason or rights.
>
> We call on the governments of the world to...
>
> - reject Sharia law, fatwa courts, clerical rule, and state-sanctioned religion in all their forms; oppose all penalties for blasphemy and apostasy, in accordance with Article 18 of the Universal Declaration of Human rights;
> - eliminate practices, such as female circumcision, honor killing, forced veiling, and forced marriage, that further the oppression of women;
> - protect sexual and gender minorities from persecution and violence;
> - reform sectarian education that teaches intolerance and bigotry towards non-Muslims;
> - and foster an open public sphere in which all matters may be discussed without coercion or intimidation.[13]

The reaction at the Muslim site *IqraSense.com* (*iqra* is "read!" or "recite," the first word of the first revelation of the Qur'an to Muhammad) was unfortunately predictable. One Muslim wrote: "This is quite clearly a 'declaration of kufr' [unbelief] and only serves to strengthen the 'umbrella of kufr' that prevents the 'rain of Islaam reaching the people."[14] Another added: "This type of declaration could only have come from those who are 'ashamed' of their faith. Or better still, those who are not even believers. Religious or spiritual matters are not 'subjectable' to scientific research or enquiry. So, the declarants of that so-called 'declaration' are not only ignorant but blatantly mischievious [sic]."[15]

Such reactions made it clear: this affirmation of women's rights, the freedom of conscience, and other principles that ran contrary to Islamic law was the St. Petersburg Declaration, and not the Islamabad Declaration or Riyadh Declaration or Tehran Declaration for a very good reason—the signers wanted to keep their heads.

The Murder of Rashad Khalifa

To be sure, Muslim reformers are not and have not been absolutely safe even on American soil. In the late 1980s, Rashad Khalifa, a Muslim from Egypt who had settled in Tucson, Arizona, began publishing complex and arcane analyses of the Qur'an, which he also translated himself. Ultimately, he declared that he himself was a prophet, which is a death-penalty offense in the religion that styles Muhammad the "seal of the prophets" (Qur'an 33:40). Enraged by what he perceived to be Khalifa's blasphemy, a convert to Islam named Glen Francis moved to Tucson and joined Khalifa's mosque. Once there, he studied Khalifa's movements, learned his schedule, and on January 31, 1990, confronted the wayward scholar in the mosque's kitchen.

He wasn't there for a theological discussion. Francis stabbed Khalifa 29 times and then doused his body with a flammable liquid while turning on the gas stove burners. When he sentenced Francis to twenty-five years to life in prison in 2013, Pima County Superior Court Judge Christopher Browning noted that Francis had committed the murder because he believed Khalifa to be a blasphemer and a heretic: this was ironic, Browning told the killer, because Islam "values peace and wholeness and denounces aggression."[16]

Where Browning gained his expertise on Islamic teaching, he did not explain, and unfortunately, all too many Muslims would disagree with his claims. But he did remind Francis that the United States valued and protected each individual's freedom of religion and right to practice and even preach it "in peace." "Finally, we punish criminals like you and crimes like yours strongly and decisively with far greater dignity and peacefulness than you afford Dr. Khalifa."[17]

Browning was rightfully indignant that Francis would dare to murder a man for blasphemy on American soil. We just don't do such things here. And it's true. Nearly thirty years after his murder, the killing of Rashad Khalifa still stands as a singular incident in U.S. history. Tashbih Sayyed died peacefully in 2007, and was never, to my knowledge, unduly worried about the prospect that he could suffer the fate of Rashad Khalifa.

But as the Muslim presence in the United States grows, this can no longer be so easily taken for granted. Certainly not all of the recent arrivals into this country who are Muslim are interested in implementing Islam's death penalty for blasphemy, but it likewise cannot safely be assumed that few or none of them ever would.

Preferring Sharia in Minneapolis

Most Americans take it for granted that the Muslims in the U.S. share American values, and simply don't believe in the same things that Muslim "extremists" believe in. Indeed, if one does not assume that Muslim communities in America are all full of loyal and productive citizens who understand and accept the value of the principles enshrined in the U. S. Constitution, you're a racist, bigoted Islamophobe.

But is it true? Or is it possible that sizable numbers of Muslims in the U.S. prefer Sharia values to American ones, even including the second-class status for women and non-Muslims, the stoning for adultery, the amputation of the hand for theft, the denial of the freedom of speech and the freedom of conscience, and all the rest?

In May 2015, filmmaker Ami Horowitz went to the Cedar-Riverside neighborhood of Minneapolis to conduct a series of man-on-the-street interviews with Muslim migrants from Somalia who lived there. Horowitz asked several, "Do you prefer American law or Sharia law?" He had no difficulty finding numerous Muslims who said they preferred to live under Sharia. He asked one: "Do you find most of your friends feel the same way?" the young man answered: "Yeah, of course, if you're a Muslim, yeah."[18]

This was shortly after the jihad attack at our free speech event in Garland, Texas, so Horowitz asked the same young man: "How do you feel, this whole controversy over the prophet Muhammad, and people depicting the prophet in cartoons. How does the whole thing make you feel?" The young man answered: "That really pisses me off, you know what I mean? Cause it's—I mean, they know it's a button to push." Horowitz followed up: "Do you understand the motivation behind the people, then, who, who, strike out violently against people who depict the prophet Muhammad?" He answered: "Yes, I understand totally where they're coming from, yep." Asked if the Garland organizers deserved to be attacked, the young man said: "Yeah. Every action has a consequence."[19]

Another responded: "I was so upset and I was so mad. They insulted our religion. They insulted our prophet. And we gotta take that." Horowitz asked: "And they shouldn't be allowed to do that." The man answered: "Oh my God. Big time, yes." Asked if he understood why jihadis felt motivated to respond violently, he answered: "Yes, because when you, when you, when you, every day you face frustration, and, you know, every day you…you mad, or somebody say that, you feel hate yourself! You do anything! You commit suicide! You don't care, because your heart is telling you, 'I don't wanna live no more,' because you can't take that much hate, or you kill someone."[20]

A third young Muslim said: "That makes me angry. It's just that, everyone gets, like, the big freedom, and then, they don't see that the freedom that they're getting is causing a problem, as chaos and hatred for other people."[21] Asked directly, "Is it right to kill somebody who insults Muhammad?," a hijab-wearing Muslim woman said: "Yeah, because she [event organizer Pamela Geller] hate the religion, I understand, but she shouldn't beat up the prophet, you know?"[22]

Horowitz asked, "Would it be better if we made it illegal in America to make fun of the prophet Muhammad?" The answer: "Definitely, yeah." Another said: "That would be better, yeah. That would be better. To stop, you know, aggression."[23]

One young Muslim who looked to be around middle school age explained why Sharia punishments were a positive good: "Sharia law, it says that if you steal something, they cut off your hand. So basically, they can leave their stores' doors open. Nobody is going to steal anything because Sharia is so tight. Usually, they don't do anything. The smallest things usually have big consequences."[24]

The Muslims Horowitz interviewed all said that they would rather live in Somalia than in the United States, but they live in the U.S. nonetheless. And in the coming years they are going to make it increasingly difficult for secularized Muslims such as Tashbih Sayyed to live here in peace. The Muslims who believe that Sharia is the immutable law of Allah and should be the law of the land in the United States are growing in number; Muslims like my old friend Tashbih who would rather have a beer and dance with his wife in the cool of the evening will find their sphere increasingly narrowing.

Ramadan Eaters and Apostates Under Threat

It is already narrowing elsewhere in the world, including in Europe. Take, for example, the observance of the Ramadan fast. This is a time when non-observant Muslims, if they dare to eat in public or are caught eating, are most visible in their disregard for Islamic requirements. And many have been made to pay for this disregard.

The Islamic State in its heyday was especially tough on Ramadan violators. During Ramadan 2015, it punished 94 people, including five who were in their teens, for violating the Ramadan fast.

According to the Syrian Observatory for Human Rights, offenders were variously flogged, crucified, or imprisoned in metal cages.[25] The punishment of crucifixion was specified in the Qur'an: "Indeed, the penalty for those who wage war against Allah and His Messenger and strive upon earth corruption is none but that they be killed or crucified or that their hands and feet be cut off from opposite sides or that they be exiled from the land" (Qur'an 5:33). The Islamic State Ramadan enforcers hung a sign around the neck of one teenage boy who was crucified, specifying the charge against him: "Broke fast without justifiable excuse under sharia."[26]

The following year, Rami Abdelrahman, director of the Syrian Observatory for Human Rights, noted that the Islamic State was crucifying people at a rapid rate for not keeping the Ramadan fast. "Every day this happen [sic], not only one day," he said. "Every day we publish it. Many times this month."[27] Also during Ramadan 2016, a Muslim in Kuwait stabbed his older brother to death. When police arrived, the killer calmly explained to them that he had done it because his brother wasn't praying and fasting during Ramadan, and that he therefore considered him to be an apostate from Islam.[28]

Such attitudes will never come West, right?

In reality, they already have. In June 2017, a group of Muslim refugees in the German city of Oldenburg stabbed another Muslim refugee, Abed Hannan Yaghoub, to death for refusing to keep the Ramadan fast, and for even daring to smoke a cigarette during the time of the fast.[29]

Another indication of the growing threat to secular Muslims in the West is the rising pressure in Europe and North America upon those who have left Islam. A Kurdish ex-Muslim who had become a Christian pastor spent much of 2016 in the refugee camps in northern France. He reported a great deal of hostility and threats due to his apostasy. "In Calais," he recalled, "the smugglers [saw] my cross [round my neck], and said: 'You are Kurdish and you are a Christian? Shame on you.' I said, 'Why? I'm in Europe, I'm free, I'm in a free country.' They said, 'No, you are not free, you are in the Jungle. The Jungle has Kurdish rule here—leave this camp.' The smugglers were from inside the camp, and were Kurdish. They said to me, 'We will tell the Algerians and Moroccans to kill you.'"[30]

They tried: "They [set] fire [to] my tent," whereupon he moved from Calais to another camp outside Dunkirk. His reputation preceded him: "You're a Kurdish pastor? I've heard about you." The pastor explained: "He was really dangerous, like a gangster. I was really scared."[31]

The pastor left Kurdistan after receiving threats there over his conversion to Christianity: "In the mosque the imams talked about me, and my father, and my little brother, who became a Christian too… The imam talked about us—'they are kafir [unbelievers], they have to die,' from the stage, into the mosque microphone. My father [a Muslim] was filled with shame. They were taught bad things about us in the mosque: 'The Christians are kafir.' Of course, they [also] say you are slaves to Israel, to the American people."[32]

The pastor moved on to Britain, where he said he felt safe. Before too long, he might have to revise that view. In 2014, a Muslim in Britain named Faisal Bashir, after hearing sermon after sermon in his mosque that he considered "hateful" and "sending out the wrong message," decided to abandon Islam. "I heard religious people say things I couldn't put up with any longer—it was all too hateful." But he didn't know what "hateful" really was until his former coreligionists discovered that he had left Islam: "These people knew I had become an atheist and soon enough my whole family was being harassed. At least once a week they would hang around near my house, shouting and swearing at me. I was called an apostate, a non-believer, I was told I had betrayed my God and my faith. Sometimes they would even say things to my children—they are far too little to know what was happening, they were very frightened."[33]

Bashir repeatedly contacted the police, but got no satisfaction. "They always said they couldn't really do anything because no physical altercation ever took place. But I'm not the kind of person to get violent with anybody. Also, it was always different people so they claimed they couldn't log it as similar complaint. Eventually a police officer told me I should just move house to get away from it all. We weren't left with any other choice. It was very distressing for all of us, not to mention the inconvenience. I used to be able to walk my children to school, now I have to drive them every day."[34]

Distance didn't bring security: "The new house is over a mile away, but they still managed to find us again."[35] Finally police acted and the situation died down, but Bashir maintained that he was by no means the only ex-Muslim in Britain to have suffered this kind of treatment: "My personal problem appears to have been solved for now, but it doesn't mean it's not still out there in society. Where there's smoke there's always fire. We need local authorities to investigate this kind of thing more thoroughly before something terrible happens."[36]

Wilson Chowdhry, the chairman of the British Pakistani Christian Association (BPCA), agreed. "Sadly Faisal's description of persecution is similar to that faced by many Muslims choosing to leave the faith who end up shunned by their community. Police and councils up and down the country just don't understand the level of animosity people choosing to leave Islam can face."[37]

Indeed. Another ex-Muslim in Britain, Nissar Hussain, suffered through an ordeal remarkably similar to that of Faisal Bashir. After what he characterized as "seven years of persecution," he and his family were relocated, under police guard. Said Hussain: "My family are distraught and extremely traumatised to be leaving. But when your life is at stake there is no other choice....This extreme persecution by certain people in the Muslim community because we are converts has broken us as a family. We are fragmented and I do not know how we will recover from this. We haven't functioned properly for years."[38] Muslims have physically attacked Hussain, smashing his kneecap and breaking his hand. One Muslim with a pick-axe handle assaulted him outside his home.[39]

One British former Muslim was threatened with death by her own mother for leaving Islam. Another said of devout Muslims: "They see us trouble-makers, deviants, apostates and blasphemers."[40] One young woman recalled: "I remember saying to my mum, I don't believe in God any more. And her saying, 'you can't tell anybody else because they'll kill you, we are obliged to kill ex-Muslims.'"[41]

This is happening all over the free world.

In March 2017 in Sydney, Australia, Uthman Badar, a spokesman for the Islamic hardline group Hizb ut-Tahrir, made his support for Islam's traditional death penalty abundantly clear. "The ruling for apostates as such in Islam is clear," he said, "that apostates attract capital punishment and we don't shy away from that….The role of apostasy in Islam is very clear. Again, this is one of the things the West doesn't like and seeks to change the role of apostasy.'[42] The West may be seeking to change that Islamic law, but that Islamic law is also seeking to change the West.

Hizb ut-Tahrir is a hardline group, but similar thinking could be found among those considered "moderate" in Australia. The imam Feizel Chothia and his congregation were given space for worship by an Anglican parish in Perth, before they had built their own building. The Anglicans no doubt took Chothia for a moderate, and considered their gesture to be a strike against "Islamophobia."

But that didn't stop Chothia for penning an article entitled "The Islamic Punishment for Apostasy," in which he justified Islam's death penalty for those who leave Islam: "Just as states such as Britain or the United States consider high treason a major crime, so Islam prescribes capital punishment for apostates. Certainly, the protection of society is the underlying principle in the punishment for apostasy in the legal system of Islam."[43]

Some Muslims in the West have shown themselves willing to translate such talk into action. This is no surprise, since these views on ex-Muslims deserving death for leaving Islam did not originate with Badar or Chothia, but are, in fact, rooted in Islamic law. In September 2016, another Muslim in Australia, Amir Darbanou, was charged with stabbing his wife, Nasrin Abek, to death because she had converted to Christianity.[44]

Another such incident took place on April 29, 2017, when a Muslim asylum seeker from Afghanistan stabbed a woman to death in the German town of Prien am Chiemsee, while her small children, ages five and eleven, looked on in horror. The killer was apparently enraged, according to the German press, because the woman had converted to Christianity several years earlier, and had been spotted attending church services. The killer also had reportedly threatened the woman because of her conversion. Police spokesman Andreas Guske said cautiously: "There is evidence of a religious motive for the deed we are pursuing."[45]

Here again, this was no isolated case. In 2016 at a refugee camp in Hamburg, Germany, an Afghan Muslim attacked an Iranian, beating him until he lost consciousness and giving him serious head injuries. Before he attacked his victim, the Afghan screamed, "I will kill you!" The Iranian's crime was, here again, conversion from Islam to Christianity, which the Afghan said was "a sin."[46]

Just weeks later, on August 17, 2016 in the German town of Maintal, near Frankfurt, four Muslims from Afghanistan began punching and kicking another Afghan, all the while screaming "Allahu akbar."[47] Their victim had committed the crime of converting from Islam to Christianity. As he tried to escape his attacker, one of them shouted, "Kill him!"[48] Another pulled a knife. The victim managed to escape. Benjamin Dauth of the local Evangelical Free Church remarked: "Who speaks openly about his faith as a convert to devout Muslims and does not hide his cross, is not safe in Germany."[49] He added that the victim of this attack was still in danger: "The Afghan Christian is still in the asylum procedure and has worked for a temporary employment agency. Three of the four attackers are housed, according to the victim in the refugee shelter in Maintal, in which he himself has worked as a translator. The fourth is allegedly living in Darmstadt." Other Muslim refugees had warned the Christian convert that he was likely to be attacked.[50]

Ex-Muslims and Secular Muslims Living in Fear...in Portland, Oregon

To be sure, some of the pressure on ex-Muslims is coming from the non-Muslim Left, in its indefatigable pursuit of an alliance with

Islamic individuals and groups, including some that are openly pro-jihad. On November 23, 2016, a secular humanist group at Portland State University in Oregon, Freethinkers of PSU, hosted a screening of a documentary film about ex-Muslims, *Islam's Non-Believers*. The screening touched off a massive controversy on campus. Many of the fliers advertising the event were torn down, and someone left a note in glass display case where Freethinkers of PSU was advertising the showing, reading: "Atheist Islamophobia is not okay."

Despite the anger it aroused, the documentary screening went off without incident; however, there were numerous ex-Muslims attending, and several asked that there be no videotaping, as they could be in physical danger from observant Muslims if their identities were known. One attendee addressed the crowd with a plea for free inquiry: "To the people who are afraid to criticize Islam ... I implore you to think about the minority within the minority. [Religion] is defended every day. The minority with the minority does not have a voice."...[51]

Indeed. But the turned-off video cameras gave the clear impression that the minority within the minority would continue not to have a voice for quite some time. Portland State University was attended by a number of ex-Muslims, including Saudis who had come to the U.S. to study and were set to return home. They lived in fear. One told Andy Ngo, a journalist for the Portland State student newspaper, the *Vanguard*: "Even if you change my name, I'm afraid they'll find out who I am. If my government finds out I am an apostate, I could be jailed when I go home. Or I could be killed....Even if my state doesn't kill me, a fellow citizen could, and he would have legal justification based on Shari'a."[52]

This young man explained that he had abandoned his faith because "Islam, as I was taught, was used to suppress human rights. I choose to follow a different path now."[53]

A secular Muslim woman, also from Saudi Arabia, also stated that she had abandoned strict adherence to Islam, although she still considered herself to be a Muslim, for reasons that should give pause to secular liberals concerned only with "Islamophobia." "I was brainwashed to hate. The Jews, Christians, non-Muslims—even Muslims not like us. There is nothing spiritual about that kind of Islam."[54] Regarding women's rights in Saudi Arabia, she added: "I'm an adult woman and my country requires me to get permission from my father to do anything. This is inhumane."[55] This young woman said wistfully: "I am most homesick when I'm actually at home. I am homesick for freedom."[56] She added a warning: "Anything I say or do here—online or offline—could have consequences back home. It's better to stay quiet."[57]

The secular Muslim and ex-Muslim students at Portland State, according to an article about their plight in the *Vanguard*, "expressed discomfort with some Islamophobia awareness campaigns. They explained that even though they are sometimes the victims of anti-Muslim bias, Islamophobia can be a problematic concept at the ontological level because it does not separate criticism of ideology and religious practice from that of Muslim people. In a Saudi Arabian context where religion and state are intertwined, they have been accused of being Islamophobic when they spoke out online against state practices."[58]

That's as instructive an insight as any into how charges of "Islamophobia" are used to manipulate and stifle necessary debate about the problematic aspects of Islam.

In any case, these students were safe in Portland, Oregon, in a way they would never be back home in Saudi Arabia. Not all recent Muslim immigrants to the U.S. would ever want to endanger them; indeed, many no doubt share their relief at being out of a Sharia-influenced environment and finally able to think and speak freely. But some also, without any doubt, would bring to the U.S. the attitudes and assumptions that made them feel unsafe back home.

Would this really enrich the putative land of the free? There was no reason why not. On April 26, 2017 at Portland State, a Muslim student participating in a panel discussion was asked if the Qur'an really called for the killing of those who left Islam. The student explained: "And some, this, that you're referring to, killing non-Muslims, that is only considered a crime when the country is based on Koranic law. That means is there is no other law than the Koran. So in that case, you are given the liberty to leave the country. I am not going to sugarcoat it. So if you go to a different country…but in a Muslim country, a country based on Koranic law, disbelieving or being an infidel, is not allowed, so you will be given the choice."[59]

Ominously, for posting a video of this statement on Twitter, Portland State student Andy Ngo was fired from his job on the *Vanguard*. Apparently to report accurately on the statements of Muslim students when they reflected poorly upon Islam was "Islamophobia." Ngo explained that the *Vanguard* editor was concerned about how he had exposed the Muslim student to danger from "Islamophobes." Ngo, said the editor, was "predatory" and "reckless." Ngo recounted, "Another person in the meeting said I should have taken into account the plight of victimized groups in the 'current political climate.' The editor claimed I had 'violated the paper's ethical standards' by not "minimizing harm" toward the speaker."[60] The editor told Ngo: "We have to ask you to step aside": his "history" of dallying with conservative media sites had hurt the "reputation of the Vanguard."[61]

This concern about "minimizing harm" toward the Muslim speaker who had spoken honestly about Islam's death penalty for apostates was not balanced by any similar concern for "minimizing harm" to those apostates and secular Muslims. The possibility that they might be in danger didn't seem to enter the editor's mind.

It wasn't just Portland State University. In January 2017, Texas state representative Kyle Biedermann asked Muslim leaders in Texas to pledge that they would protect the safety of ex-Muslims in the state. Rather than readily avow that they would and affirm the freedom of conscience, the mosque generally ignored the request, and the explicit demand of the Council on American-Islamic Relations (CAIR).[62]

Apparently pledging support for the freedom of conscience and the right of ex-Muslims to live without fear would have been "Islamophobic."

So who would stand for ex-Muslims and secular Muslims in the U.S.?

It must be acknowledged that because of Islam's death penalty for apostasy, its formidable numbers ("1.6 billion Muslims" is a figure we often hear in the establishment media) are not as formidable as they seem. There is an unknowable number of Muslims who are Muslims in name only, and who do only as much as they have to so as to stay out of danger.

These people are essentially prisoners of Islam, and they are truly the most downtrodden people in the world, with no voice, no advocate, no support of any kind from any quarter. They deserve better.

The Threat to Secular Muslims from Converts to Islam

It also does not bode well for secular Muslims in the U.S. that so many converts to Islam have turned to jihad. Not only might they themselves be threatened as hypocrites or apostates, but the frequent incidence of converts becoming jihad terrorists reflects poorly upon what is taught in American mosques.

John Georgelas, the Texas-born son of a U.S. Air Force doctor and grandson of a World War II veteran, now calls himself Yahya Abu Hassan, and reportedly became one of the top leaders of the Islamic State (ISIS).[63] Nor was he by any means the only convert to Islam to have gotten the idea that his new religion, while touted as peaceful by almost all American authorities, actually commands him to commit treason and mass murder.

Those peaceful teachings also eluded Joshua Cummings, another convert to Islam, who murdered Denver Regional Transportation District (RTD) security guard Scott Von Lanken on January 30, 2017. Cummings explained: "I give my bay'ah (pledge) to Abu Bakr al-Baghdadi and I am committed to being a soldier for the Islamic State."[64] However, "on the night in question, what I did do, I didn't do that for the Islamic State. I did that purely and solely for the pleasure of Allah."[65] He didn't explain where he got the idea that Allah would be pleased by the murder of a Denver security guard, but maybe it had something to do with the Qur'an's exhortations regarding unbelievers, to "kill them wherever you find them" (2:191, 4:89, and 9:5).

Not long after that, a convert to Islam in Kansas City named Robert Lorenzo Hester, Jr. (who called himself Ali Talib Muhammad and Rami Talib) planned a jihad massacre on President's Day, involving coordinated attacks on buses, trains, and a train station. President's Day, he told people he thought were accomplices but who were actually FBI informants, was "going to be a good day for Muslims worldwide" and said that it was "good to help strike back at the true terrorist."[66] U.S. Attorney for the Western District of Missouri Tammy Dickinson said that Ali Talib Muhammad "believed he was part of an ISIS-sponsored terrorist attack that would result in the deaths and injuries of many innocent victims."[67]

While the plot was foiled, the questions remained: where did this convert learn about Islam? From whom? How many other American converts were taught by the same people? Where are they now? Generally media reports about jihad plotters tell us that they were "radicalized on the Internet." These reports never explain why the supposedly peaceful Islam that these Muslims presumably learned at the local mosque was unable to withstand the appeal of the allegedly twisted and hijacked online version.

The same questions could be asked about 27-year-old Garrett Grimsley of Cary, North Carolina, who was charged with threatening non-Muslims. In February 2017, Grimsley posted a warning online: "Don't go to Cary tomorrow." He explained to a friend: "For too long the kuffar [non-Muslims] have spit in our faces and trampled our rights. This cannot continue. I cannot speak of anything. Say your dua [prayers], sleep, and watch the news tomorrow. It will only be the beginning..."[68]

These were not empty words. According to WTVD, "a search of Grimsley's apartment by the FBI, SBI, and the Cary Police Department revealed an AK-47 assault rifle, four 30-round magazines, and approximately 340 rounds of 7.62 millimeter ammunition."[69]

Clearly Grimsley meant business, as did Emanuel Lutchman, another convert to Islam who plotted to attack patrons at Merchants Grill in Rochester, New York, with a machete. When he was sentenced to twenty years in prison, he screamed out in court: "There's going to be more of us....You think because I'm going to be incarcerated there aren't going to be more of us that rise up?"[70] Lutchman had previously made a video in which he said: "The blood that you spill of the Muslim overseas, we gonna spill the blood of the kuffar."[71]

On March 22, 2017, a convert to Islam in London named Khalid Masood drove a car into a crowd on London's Westminster Bridge, killing four people and injuring more than fifty. Then Masood got out of the car and stabbed a policeman to death. The Islamic State (ISUS) claimed responsibility for the attack, although British police discounted that, apparently because Masood wasn't carrying an ISIS membership card.[72] Later it was revealed that in a final text message, Masood had explicitly stated that his was a jihad attack.[73]

British authorities ignored, of course, the fact that the Islamic State had called upon Muslims in the West to attack non-Muslim civilians, specifically mentioning vehicular jihad attacks: "If you are not able to find an IED or a bullet, then single out the disbelieving American, Frenchman, or any of their allies. Smash his head with a rock, or slaughter him with a knife, or run him over with your car, or throw him down from a high place, or choke him, or poison him."[74] One need have contact with ISIS members to believe that the Islamic State is the caliphate and that its calls must be obeyed.

A few days later another soldier of the caliphate, like Masood a convert to Islam, appeared in court in Detroit. According to the *Detroit News*, "a Detroit man accused of plotting jihad on behalf of the Islamic State accepted a plea deal with federal prosecutors Thursday and could spend up to five years in prison. Sebastian

Gregerson admitted he acquired a fragmentation grenade last summer from an undercover FBI employee, a crime because the grenade was an unregistered destructive device."[75] Gregerson calls himself Abdurrahman Bin Mikaayl.

The following week, yet another convert to Islam was in court in Germany. The Associated Press reported that four jihadis were given "lengthy prison sentences," including a convert identified only as Marco G. The zealous Marco was found guilty "of attempted murder for placing an explosive device at the main train station in the western city of Bonn in December 2012."[76]

Several days the same scenario played out in Philadelphia. According to AFP, a "New Jersey teen pleaded guilty…to a plot allegedly inspired by the Islamic State group to kill Pope Francis during his 2015 visit to the United States. The US Justice Department said Santos Colon, 15 years old at the time, sought to recruit a sniper to shoot the pope as he celebrated mass in Philadelphia on September 27, 2015. Colon also allegedly planned to set off explosives."[77]

There are so many other lethal converts to Islam, some of them quite high profile, including John Walker Lindh, the "Marin County Mujahid" who was discovered fighting alongside the Taliban and al-Qaeda against American troops in Afghanistan, and Adam Gadahn, the self-described "revolting geek of mass proportions" who rose high in the ranks of al-Qaeda until he was liquidated in a U.S. drone strike.

Western authorities, despite the ever-growing list of converts to Islam who have turned to jihad, remain resolutely uncurious as to why so many converts to Islam seem to miss the peaceful teachings of the Qur'an that are so patently obvious to learned imams such as Pope Francis, John Kerry, and George W. Bush. Yet all these converts to Islam learned their Islam somewhere. It strains credulity that they were all, as police usually announce when they're apprehended, "radicalized on the Internet." Many of them almost certainly learned Islam at the local mosque, and the Islam they learned would lead them not only to wage jihad against infidels, but to view secular and peaceful Muslims as apostates, heretics and hypocrites, deserving the wrath of Allah of which they were the rightful executor.

One woman of Muslim background in Canada was painfully aware of this.

At Masjid Toronto, an imam garnered headlines for praying that Allah would kill unbelievers "and spare not one of them," and "purify Al-Aqsa Mosque from the filth of the Jews."[78]

An ex-Muslim named Sandra Solomon showed up at that mosque in February 2017 with some requests of her own:

> I am standing here in your mosque today, asking for you to show me the tolerance you ask of all Canadians. To accept me for whom I am and the free choices I made to be something other than Muslim....
>
> I have concern about my life and I would love to get an answer from you Muslims to tell me: Am I going to be killed, or my child is going to be killed or harmed by anyway for me openly criticizing Islam?[79]

It was a fair question, and a poignant one coming at a time when the Canadian Parliament was considering a motion, which it eventually passed, condemning an undefined "Islamophobia." While Canada mulled officially designating Muslims as a victim class, Sandra Solomon was worried about being victimized by those supposed victims.

CIJ News reported that "a member of the mosque congregation said to Sandra that she is free to choose her faith emphasizing that her problem is not with Islam but with the Saudi regime."[80]

This was, unfortunately, not true. We may surmise this from how Islamic tradition records Muhammad himself dealing with criticism.

Abu Afak was a poet who was over one hundred years old, and he had mocked Muhammad in his verses. Muhammad asked the "companions" (*sahaba*), his closest followers: "Who will deal with this rascal for me?" One of the companions murdered Abu Afak in his sleep.[81]

Likewise, with another poet who mocked him, Asma bint Marwan. Muhammad cried out: "Who will rid me of Marwan's daughter?"[82] One of the companions, Umayr ibn Adi, went to her house that night, where he found her sleeping next to her children. The youngest, a nursing babe, was in her arms. But that didn't stop Umayr from murdering her and the baby as well. Muhammad commended him: "You have helped Allah and his apostle, O Umayr!"[83]

Then there was Ka'b bin Al-Ashraf. Muhammad again asked his companions: "Who is willing to kill Ka'b bin Al-Ashraf who has hurt Allah and His Apostle?"[84] One of the Sahaba, Muhammad bin Maslama, answered: "O Allah's Apostle! Would you like that I kill him?"[85] Muhammad said that he would. Muhammad bin Maslama said: "Then allow me to say a (false) thing (i.e. to deceive Kab)."[86] Muhammad responded: "You may say it."[87] Muhammad bin Maslama duly lied to Ka'b, luring him into his trap, and murdered him.

In light of such accounts, Sandra Solomon had every reason to be concerned, and Canadian authorities would do well to worry also. What are the implications of allowing into North America large numbers of people who don't believe in the freedom of expression, an indispensable prerequisite of any free society? No Canadian or American authorities appear to be considering that question.

Nor are they pondering the fact that the Toronto mosque member was wrong when he said that Sandra Solomon was "free to choose her faith." In reality, the death penalty for apostasy is part of Islamic law. It's based on the Qur'an:

> They wish you would disbelieve as they disbelieved so you would be alike. So do not take from among them allies until they emigrate for the cause of Allah. But if they turn away, then seize them and kill them wherever you find them and take not from among them any ally or helper. (Qur'an 4:89)

A hadith depicts Muhammad saying: "Whoever changed his Islamic religion, then kill him."[88]

The death penalty for apostasy is part of Islamic law according to all the schools of Islamic jurisprudence, even today. Both Sunni and Shi'ite. Sheikh Yusuf al-Qaradawi, the most renowned and prominent Muslim cleric in the world, has stated:

> The Muslim jurists are unanimous that apostates must be punished, yet they differ as to determining the kind of punishment to be inflicted upon them. The majority of them, including the four main schools of jurisprudence (Hanafi, Maliki, Shafi'i, and Hanbali) as well as the other four schools of jurisprudence (the four Shiite schools of Az-Zaidiyyah, Al-Ithna-'ashriyyah, Al-Ja'fariyyah, and Az-Zaheriyyah) agree that apostates must be executed.[89]

Qaradawi also once famously said: "If they had gotten rid of the apostasy punishment, Islam wouldn't exist today."[90]

But it does, in Toronto and all over. Canada and the U.S. government officials in both countries would do well to consider very carefully Sandra Solomon's question at the Toronto mosque: "Can I criticize Islam without fearing for my life?"

Even the fact that it had to be asked ought to be a spur for reconsideration of some cherished assumptions, for the health and safety of secular Muslims all over the West. But of course, it will not be.

CHAPTER 9

MODERN MAN VERSUS REALITY

Flying While Islamophobic

In a fawning September 2016 write-up in *The New York Times*, Roula Allouch of the Council on American-Islamic Relations (CAIR) said that she was worried about "Islamophobia" in airports because, she claimed, people sometimes gave her "a hard, strong stare and a stern look."[1]

Horrors!

People give me "a hard, strong stare and a stern look" in airports all the time. I've always thought that it was because they weren't thinking about me at all, but were preoccupied with making their flight and other pressing matters. But Roula Allouch was apparently sure that everyone who didn't give her a cheery grin was an "Islamophobe" who disapproves of her hijab, and her religion, and of her very presence in this country, and possibly on the planet as a whole.

Allouch elaborated: "Our main concerns during this time of heightened Islamophobia are mosque attacks, bullying against students and traveling—they're equally discussed. More and more people are being deplaned because they're Muslim. For instance, one student was asked to leave a flight because he was speaking Arabic. What seems to be happening frequently is if another passenger on the plane has a complaint, the person they're complaining about is asked to deboard. We're a country that operates with civil rights. It's very arbitrary and very troubling."[2]

In reality, the claim that Muslims are singled out for special examination or harassment in airports is wholly baseless. Many who claim they were persecuted for "Flying While Muslim" really were acting suspiciously.

For example, Allouch said that "one student was asked to leave a flight because he was speaking Arabic."[3] This was the case of a young Muslim named Khairuldeen Makhzoomi. According to the *Dallas Morning News*, "Makhzoomi, an Iraqi refugee and senior at the University of California Berkeley, was removed from an April 6 flight from Los Angeles to Oakland after another passenger told crew she overheard 'potentially threatening comments.' Makhzoomi's comments came during a conversation with his uncle."[4]

There was just one catch: "A Southwest Airlines passenger who overheard a college student's conversation also spoke Arabic and perceived the comments to be threatening, according to a new Southwest Airlines statement."[5] Strangely, Roula Allouch didn't seem to have apprised her *New York Times* interviewer about that detail.

If Roula Allouch really wants to know what it is like to be gratuitously harassed while flying, let her declare that she doesn't think Islam is a religion of peace.

For two years now, every time I fly American Airlines, which up until this began had been almost every week, I have been subjected to extensive and time-consuming extra security checks. This never happened when I flew any other airline—but I was a Platinum frequent flyer on American, so it happened often.

After repeated inquiries, I finally found that it was because American Airlines and British Airways are partner airlines, and British Airways was requiring that I be subjected to these extra security checks to make sure I wasn't flying to Britain. I am, of course, banned by the British government from traveling to Britain because

I noted (correctly) that Islam is "a religion and is a belief system that mandates warfare against unbelievers."[6]

I wasn't banned due to any criminal activity and I have no criminal record. It was and is, moreover, perfectly clear from my flight ticket in every case that I am not traveling to Britain. Hence these extra security checks simply constitute harassment, mandated by British Airways and perpetrated by American Airlines, because I am considered an "Islamophobe," and there is no class more despised among the political and media elites today.

I wrote to American Airlines explaining the situation, noting that I had been a loyal and frequent customer for many years, and asking that they stop the extra security checks. All I got back was a form letter.

So it is clear: American Airlines only wants the business of those who believe Islam is a religion of peace. Very well. I have taken my business elsewhere. If American Airlines is going to harass people for "Flying While Islamophobic," then I will fly Delta.

That's harassment. But as far as the intelligentsia goes, the real victims in Western society today are, chief among other downtrodden classes, Muslims.

Beyond Civilizational Conflict?

One would think that the truth of the things I write about would be more immediately clear. Yet even as the world is increasingly in flames because of jihad, the fog of deception is thicker than ever.

If you have ever tried to point out to friends or coworkers the violent texts and teachings of Islam that jihadists use to justify violence and supremacism, you may have experienced its effects yourself: charges of "racism," "bigotry," and "hatred"; invocations of the violent passages of the Bible; denunciations of American imperialism; attacks upon Donald Trump.

Yet the unpleasant fact remains: Muslims, not Christians or Jews or Hindus or Buddhists, are committing acts of violence today on a global scale, and justifying those acts and making recruits by pointing to their own sacred texts. When foes of jihad terror point this out, however, they become the problem. They become enemies of the people, as Henrik Ibsen pointed out so long ago.

This fog of deception and willful ignorance is only hindering genuine attempts to formulate positive and effective ways to limit the power of Islamic teachings to incite to violence. But it doesn't look as if it is going to clear anytime soon.

One reason for this is that the prevailing wisdom is that we are above all that. We are beyond war and conflict. Take Donald Trump's July 2017 speech in Warsaw, Poland. Interrupted repeatedly by chants of "Donald Trump! Donald Trump! Donald Trump!" as he was speaking, President Trump delivered a ringing affirmation that he would defend Western civilization: "Just as Poland could not be broken, I declare today for the world to hear that the West will never, ever be broken. Our values will prevail, our people will thrive, and our civilization will triumph."[7] He also said: "We are fighting hard against radical Islamic terrorism," he declared. "And we will prevail. We cannot accept those who reject our values and who use hatred to justify violence against the innocent."[8]

Trump summed up the challenge facing the West today: "The fundamental question of our time is whether the West has the will to survive. Do we have the confidence in our values to defend them at any cost? Do we have enough respect for our citizens to protect our borders? Do we have the desire and the courage to preserve our civilization in the face of those who would subvert and destroy it?"[9]

To many in the establishment media, the answer was no. *The Daily Beast* sneered at Trump with the headline "Trump in Poland: A Clash of Civilizations Battle Cry, or, Reality TV as Policy."[10] *The Guardian* painted Trump as a Crusader: "Donald Trump's warning about 'western civilisation' evokes holy war: About all that was missing from Trump's Warsaw war cry was a rousing chorus of 'Onward Christian Soldiers.' "[11] According to *Vox*, Trump's remarks were something even worse than reality TV: "Trump's speech in Poland sounded like an alt-right manifesto."[12] *Slate* went all the way:

"Trump's speech in Poland defending 'Western civilization' from its enemies sounded less like Reagan's Cold War-era speeches than white nationalist rhetoric."[13]

These journalists didn't appear concerned for the future of Western civilization. They are beyond fighting; they are Modern Men. In October 2015, *The New York Times* published an article entitled "27 Ways to Be a Modern Man."[14] It appeared in the Men's Style/Self-Help section, but it had a much larger significance.

Author Brian Lombardi fills his list with hipness, as in "the modern man listens to Wu-Tang at least once a week."[15] Modern Man also uses a melon baller to make sure that "the cantaloupe, watermelon and honeydew he serves" are "uniformly shaped."[16]

But there is also this: "the modern man lies on the side of the bed closer to the door. If an intruder gets in, he will try to fight him off, so that his wife has a chance to get away."[17] Yet despite this anticipation of conflict and vow of gallantry, "the modern man has no use for a gun. He doesn't own one, and he never will."[18]

All right. If Modern Man must never own a gun, that's his choice. But is it true he "has no use" for one? What if the intruder who storms into his bedroom is too strong for Modern Man to fight off barehanded? What if the intruder has a knife, or is even so much of an Antiquated Man as to have a gun? What can Modern Man do then? Reach for the melon baller?

A clue as to how all this sage advice hangs together comes in the oracle's penultimate utterance: "The modern man cries. He cries often."[19] Perhaps the Modern Man is so given to such displays because the intruder was indeed armed, and Modern Man wasn't, and Modern Man's wife had no chance to get away.

That possibility, however, almost certainly didn't occur to Brian Lombardi or his *New York Times* editors. They no doubt all agree: "the Modern Man has no use for a gun." Barack Obama and John Kerry are quintessential examples of this Modern Man. They live in a world where all people are rational, gentle, and peace-loving, and concerned about saving the planet and sharing her resources.

That includes the Ayatollah Khamenei and Hassan Rouhani. Hell, it includes Kim Jong-un and Abu Bakr al-Baghdadi.

Brian Lombardi could have added a 28th characteristic of the Modern Man: The Modern Man assumes that everyone he ever encounters in any situation, no matter how threatening, irrational, or actively violent, is also a Modern Man. There is, in other words, no one who cannot be talked to, no one who cannot be negotiated with, no one who doesn't prize Peace above all things, and no one who isn't willing to make concessions and receive them in turn, in order to bring about and preserve that Peace.

This is a core assumption of the Leftist worldview. It founders on reality every day, but no matter: The Modern Man is impervious to disconfirming evidence. In the world of the Modern Man, there are no enemies. Oh, and there are a few "bad guys"—the now universally employed appellation in the military and the State Department for those who wish to destroy and subjugate us—who are really good people who just so far have not succumbed to the kindness and rationality of the Modern Man. But they will.

The Modern Man faces no jihad threat. The Modern Man faces no threat at all. All he faces are dissatisfied pre-Modern Men who, with a bit of money and a few good job opportunities, will become happy and productive Modern Men themselves. Those who dissent from this view are "Islamophobes," who will soon be relegated to the dustbin of history.

What will the modern man do when the Islamic State threat that he (and *The New York Times*) has ignored, denied, and dismissed as an "Islamophobic" hobby-horse for so many years becomes undeniable reality staring him in the face? He will cry. He will cry often.

The Modern Man is everywhere today, and so it's really no surprise that rational discussion of the information I have presented in the foregoing chapters is so hard to come by. Concern about these matters has been dismissed as a concern of the "right wing" or even of "white nationalists" at a time when the centers of political and media power are all firmly in the hands of the Left. Deeply shaken by the Brexit vote in Britain and the victory of Donald Trump in the United States presidential election of 2016, those elites are rapidly becoming more authoritarian than ever, closing off social media and other outlets for the broad dissemination of information to those considered "right-wing," under the guise of cracking down on "hate speech."

This action, however, is nothing new. As long ago as 1952, when Hannah Arendt was preparing her scathing review of Whittaker Chambers' *Witness*, which quickly became a landmark of contemporary conservative thought, the novelist Mary McCarthy wrote to Arendt that *Witness* "can't be treated simply as a book. The great effect of this new Right is to get itself accepted as *normal*, and its publications as a *normal* part of publishing....and this, it seems to me, must be scotched, if it's not already too late. What do you think? I know you agree about the fact, the question is how it's to be done."[20]

Over fifty years later, the Left is committed to the same program. The "Islamophobia" program is an effort to make sure that opposition to jihad terror is never accepted as *normal*.

But in reality, there is nothing abnormal about wanting to preserve free and genuinely pluralistic societies. And the dismissal of such a desire as "Islamophobia" requires increasingly absurd intellectual contortions. In February 2017, not long before he became embroiled in a controversy over his meal of human brain tissue on his CNN show and was then fired after calling President Trump a "piece of shit," the "scholar of religions" Reza Aslan spoke at the University of Pennsylvania, where he railed against a handful of "clowns" and "fringe figures" who, despite their idiocy, had managed to create a prevailing climate of "Islamophobia" against Muslims in the United States.[21]

According to *The Daily Caller*, at Penn Aslan spoke to a crowd of around 750 people, including many who show that his message is treated on campus with the utmost respect. In attendance was "a diverse mix of students, attentive adults, and prominent Penn faculty and alumni, most notably NBC's Andrea Mitchell. The significance of the turnout was clear: fearmongering about rising 'Islamophobia' is trending, and a young, hip Muslim-American with cable TV producing credentials has the answers."[22]

Aslan claimed, according to Gregg Roman in the Caller, that "Islamophobia" as a phenomenon is only three years old: "a few fringe groups, or 'clowns' as he put it, supposedly created it in 2014."[23]

2014? "Islamophobia" was invented in 2014? That would come a surprise to the Reza Aslan who gave an extensive interview about "Islamophobia" in December 2010, but you know what they say about consistency being the hobgoblin of small minds.[24]

And Aslan's mind is very large indeed—large enough to admit of the possibility that a rogue's gallery of hacks and psychopaths have been able to hoodwink a huge segment of the American people into thinking there is something wrong with their entirely benign, friendly, cuddly Muslim neighbors.

These idiot masterminds, Roman noted, "allegedly include authors Robert Spencer, whom Aslan charmingly called a 'moron,' Pamela Geller, Frank Gaffney (a 'wackjob!'), and Middle East Forum president Daniel Pipes.... Aslan encouraged the audience to 'laugh at these guys' and ostracize them as 'fringe figures, hate group leaders... and people who have no business in the mainstream on any topic, much less Islamism.'"[25]

So a group of group of four "clowns," including a "moron" and a "wackjob," who besides being stupid are also evil "hate group leaders," have despite our bumbling idiocy and manifest malevolence been able to make "Islamophobia" a large enough problem that it requires Reza Aslan to traverse the country attempting to undo the damage we have done.[26]

So yes, sure, "laugh at these guys," but the laughter appears to be catching in Aslan's throat. Why is it that Aslan, with his massive platform (on CNN, until he blew it, and elsewhere) and the unstinting adulation of the entire establishment, has been unable to prevent this sudden three-year spread of "Islamophobia" across the land? Why has he not been able to outwit and out-charm us in the court of public opinion? How could my henchmen and I have managed to pull this off, as moronic and mean-spirited as we are?

Aslan's Penn speech was in essence an admission of defeat. Aslan, after all, represents, in the eyes of the establishment media, everything that is good and true. He is also unarguably Muslim and Leftist. He hates and ridicules Trump with the best of them. He heaps scorn on all the right people (i.e., anyone to his right). He refuses to engage us intellectually in discussion or debate, because he knows in his heart of hearts that he is smarter than we are, and better than we are, and that we are beneath contempt.

And yet, for all his pride in being the voice of reason against the sinister "Islamophobic" forces, he has failed. He has all the influence and all the access, and has denounced the "Islamophobes" from his bully pulpit multiple times, and yet "Islamophobia" persists.

There is, of course, a very good reason why he has failed. And that is because the real originators of "Islamophobia" in the U.S. are not Geller, Gaffney, Pipes and me, or any other moron or wackjob, but Nidal Malik Hasan, Mohamed Atta, Osama bin Laden, Anwar al-Awlaki, Tamerlan and Dzhokhar Tsarnaev, Mohammed Abdulazeez, Syed Rizwan Farook, Tashfeen Malik, Omar Mateen, and all the other Muslims who have plotted and/or carried out jihad massacres on American soil.

Propaganda may be effective in the short term, but reality cannot be hidden forever.[27]

The "Islamophobia" Mindset: A Thought Experiment

If the run-up to World War II, and World War II itself, had been reported the way the establishment media writes about the global jihad today, the outcome would have been very different.

Imagine if this were 1930, and the Southern Poverty Law Center existed, and it issued a lavishly illustrated, apparently meticulously documented report on critics of the Nazis, dubbing them "anti-German hate group leaders." There were profiles of Winston Churchill, Edgar Mowrer, and other early critics of Hitler, noting when they had made false claims about Hitler (false, that is, according to the Nazis) and charging them with "hate" and "anti-German bias."

Certainly, there was a great deal of actual sympathy for Hitler in Britain and the U.S. before the war, and many did regard Churchill as something of a crank. But if he were speaking out about the jihad threat today, he would likely be treated even more roughly. Imagine then that the mainstream media, whenever it quoted Churchill, Mowrer, or the others, described them as "anti-German," and noted that the Southern Poverty Law Center said that they were hate group leaders. It would call them "rabble rousers" and "wide boys" and "demogogues." Quotes from Goebbels and Göring would also invariably be included, calmly explaining the truth of the matters at hand and patiently answering questions about what a shame it was that they had to deal with the likes of Churchill.

This kind of coverage would be universal: critics of Nazism were never described in the mainstream media in anything but pejorative terms. Whenever they got mainstream media attention, they were challenged to respond to charges that they were "anti-German" and "spreading hate." Their views were more often presented by the SPLC and others who dubbed them "anti-German" than by themselves. The leading authorities the media consulted about Hitler and Nazism were favorable to both, and opposed only to excessive violence by the Brownshirts, which they stressed was inconsistent with the spirit of Nazism, and had nothing whatsoever to do with it.

Meanwhile, the critics were constantly vilified, ridiculed, and mocked, and likened to the Ku Klux Klan and other genuinely hateful groups. People wrote that they wanted to attack them physically, and that it would be legitimate to do so.

Imagine that this situation prevailed, without any cracks in the edifice, for five years. Ten years. Fifteen years.

Imagine that it prevailed as Hitler came to power, as he began persecuting the Jews, as he began his rearmament of Germany, as he bullied weak Western leaders, who were anxious to appease him anyway, into allowing him to take Austria and Czechoslovakia, and finally as he invaded Poland and the Western powers finally decided to fight back.

Imagine then that every step that Britain, France, and ultimately the Soviet Union and the United States took to defend themselves against Hitler and the Nazis was decried by the mainstream media and a huge segment of the American public as "anti-German" and a manifestation of hatred and bigotry. Every step FDR took to prosecute the war was denounced and even voided by federal court orders; he was derided as a fool, a criminal, an authoritarian ruler, and there were open calls not only for his impeachment, but for a coup to remove him from power, and even numerous calls for his assassination.

In that scenario, which side do you think would have won the war?

This is how "Islamophobes" are treated today. The thoroughgoing and honest public discussion of the acceptable parameters of criticism of Islam, in light of genuine interests not only of national security but of civilizational survival, is long overdue. Our lives, quite literally, could depend on it, as could those of our children and our children's children.

Defaming Islamophobes and Driving Them Out of Polite Society

Many liberals would sneer at my analogy, as they have determined that it is those who oppose jihad terror, not they, who are the new Nazis. And these defenders of tolerance are determined to drive us completely out of their society.

Consider a recent incident that raised the question, "Should actual neo-Nazis be allowed to use gym facilities?"

It is an odd question, but it has larger implications for the future of dissenters in the public square, and for America's prospects of staving off a new civil war.

The question about neo-Nazis and the gym came up in May 2017 when Georgetown University professor Christine Fair happened upon neo-Nazi Richard Spencer, who is not me, at a gym and began berating him. The gym then revoked Richard Spencer's membership.[28]

I have scant regard for Richard Spencer, as often as I am confused with him. He has more than once demanded that I reveal my "real" name, as he is convinced that I am secretly a Jew who has changed my name to fool good white folks like him. He has become notorious for openly espousing a white nationalism that most people would have rather remained a relic of history.

But does that mean he can't even use gym facilities that he paid for, and in which he wasn't bothering anyone?

Like the Nazis, Christine Fair wants those whom she hates destroyed, full stop. Just destroyed. She doesn't want them to be able to speak in public. She doesn't want them to be able to hold memberships in gyms. She doesn't want them to be allowed to live in the city she lives in. She told Richard, among other things: "I find your presence in this gym to be unacceptable, your presence in this town to be unacceptable."[29]

Is there *anything* that Christine Fair thinks Richard Spencer ought to be allowed to do? Does she find his breathing unacceptable?

Fair's berating of Richard Spencer, and getting him kicked out of his gym, was quintessentially Nazi behavior, and was in direct contradiction to the principles that make a society free.

While Richard Spencer is indeed a Nazi or something very close to one, albeit in a different way from how Fair is one, there is no excuse for what she did. As long as he was not breaking any laws, he had as much right to be in that gym as Christine Fair has.

Christine Fair had apparently not reflected upon the precedent she was setting, or on the possibility, as remote as it was, that one day her views could be out of favor, and she could find herself getting poisoned, and prevented from speaking by riots, and screamed at by campus fascists, and driven out of gyms, and the like, and that a healthier and freer society allows for the freedom of expression and doesn't persecute or hound those whose ideas are unpopular or even unarguably obnoxious.

Instead, she believes we need ideological purity tests even for gym memberships. Once the precedent is set that one must hold a certain set of beliefs and shun others in order to be able to work out at the gym, the required beliefs could shift, and any individual or group could be victimized.

Another example of the Left's determination to destroy utterly everyone who opposes it, and one that has to do directly with "Islamophobia," is the brief career of Terry Jones, the infamous Qur'an-burning pastor, as a driver for Uber.

I am not a supporter of Terry Jones; I oppose burning books. I believe in free speech and free discourse. The thuggish, authoritarian Left shuts down opposing views and censors those whom it hates. Burning books is the kind of thing they do, if not literally, then by shutting down, smearing, and defaming those whom they hate. I am not inclined to emulate them.

All that said, however, Terry Jones lives in a nation that has the First Amendment in its Constitution. It is not illegal for him to dislike Islam or to burn Qur'ans. But in early February 2017, the *Washington Post* wrote a gleeful story about how Jones had been working as an Uber driver, but had been fired by Uber after the *Post* reporter, a Muslim named Faiz Siddiqui, called Uber and alerted them to who Jones was.[30]

So now your Uber driver has to love Islam. If he doesn't appreciate Islam sufficiently, he could be fired. Uber's job is not just carrying people from one place to another, but guarding against "Islamophobia."

What does loving Islam have to do with driving for Uber? About as much as being a neo-Nazi has to do with holding a gym membership. Is it acceptable for your plumber to take a dim view of Buddhism?

The Left is becoming so totalitarian, so inhospitable to the slightest dissent, that even when a critic of Islam is doing something that has nothing to do with Islam, Leftists move to shut him down. Jones had to close down a French fry stand he was running in a Florida mall, and he can't drive for Uber.

What *can* he do? The Left just wants him dead—that's all.

Similarly, when I was scheduled to speak several years ago at an education conference that had nothing to do with Islam, Christine Fair's colleague Nathan Lean of Georgetown University (who has several times posted a link on Twitter to what he erroneously thought was my home address, in an obvious attempt to get me killed by jihadis and/or frighten me into silence) successfully got the host, a Catholic bishop, to cancel the event because of my work on Islam, even though Islam had nothing to do with what I was set to discuss. (The event was held at another location, and I spoke as planned.)

The Left, quite simply, wants to make it impossible for those whom it hates to do anything. Leftists want to make it impossible for us to make a living, impossible for us to exist. Leftists want us dead. Just for being "Islamophobic."

Christine Fair, Faiz Siddiqui, Nathan Lean, and their ilk are quintessential totalitarians, and they are dragging our once free society toward a new barbarism. And they represent the mainstream.

And so it was that when I was shouted down on a campus and *The New York Times* wrote up the incident, I was the villain of the piece, not the campus fascists.

The real story of my appearance at the University at Buffalo on April 21, 2017, was how campus Left-fascists and Islamic supremacists screamed abuse at me for an hour and a half, such that I was able to say very little. The real story, in other words, was about how Left-fascists on campuses nationwide are increasingly authoritarian, unwilling to allow views that depart from the Leftist establishment agenda to be heard. It was about how campus Leftists and their Muslim allies are emulating the Nazi Brownshirts, shouting down and physically menacing campus speakers whose views they hate.

University campuses today are radioactive wastelands of hard-Left indoctrination, in which any views that dissent from the Leftist line are stigmatized, demonized, and not allowed a fair hearing.

But that was not the story that got into *The New York Times*. In its story, "The Conservative Force Behind Speeches Roiling College Campuses," the *Times* didn't devote a word to the decline of civil discourse and the freedom of inquiry on university and college campuses today, and to the increasingly demonization and marginalization of thought that deviates from the Left's line.[31] For the *Times*, the real story was the wealth of and donors to the Young America's Foundation, an organization that labors tirelessly to try to bring some small measure of free inquiry to university campuses by sponsoring speakers who invite consideration of ideas that are usually forbidden at these Leftist indoctrination centers.

The *Times*'s approach was laughably ironic in light of the massive amounts that Leftist philanthropist George Soros lavishes upon activist groups such as the Center for American Progress that further the hard-Left agenda. YAF's money is a pittance compared to the money Leftist organizations have, and Leftist speakers such as Reza Aslan command speaker fees much larger than mine and Ann Coulter's as well.

Where was the *Times* article about the Leftist money machine sending hard-Left speakers to campuses to reinforce the propaganda students are being fed by their professors?

Instead, we are told that efforts to bring alternative points of view to campus were "'part of a larger systematic and extremely well-funded effort to disrupt public universities and create tension among student groups on campus,' said Alexandra Prince, a doctoral student at Buffalo who circulated a petition to block Mr. Spencer."[32] Create tension? Yes, by making students think about uncomfortable truths, issues and perspectives they have been told to ignore and shun as evil.

The one good thing about this ridiculous article was that it featured a wonderfully villainous photo of me. The University at Buffalo, not content to let the fascist Brownshirts scream at me unimpeded, also turned up the heat in the room; it was sweltering in there, and university officials refused requests from YAF chapter members to turn the heat down. So the *Times* got a marvelous photo of a sweaty, sneering, disheveled thought criminal, fiendishly poisoning the students' pure minds, and planning to stop on the way out of town to tie a few maidens to the railroad tracks.

The *Times* article concluded: "Mr. Spencer warned that the audience would live to regret its behavior. 'The forces you are enabling are going to come back to haunt you,' he said."[33]

Indeed.

Those who value free societies and prize free discourse should take note of what is happening. The Western intelligentsia has decided that "Islamophobia," not jihad terrorism, is the real problem, and the Western world is reaping the consequences.

Consider, for example, the aftermath of the jihad attack at an Ariana Grande concert in Manchester, England, that murdered 22 people and injured 59, a little over a month after I played the villain at the University at Buffalo. For some time after that attack, the United Kingdom remained on high alert as police uncovered and hunted for the members of an entire jihadi network connected with the Manchester massacre.[34] Then there quickly followed the jihad attacks at the London Bridge and elsewhere in the city.

MI5 revealed shortly after the Manchester attack that there were as many as 23,000 jihad terrorists on the streets of Britain today.[35]

That is an army. And Britain is indeed at war. But this was not just a problem that Prime Minister Theresa May had the responsibility to solve. It was also a problem that she and her colleagues created.

This Britain of troops on the streets and high tension over another imminent jihad attack is the Britain that Theresa May and her ilk have chosen.[36] Today's Britain is the Britain of the policies that she and her predecessors, David Cameron, Gordon Brown, and Tony Blair have followed for years. They chose jihad over "Islamophobia." They now have the Britain they have made. In getting to today's traumatized, bloodied, nervous, frightened Britain, they followed a multi-pronged strategy.

One chief element of this strategy was to demonize and marginalize anyone who spoke too clearly about the motivating ideology behind jihad terrorism.

For years, May and her cohorts hounded, stigmatized, and demonized foes of jihad terror, falsely claiming that they represent a "far-right" equivalent to jihad terrorists, while appeasing and accommodating Muslim groups in Britain, many of which were by no stretch of the imagination "moderate," and allowing numerous jihad preachers to operate without hindrance.[37]

In December 2016, May spoke at a luncheon of the Conservative Friends of Israel Monday, and boasted about banning me and others from the country. May said:

> Indeed, when I was Home Secretary we took what I believe was an important step in gauging a truer picture of the problem, requiring all police forces to record religious hate crimes separately, by faith.
>
> And I made sure we kept extremism—including the sort that peddles anti-Semitic vitriol—out of our country.
>
> That is why I said no to so-called comedians like Dieudonne coming to Britain.
>
> It's why I stopped Pamela Geller, Robert Spencer, and Pastor Terry Jones coming too—since Islamophobia comes from the same wellspring of hatred.
>
> It is why I kicked out Abu Hamza and Abu Qatada as well.[38]

So as far as May was concerned, I was the "Islamophobic" equivalent of Abu Hamza and Abu Qatada. Abu Hamza was placed in solitary confinement in a super-max U.S. for, among other things, conspiring to set up a training camp for jihad terrorists in Bly, Oregon.[39] Abu Qatada was convicted of plotting the jihad massacre of Americans and Israelis in Jordan.[40]

I've never plotted, called for, or approved of any kind of terrorist or vigilante violence against anyone. And thus, May's speaking of me as the flip side of Abu Hamza and Abu Qatada was beyond outrageous: it was so ridiculous that it should have led any competent member of the British Parliament to question her fitness, if not her sanity.

An examination of May's mental state might have been particularly appropriate in light of the fact that the British government has admitted numerous jihadis into the country. The UK Home Office admitted the Pakistani Muslim cleric Syed Muzaffar Shah Qadri, whose preaching of hatred and jihad violence was so hardline that he was banned from preaching in his native Pakistan. However, the negative publicity over this move was such that even the mosque that had planned to host him canceled his appearance, claiming that they were shocked! shocked! to learn that Qadri preached intolerance, hatred, and violence.[41]

This was the comic opera that is contemporary Britain: The Home Office was so bent on appeasing Islamic supremacists that it went even farther than mosques in the country are willing to do.

Qadri was not a singular case. The Home Office admitted Shaykh Hamza Sodagar into the country, despite the fact that he has said: "If there's homosexual men, the punishment is one of five things. One—the easiest one maybe—chop their head off, that's the easiest. Second—burn them to death. Third—throw 'em off a cliff. Fourth—tear down a wall on them so they die under that. Fifth—a combination of the above."[42]

The Home Office also admitted two jihad preachers who had praised the murderer of a foe of Pakistan's blasphemy laws.[43] One of them was welcomed at the airport by no less illustrious a personage than the Archbishop of Canterbury.[44] It admitted South African imam Ebrahim Bham, who once likened Jews to "fleas," favorably invoking Nazi propaganda about them.[45]

What can one conclude from all this than that the British government was indifferent to the preaching of jihad terror and Sharia oppression in the country?

But toward Christian preaching it was not so charitable. The Home Office banned three bishops from Iraq and Syria—leaders of Christian populations that have been decimated by Muslim persecution—from entering the country.[46]

May's other remarks were equally bad.

"Islamophobia," she said, of which I was guilty and thus barred from the U.K., "comes from the same wellspring of hatred" as anti-Semitism.

The implication was that "anti-Muslim rhetoric"—that is, public discussion of the jihad threat and what can be done about it—led inexorably to the demonization of Muslims and ultimately to genocide. This was ridiculous, overheated rhetoric that only hindered the prospects of any genuine discussion of the salient issues, and that was probably the goal all along. It also denies any rational basis for members of liberal Western societies to be fearful of Muslim extremists.

The clear purpose of May's equivalence of "Islamophobia" with anti-Semitism was to intimidate people into thinking that criticism of Islamic supremacism led to the concentration camps, and thus there must be no criticism of Islamic supremacism. The unstated assumption was that if one group was unjustly accused of plotting subversion and violence, and was viciously persecuted and massacred on the basis of those false accusations, then any group accused of plotting subversion and violence must be innocent, and any such accusation must be in service of preparing for their subversion and massacre.

It was simply a method to foreclose on any criticism of jihad terror and Islamic supremacism.

Adding bitter irony to all this was the fact that one of the reasons underlying our ban from the country was our support for Israel—although that material was removed from the records in an attempt by the British government to cover up its own venomous opposition to Israel, as if that opposition weren't obvious.[47]

This issue was larger than me, or Pamela Geller, or Abu Hamza, or Abu Qatada. It was this: would the British people continue to allow their Prime Minister to equate legitimate opposition to an obvious and genuine threat with that threat itself, as well as with scapegoating that leads to genocide? If they do, they would be continuing to hamstring any opposition to that threat, and it would advance unimpeded and unopposed.

When you ban foes of jihad and allow jihad preachers to enter and preach all over the country, you're going to get more jihad. And so that is what Britain has today, and will have a great deal more of in the near future.

Events canceled for security concerns, heavily armed troops roaming the trains and the streets, the candle and flower industries booming as more and more impromptu monuments spring up to an ever-rising number of victims of jihad—this is Theresa May's Britain. This is the Britain she wanted. This is the Britain she has.

Jihadis vs. Islamophobes

Consider the Manchester jihad massacre in May 2017.

The perpetrator of that massacre was a man named Salman Ramadan Abedi, whom friends described as a "devout" Muslim who had memorized the entire Qur'an.[48] He was known to British authorities as a terror threat and had been in touch with a recruiter for the Islamic State (ISIS).[49]

I hadn't heard of Salman Abedi before he murdered all those little girls and their friends and family members at the Ariana Grande concert, but when I spoke, not long before that massacre, at Truman State University, the University at Buffalo, Gettysburg College, and then in Iceland, I discussed the belief system that incites people such as Abedi to violence. I explored the ways in which jihad terrorists use the texts and teachings of Islam to justify violence and make recruits among peaceful Muslims, and the texts of the Qur'an and Islamic law that call upon Muslims to wage war against those who do not believe in Islam.

For this, the three universities and the Icelandic press treated my presence in the country as if Josef Goebbels had stopped by for a visit. A petition demanding that my Truman State appearance be canceled called me "rabble rouser, inflammatory speaker, and outright Islamaphobe [sic]," and claimed that I have "an agenda of hate and violence."[50] It further claimed that "allowing Spencer on this campus is detrimental to the safety and well-being of this university's community members." There followed the calls for me to be physically attacked.

A similar petition at the University at Buffalo charged: "Spencer's scheduled talk poses the very real risk of inciting acts of violence on campus between student communities."[51] A Gettysburg College student claimed, without providing any evidence, that my work has been "used as a basis for hate crimes against Muslims in the United States."[52]

The Icelandic press wrote in the same vein. The *Reykjavik Grapevine* warned: "Known Islamophobe To Hold Conference At Grand Hotel, Protest Likely."[53] After I left, the *Iceland Monitor* observed that "US lecturer and Islamophobe Robert Spencer…gave a lecture on what he calls the 'Jihad Threat' in Reykjavik recently."[54]

While I was there, several interviewers accused me of casting unjust suspicion upon the small Muslim community in Iceland, and worried that Muslims in Iceland might be attacked by vigilantes in the wake of my lecture. Virtually every news story about my Icelandic visit, like the petitions and news stories about my visits to those three universities, contained the information that Norwegian mass murderer Anders Breivik, who killed 77 people in two attacks on July 22, 2011, to kill, since he quoted me (along with many others, including Gandhi and Barack Obama) in his voluminous and incoherent "manifesto." In reality, I'm no more responsible for Breivik's murders than the Beatles are for Charles Manson's.[55]

After the event, one article even featured a big photo of Breivik but quoted not a single syllable of what I said that evening. None of them noted the differences between his beliefs and mine; or the fact that he started planning violence in the 1990s, before I had published anything about the jihad threat; or the fact that he criticized me in that same manifesto for not inciting violence; or the fact that he also quoted many people across the ideological spectrum, including Barack Obama, Tony Blair, and Condoleezza Rice, who are never questioned about their possible role in inciting him to kill.

The message was consistent and clear: Spencer was a dangerous person whose work threatened the safety of innocent people. He speaks about a threat where there is none.

Yet while I was vilified at those universities and poisoned in Iceland, and my words were claimed to endanger innocent Muslims everywhere I went, were any Muslims at Truman State, the University at Buffalo, Gettysburg College or anywhere in Iceland brutalized by people who heard me speak? No.

But thirty were dead in Britain not long after those speaking events, at the hands of men who were manifestations of, as the *Iceland Monitor* put it, *what I call* the jihad threat.

Anders Breivik was a madman, a psychopath with no coherent worldview. Those who disagree should try to account for the fact that this murderous "Islamophobe" counseled collaboration with the jihad terror groups Hamas and al-Qaeda.[56] He did not represent the violent outcome of "Islamophobic" rhetoric. That there were no other "Islamophobic" mass murderers either before or after him, with the arguable exception of the Finsbury Park Mosque attacker, is further evidence of this.

What his continuing notoriety actually represents is the avidity of the Left and the establishment media to stigmatize and demonize, and thereby marginalize and silence those who are calling attention to what is an actual threat: that of Islamic jihad.

Within the year before my appearances at those universities and in Iceland, there were murderous jihad attacks in Orlando, Florida; Magnanville, France; Würzburg, Germany; Ansbach, Germany; Rouen, France; Ohio State University; Berlin; and then Manchester and London.[57]

I listed only the attacks in Europe and the U.S.; there were many others elsewhere in that span as well. In the ones I listed, 90 people were killed, all by Muslims who took the exhortations to kill that are contained in the Qur'an and Sunnah to heart.

There remain no casualties by anyone who took my exhortations to heart, anywhere at any time. I don't call for or condone violence. Yet I am certain that those institutions of higher learning and the Icelandic media were far more hostile to me than they would have been if, say, a jihad terrorist freed from Guantanamo had come to speak.

Clearly Britain, like Truman State University, the University at Buffalo, Gettysburg College, and the Icelandic media, believes that the "jihad threat" is imaginary and the "Islamophobia" threat is real. And this view is the dominant mainstream one all over the West.

Endgame

I want free societies to continue and prosper. I don't want to see future generations of American women subjugated, gays brutalized, Jews and Christians living in a harassed and precarious state. That seems to be what our leaders are choosing for our future. I am among those who are trying to head it off.

This goal has made me a hated "Islamophobe." Nonetheless, in service of that goal, I'm willing to take risks.

And so it was that on a brilliantly sunny day in June 2011, I spoke at an outdoor rally in Stuttgart, Germany. Hundreds of police were present. Before I spoke, I was standing in front of the massive police phalanx with some members of the German group that had invited me; among them was a young man who I took to be one of their number until I shook his hand and smiled and he responded, "If it weren't for all these police here, I would have knifed you by now."

The Leftist "Antifa" group was out in force, throwing things and screaming, "Nazis *raus*." Like Christine Fair with Richard Spencer, however, they were behaving much more like Nazis than those they were screaming at.

The police pushed them back, but not so far that they couldn't throw things at the stage, and they did: rocks, bottles, bags of manure, and more. In the midst of this barrage, I stood at the front of the stage and addressed the Leftists, while they blew their vuvuzelas and booed to try to drown me out:

> I came from the United States of America to stand for freedom, with all free people, against the forces of oppression and darkness which you are representing.

I came here in order to stand with the people who are fighting for the freedoms that make it possible for you to do what you are doing today.

Not the violence and hatred, but to stand and dissent, but you can't stand to have any kind of rational discussion, you can't stand having dissent, you have to try to throw bottles, and drown us out, because you are cowards, because you know that you stand for nothing except for oppression and darkness and hatred, and that is why you are there.

And that is why I am here.

You are fronting for the most radically intolerant and hateful ideology on the planet. Everywhere in the world, everywhere in the world, where there are Muslims and non-Muslims, there is conflict because the Muslims attack the non-Muslims. The Qur'an teaches to make war against the unbelievers, and to subjugate them.

And you are already subjugated! You are already their useful idiots. You are already their tools. You are out here in their service.

And you think you're fighting for freedom. You are fighting for your own slavery!

You are fighting for your own enslavement.

And it will come. It will come to you.

You are fighting for an ideology that denies the freedom of speech, and one day you will wish you had the freedom of speech, and one day, you will wish you had the freedom of speech that you are trying to fight against today.

You are fronting for an ideology that denies the freedom of conscience and will kill you if you disagree, which is exactly what you want to do already.

You are fighting on behalf of an ideology that denies equality of rights for women, and all the women among you will one day be enslaved, if you get what you want.

You are fighting for the destruction of all the freedoms that you enjoy.

> You are fighting for the utter defeat of your own selves, and your own life.
>
> You are slaves seeking slavery. You are the oppressed loving your oppression, and thinking that you are standing for freedom.
>
> You are the most foolish, you are the most evil, foolish, people on Earth.
>
> We are standing for the human rights of all people. Of the oppressed Christians in Indonesia, in Pakistan, in Egypt, in the Sudan that you just heard about.
>
> We are standing for the oppressed people who are targeted by Islamic jihad everywhere around the world. In Israel. Everywhere around the world.
>
> And so, in closing, I have to say: Shame on you![58]

I can't say that any of the Antifa members came out of the crowd, shook my head, and told me that I had changed his or her mind. Nonetheless, those words sum up why I became an "Islamophobe." I prefer freedom to slavery, and peace to violence. It isn't really any more complicated than that. Leftists and their allies can claim that the increased presence of Muslims will not mean more violence and civil strife, and more erosion of women's rights and gay rights and the freedom of speech and all the rest, but the record, in Europe and increasingly in North America, is clear.

All these years later, it isn't just Antifa, but the entire political and media establishment has determined that my colleagues and I are way beyond the bounds of acceptable discourse, and must be stopped.

But I can't stop.

At the end of Eugène Ionesco's marvelous play *Rhinoceros*, every human being has become a rhinoceros and joined the herd, except for one holdout, Berenger, and even he is starting to waver: "I'm not good-looking. I'm not good-looking. They're the good-looking ones. I was wrong! Oh, how I wish I was like them! I haven't got any horns, more's the pity! A smooth brow looks so ugly. I need one or two horns to give my sagging face a lift."[59]

Unlike Berenger, I am not wavering, but I know it's true. They're the good-looking ones: the darlings of the Left, Linda Sarsour and Reza Aslan and the other purveyors of the idea that "Islamophobia" is a greater threat than jihad terror are the apple of the eye of the political and media establishment. Even Antifa has friends and supporters in the highest corridors of power. The more respectable foes of "Islamophobia," meanwhile, are everywhere, or nearly everywhere, celebrated, hailed, feted, adored.

A smooth brow looks so ugly. They are the beautiful people. They stand, or are perceived as standing, for everything our culture values most: diversity, tolerance, openness to other cultures, broad-mindedness, generosity, magnanimity.

I, on the other hand, am the ugly one: listed as a hate group leader, a notorious exponent of what is regarded as hatred and bigotry. As Berenger says: "Now I'm a monster, just a monster."[60] As Reza Aslan and Faizan Syed of CAIR and no doubt others have said of me, I am on the wrong side of history.

I may well be on the wrong side of history. But that doesn't mean I'm wrong. History, unfortunately, is not a proposition in which those who are right, or those who are defending freedom and human rights, always win. I'm not a Trotskyite; I don't believe that history moves in mechanical, identifiable and predictable patterns. I'm not a progressive. I don't believe that every day and in every way we're getting better and better, and that history is progressing inexorably toward an age of greater enlightenment and peace and sweet reason than what prevailed before.

Whittaker Chambers, when he left the Communist underground and stepped back into the light, said that he believed he was joining the losing side. That may be true of me as well, in being an Islamophobe in a Western world that has determined that Islam is wonderful, and to be encouraged, and those who oppose this are to be vilified and excoriated.

I am fully aware that I may be on the losing side. With leaders in the West such as Theresa May, Jeremy Corbyn, Justin Trudeau,

Emmanuel Macron, and Angela Merkel, that may very well be the case.

Still, I can't stop.

As another famous heretic once said: "I cannot and will not recant anything, for to go against conscience is neither right nor safe. Here I stand, I can do no other, so help me God. Amen."

I'm no Luther. I'm not leading some immense revolution. But like him, I simply cannot renounce what I am doing, because I believe it to be right. If it means taking abuse and opprobrium and humiliation, so be it.

As Berenger puts it in his last despairing determination to make a stand: "People who try to hang on to their individuality always come to a bad end! Oh well, too bad! I'll take on the whole lot of them! I'll put up a fight against the lot of them, the whole lot of them! I'm the last man left, and I'm staying that way until the end. I'm not capitulating!"[61]

People who try to hang on to their individuality may always come to a bad end, but following the herd off the cliff is even worse.

I'm not capitulating because I cannot capitulate. Stéphane Charbonnier, or "Charb," the editor of *Charlie Hebdo* whom Islamic jihadis murdered in January 2015, said it in 2012: "What I'm about to say is maybe a little pompous, but I'd rather die standing up than live on my knees."[62] Well, yes. I'm aware of sounding a little pompous myself, and I can only hope to have Charb's courage, but I share his sentiment: I'd rather die standing up than live on my knees.

I'd love to give all this up and take up jazz record reviewing, but I can't. I have to keep speaking out while I can. For once every foe of jihad terror is demonized and silenced, who will be left to speak out in resistance as the jihad advances? No one—and then the jihad will continue to advance, unopposed and unimpeded, while those who might have spoken out remain silent for fear of charges of "Islamophobia."

And so, despite all the vilification, all the marginalization, all the peer pressure and all the shaming, this Islamophobe is not ashamed, and will never be ashamed, of sounding the alarm.

Being a notorious "Islamophobe" has been an exciting, exhilarating, horrifying, dangerous, and dispiriting experience. I have met some of the most heroic people in the world, and had experiences I never expected to come close to having, and would not wish on anyone.

"Everywhere I go," Simon and Garfunkel sang long ago, "I get slandered! Libeled!" I know how they feel. I've been slandered, libeled, banned, threatened with death, and poisoned.

I am proud of my work.

I have no regrets.

How can I regret telling the truth?

ENDNOTES

Preface

1 Niall Ferguson, *The War of the World: Twentieth-century Conflict And the Descent of the West*, Penguin, 2006, p. 180.
2 Manus I. Midlarsky, *The Killing Trap: Genocide in the Twentieth Century*, Cambridge University Press, 2005, p. 342.

Chapter 1

1 "CAIR Asks NYPD to Probe Use of Anti-Muslim Training Film," Council on American-Islamic Relations, January 19, 2011.
2 Kyle Swenson, "Muslim Hunting: David Horowitz's Antagonistic Career," *SF Weekly*, December 5, 2012.
3 Kecia Ali, *The Lives of Muhammad*, Harvard University Press, 2014, p. 190.
4 "May's speech to the Conservative Friends of Israel—full text," *Conservative Home*, December 12, 2016.
5 Encounter Books, 2002.
6 Booklist Review, *Islam Unveiled: Disturbing Questions About the World's Fastest-Growing Faith*, *Booklist*, September 1, 2002.
7 Muhammad Hisham Kabbani, "Islamic Extremism: A Viable Threat to U.S. National Security," U.S. State Department Open Forum, January 7, 1999.
8 "Letter to DHS John Brennan on FBI's Use of Biased Experts and Training Materials," Muslim Advocates, October 19, 2011.
9 Robert Spencer, "Bishop cancels 'foremost Catholic expert on Islam in our country' from Catholic conference, but Kolbe Academy stands firm, will still host Robert Spencer talks," Jihad Watch, July 9, 2013.
10 Robert Spencer, "Britain capitulates to jihad," Jihad Watch, June 26, 2013; Robert Spencer, "Saint Anselm College: The Most Unsafe Campus In the U.S.?," *FrontPageMag.com*, November 16, 2015.
11 Robert Spencer, "Flying While Counter-Jihad," *FrontPageMag.com*, October 4, 2016.
12 Helena Horton and Emily Allen, "Everything we know about the Finsbury Park mosque terror attack," *The Daily Telegraph*, June 20, 2017.

13 Muddasar Ahmed, "Finsbury Park Mosque Attack: The Media's Islamophobia Addiction Will Only Lead to More Violence Against Muslims," *Newsweek*, June 19, 2017.
14 "Pamela Geller," Southern Poverty Law Center, n.d.
15 Rukmini Callimachi, "Defame Islam, Get Sued?," Associated Press, March 14, 2008.
16 Jeffrey Goldberg, "Obama on What Trump and Cruz Get Wrong About Islam," *The Atlantic*, March 29, 2016
17 Imam Muslim, *Sahih Muslim*, Abdul Hamid Siddiqi, translator, Kitab Bhavan, revised edition 2000, no. 30.
18 There are numerous exhortations in the Qur'an to obey not just Allah, but his messenger—Muhammad—as well: see Qur'an 3:32; 3:132; 4:13; 4:59; 4:69; 4:80; 5:92; 8:1; 8:20; 8:46; 9:71; 24:47; 24:51; 24:52; 24:54; 24:56; 33:33; 47:33; 49:14; 58:13; 64:12.
19 Muhammed Ibn Ismaiel Al-Bukhari, *Sahih al-Bukhari: The Translation of the Meanings*, translated by Muhammad M. Khan, Darussalam, 1997, vol. 1, book 6, no. 304.
20 There is considerable reason to believe that the Qur'an's violent texts were written after the initial Arab conquests in order to justify them, rather than beforehand in order to incite them; I wrote a book-length exploration of this and related questions, *Did Muhammad Exist?: An Inquiry Into Islam's Obscure Origins* (ISI Books, 2011).
21 Bat Ye'or, *The Decline of Eastern Christianity Under Islam*, Fairleigh Dickinson University Press, 1996, p. 274.
22 Philip K. Hitti, *The Arabs: A Short History*, Regnery, revised edition, 1970, p. 90.
23 Sita Ram Goel, *The Story of Islamic Imperialism in India*, Voice of India, revised edition 1994, pp. 70-71.
24 Steven Runciman, *The Fall of Constantinople 1453*, Cambridge University Press 1965. p. 124.
25 Imam Muslim, *Sahih Muslim*, Abdul Hamid Siddiqi, translator, Kitab Bhavan, revised edition 2000, no. 4294.
26 Averroes, *Al-Bidaya*, excerpted in Rudolph Peters, *Jihad in Classical and Modern Islam*, Markus Wiener Publishers, 1996, p. 40.
27 Ibn Taymiyya, "Jihad," excerpted in Rudolph Peters, *Jihad in Classical and Modern Islam*, Markus Wiener Publishers, 1996, p. 40.
28 Ibn Khaldun, *The Muqaddimah: An Introduction to History*, translated by Franz Rosenthal; edited and abridged by N. J. Dawood, Princeton University Press, 1967, p. 183.
29 Muhammed Ibn Ismaiel Al-Bukhari, *Sahih al-Bukhari: The Translation of the Meanings*, translated by Muhammad M. Khan, Darussalam, 1997, vol. 9, book 88, no. 6922; cf. vol. 4, book 56, no. 3017.

30 Manasi Gopalakrishnan, " 'Islamic State' reportedly training terrorists to enter Europe as asylum seekers," *DW*, November 14, 2016.

31 Jacob Bojesson, "German Intel Agency Says Hundreds of Jihadis Arrived Among Refugees," *Daily Caller*, July 5, 2017.

32 Julian Robinson, "Angela Merkel under more pressure over refugee policy as it is revealed migrants committed 142,500 crimes in Germany during the first six months of 2016," *MailOnline*, November 1, 2016.

33 Ivar Arpi, "It's not only Germany that covers up mass sex attacks by migrant men… Sweden's record is shameful," *The Spectator*, December 27, 2016.

34 "Opinion: Welcome to Sweden, the rape capital of the world," NA.se, February 28, 2017.

35 Michael Qazvini, "How Muslim Migration Made Malmo, Sweden A Crime Capital," *Daily Wire*, January 16, 2017.

36 Nicolai Sennels, "Dangerous refugees: Afghan Muslim migrants 79 times more likely to rape," *Jihad Watch*, July 1, 2017.

37 "Rotherham child abuse scandal: 1,400 children exploited, report finds," BBC, August 26, 2014.

38 Przemek Skwirczynski, "Polish MP: Germans Going to Great Lengths to Cover Crimes Of Their Arab Guests," *Breitbart*, July 30, 2016.

39 Liam Deacon, "Claim: Dutch Police Bribe Newspaper to Bury Data on Criminal Asylum Seekers," *Breitbart*, May 4, 2017; Donna Rachel Edmunds, "Swedish Police Stop Reporting Suspects' Ethnicity For Fear of Being Branded Racist," *Breitbart*, January 15, 2016.

40 Sue Reid, "Rabble rouser who could be the next nail in EU's coffin: Geert Wilders is the virulently anti-Islam," *Daily Mail*, February 4, 2017.

41 "Bardot Fined Over Racial Hatred," *BBC News*, June 3, 2008.

42 Tunku Varadarajan, "Prophet of Decline," *Wall Street Journal*, June 23, 2005.

43 Jenna Johnson, "Trump calls for 'total and complete shutdown of Muslims entering the United States,'" *The Washington Post*, December 7, 2015.

44 James L. Robart, State of Washington v. Trump, Motion for Stay of an Order of the United States District Court for the Western District of Washington, United States Court of Appeals for the Ninth Circuit, February 9, 2017, p. 25.

45 Derrick K. Watson, State of Hawai'i and Ismail Elshikh vs. Trump, Order Granting Motion for Temporary Restraining Order, United States District Court for the State of Hawai'i, March 15, 2017, pp. 35, 36.

46 Robert Spencer, "Federal appeals court upholds block on Trump's temporary immigration ban," *Jihad Watch*, May 25, 2017.

47 Eric Tucker, AP FACT CHECK: No arrests from 7 nations in travel ban? Nope, *Associated Press*, February 6, 2017.

48 Max Greenwood, "WH releases list of terror suspects admitted to US from travel ban countries," The Hill, February 8, 2017.

Chapter 2

1 thereligionofpeace.com; Joseph Curl, "Ramadan 2017: 161 Terror Attacks, 1,483 Dead, 1,557 Wounded," *Daily Wire*, June 23, 2017.
2 "Manchester bombing latest: Investigation making 'immense' progress as police 'get hold of' large part of terror network," *The Telegraph*, May 26, 2017.
3 Fraser Moore, "MI5 reveal 'up to 23,000 jihadis living in Britain' ahead of Bank Holiday security boost," *Express*, May 27, 2017.
4 "UK to deploy troops after attack, risk now 'critical': May," *Reuters*, May 23, 2017.
5 Raymond Brown, "Security stepped up at Cambridge mosques after early morning bacon hate crime," *Cambridge News*, June 9, 2017.
6 Julia Ebner, "The far right thrives on global networks. They must be fought online and off," *The Guardian*, May 1, 2017.
7 Paul Sperry, "The purge of a report on radical Islam has put NYC at risk," *New York Post*, April 15, 2017.
8 Ibid.
9 Ibid.
10 Ashley Soley-Cerro, Chris Burrous and Chip Yost, "San Bernardino Shooting Suspects Were Married, Had Baby; Their Redlands Home Being Searched," KTLA, December 3, 2015.
11 Jana Winter, "Clerk Rings Up N.J. Jihad Jerks," *New York Post*, May 13, 2007.
12 Ibid.
13 Paul von Zielbauer, "5 Men Are Convicted in Plot on Fort Dix," *The New York Times*, December 22, 2008.
14 Stephen Schwartz, "Reductio ad Jihadam," *TCS Daily*, February 17, 2005.

Chapter 3

1 Laurie Penny, "This isn't 'feminism'. It's Islamophobia," *The Guardian*, December 22, 2013.
2 Ibid.
3 Ibid.
4 Ibid.
5 Jim Garrison, "Muhammad Was A Feminist," *Huffington Post*, October 28, 2016.
6 Theresa Corbin, "I'm a feminist, and I converted to Islam," CNN, October 14, 2014.
7 Ibid.
8 Ibid.
9 Canadian Imam: 'Islam is the most feminist religion,'" CIJ News, April 3, 2017.
10 Naomi Wolf, "Behind the veil lives a thriving Muslim sexuality," *The Sydney Morning Herald*, August 30, 2008.
11 Ibid.
12 Ibid.

13 Ibid.
14 "Full text: bin Laden's 'letter to America,'" *Observer*, November 24, 2002.
15 Naomi Wolf, "Behind the veil lives a thriving Muslim sexuality," *The Sydney Morning Herald*, August 30, 2008.
16 Barack Obama, Remarks By The President On A New Beginning, Cairo, June 4, 2009.
17 Alice Foster, "What is the hijab? Non-Muslim women asked to wear the hijab for World Hijab Day TODAY," *Express*, February 1, 2017.
18 "World Hijab Day is Here!," *worldhijabday.com*, February 1, 2014.
19 "'I also wear the Hijab, it's beautiful!' Bizarre German TV Ad Campaign advertises Veil to Girls," YouTube, September 14, 2016.
20 Oli Smith, "Hijab-wearing students activists SHOCK Christian university with Islamic protest," *Express*, December 17, 2016.
21 Kristine Phillips, "University of Michigan student wearing a hijab was threatened with being set on fire, police say," *Washington Post*, December 21, 2016.
22 Jennifer Dixon, "Hijab-wearing U-M student threatened with being set on fire," *Detroit Free Press*, November 12, 2016.
23 University of Michigan Division of Public Safety and Security, "CRIME ALERT—UPDATE—ALERT CANCELED," December 21, 2016. www.dpss.umich.edu/news/?id=415
24 David Krayden, "No Charges For Suspected Muslim Hate-Crime Hoaxer," *The Daily Caller*, February 14, 2017.
25 Andrew Buncombe, "Muslim woman says she was called a terrorist on New York Subway by three men chanting 'Donald Trump,'" *Independent*, December 4, 2016.
26 Ibid.
27 "Muslim teen verbally attacked on NYC subway," CBS News, December 3, 2016.
28 Laura Dimon, Ross Keith, Rocco Parascandola, and Graham Rayman, "Drunk men screaming Trump's name try to rip off Muslim student's hijab as straphangers stand idly by on East Side subway, cops say," *New York Daily News*, December 3, 2016.
29 Daniel Politi, "NY Subway Riders Stand By as Three Men Verbally Assault Muslim Teenager," *Slate*, December 4, 2016.
30 Rocco Parascandola and Leonard Greene, "Muslim college student made up Trump supporter subway attack story to avoid punishment for missing curfew," *New York Daily News*, December 15, 2016.
31 Hank Berrian, "Muslim Teen Who Claimed Trump Supporters Assaulted Her ARRESTED For Lying," *Daily Wire*, December 14, 2016.
32 Rocco Parascandola and Leonard Greene, "Muslim college student made up Trump supporter subway attack story to avoid punishment for missing curfew," *New York Daily News*, December 15, 2016.
33 Ibid.

34 May Bulman, "We should wear hijabs for Donald Trump's inauguration in support of 'Muslim sisters', says US actress," *The Independent*, January 19, 2017.

35 Ann Abel, "The 10 Coolest Places to Go in 2017," *Forbes*, March 2017.

36 Ibid.

37 Melissa Biggs-Bradley, "Just Back From…Iran," *Indagare*, January 17, 2017.

38 "Our Mission," Women's March on Washington, www.womensmarch.com/mission/.

39 Ibid.

40 Ibid.

41 Ibid.

42 Kelly Riddell, "Pro-life women banned from anti-Trump Women's March on Washington," Washington Times, January 17, 2017.

43 "Linda Sarsour," National Co-Chairs, Women's March on Washington, www.womensmarch.com/team/.

44 Andrew Eicher, "Women's March National Co-Chair: Sharia Law is 'Reasonable,' 'Misunderstood,'" CNS News, January 25, 2017.

45 Ibid.

46 Ibid.

47 Qasim Rashid, "The Islamic Solution to Stop Domestic Violence," *Huffington Post*, March 5, 2012.

48 "Egyptian Cleric Abd Al-Rahman Mansour Gives Guidelines for Wife Beating in Islam," Middle East Media Research Institute (MEMRI), September 3, 2012; "Ramadhan TV Show: Saudi Cleric Muhammad Al-'Arifi Explains Wife-Beating in Islam to Young Muslims," Middle East Media Research Institute (MEMRI), November 13, 2007.

49 Andrew Bushell, "Child Marriage in Afghanistan and Pakistan," America, March 11, 2002, p. 12.

50 Muhammed Ibn Ismaiel Al-Bukhari, *Sahih al-Bukhari: The Translation of the Meanings*, translated by Muhammad M. Khan, Darussalam, 1997, vol. 1, book 8, no. 511.

51 Muhammed Ibn Ismaiel Al-Bukhari, *Sahih al-Bukhari: The Translation of the Meanings*, translated by Muhammad M. Khan, Darussalam, 1997, vol. 1, book 81, no. 6546; Imam Muslim, *Sahih Muslim*, Abdul Hamid Siddiqi, translator, Kitab Bhavan, revised edition 2000, no. 2737.

52 Muhammed Ibn Ismaiel Al-Bukhari, *Sahih al-Bukhari: The Translation of the Meanings*, translated by Muhammad M. Khan, Darussalam, 1997, vol. 1, book 2, no. 29.

53 Muhammed Ibn Ismaiel Al-Bukhari, *Sahih al-Bukhari: The Translation of the Meanings*, translated by Muhammad M. Khan, Darussalam, 1997, vol. 3, book 30, no. 1951.

54 "According to Islam is it permissible for women to drive?," Islamquest, September 24, 2006.

55 Adam Taylor, "The facts—and a few myths—about Saudi Arabia and human rights," *Washington Post*, February 9, 2015.

56 "Women and men are different in some cases, similar in others," Khamenei.ir, March 19, 2017.

57 Ibid.

58 "Women's Rights In Iran," Human Rights Watch, October 28, 2015.

59 Benjamin Weinthal, "Iran Sentences Woman to Death by Stoning," *The Jerusalem Post*, December 10, 2015.

60 "Alarming rates of acid attacks in Iran back on the rise," Al Arabiya, March 20, 2017.

61 Benjamin Weinthal, "Iran Sentences Woman to Death by Stoning," *The Jerusalem Post*, December 10, 2015.

62 Golnaz Esfandiari, "Iranian Female Soccer Star Faces Husband-Imposed Travel Ban," Radio Free Europe/Radio Liberty, September 14, 2015.

63 Ibid.

64 Linda Sarsour, Facebook, December 21, 2015. www.facebook.com/linda.sarsour/posts/10153936083745572

65 Linda Sarsour, Twitter, December 3, 2016. twitter.com/lsarsour/status/805085370631200768?lang=en

66 Linda Sarsour, Twitter, December 21, 2015. twitter.com/lsarsour/status/679051328967036928

67 Matthew North, "SJW Feminists Chant Allahu Akbar at 'Women's March' In Berlin," YouTube, January 29, 2017.

68 "Transcript: Donald Trump's Taped Comments About Women," *The New York Times*, October 8, 2016.

69 Hank Berrian, "Muslim Women's March Organizer Attacks Female Genital Mutilation Survivor Hirsi Ali: I Would Take Her 'Vagina Away,'" *The Daily Wire*, January 26, 2017.

70 Ayaan Hirsi Ali, *Infidel*, Free Press, 2007. Pp. 31-3.

71 Geraldine Coughlan, "Somali woman heads for Dutch parliament: Pim Fortuyn's murder made tolerance a key issue," *BBCNews*, January 3, 2003.

72 Chuck Ross, "Women's March Organizer Recently Met Ex-Hamas Operative, Has Family Ties To Terror Group," Daily Caller, January 21, 2017; John Perazzo, "The Anti-Semite Who Organized the 'Women's March on Washington,'" *FrontPage Magazine*, January 23, 2017.

73 Mattie Kahn, "Women's March Organizer Linda Sarsour Is Under Attack on Social Media: Less than 48 hours after the worldwide event, one of the women who helped plan it is facing Islamophobic attacks," *Elle*, January 23, 2017.

74 Ibid.

75 Bernie Sanders, Twitter, January 23, 2017. twitter.com/berniesanders/status/823682138000293892?lang=en

76 "Liberal Linda Sarsour 'Fighting Trump is JIHAD...Muslims have 'NO need to assimilate,'" YouTube, July 6, 2017.

77 Ibid.
78 Ibid.
79 Ibid.
80 Abigail Abrams, "Women's March Organizer Linda Sarsour Spoke of 'Jihad.' But She Wasn't Talking About Violence," *Time*, July 6, 2017.
81 Ibid.
82 Ibid.
83 Ibid.
84 Ashley Eady, "3 Things Conservatives Got Very Wrong About Linda Sarsour's Speech," *The Wrap*, July 6, 2017.
85 Antonia Blumberg, "Linda Sarsour Said 'Jihad' In A Speech And Conservatives Freaked Out," *Huffington Post*, July 6, 2017.
86 Jack Jenkins, "A Muslim activist referenced jihad and the right freaked out because they don't know what it means," *ThinkProgress*, July 7, 2017.
87 Abigail Abrams, "Women's March Organizer Linda Sarsour Spoke of 'Jihad.' But She Wasn't Talking About Violence," *Time*, July 6, 2017.
88 Antonia Blumberg, "Linda Sarsour Said 'Jihad' In A Speech And Conservatives Freaked Out," *Huffington Post*, July 6, 2017.
89 Ashley Eady, "3 Things Conservatives Got Very Wrong About Linda Sarsour's Speech," *The Wrap*, July 6, 2017.
90 Ahmed ibn Naqib al-Misri, *Reliance of the Traveller ('Umdat al-Salik): A Classic Manual of Islamic Sacred Law*, Nuh Ha Mim Keller, translator. Amana Publications, 1999, o9.8.
91 Tanya Chen, "After Someone Claimed This Teen's Dad Would 'Beat Her' For Taking Off Her Hijab, She Texted Her Dad," *BuzzFeed*, April 17, 2017.
92 Ibid.
93 Ibid.
94 Ibid.
95 Ibid.
96 Ibid.
97 Ibid.
98 Sami Aboudi, "Saudi police arrest young woman for removing abaya," *The Independent*, December 12, 2016; Tom Embury-Dennis, "Saudi woman pictured not wearing hijab faces calls for her execution," *The Independent*, December 1, 2016.
99 Sunan Abu Dawud 4092.
100 Sawsan Morrar, "When I'm honored for my journalism, everyone will see one thing: My headscarf," *Washington Post*, April 28, 2017.
101 Ibid.
102 Ibid.
103 Ibid.
104 "Father, son get life terms in Aqsa Parvez slaying," CBC News, June 16, 2010.

105 "BREAKING NEWS: Somalia Militants Kill Christian Woman For Refusing To Wear Veil," BosNewsLife, October 28, 2009.
106 Sinan Salaheddin, "Vigilantes kill 40 women in Iraq's south," Associated Press, December 10, 2007.
107 Colin Fernandez, "'Wear the hijab or I'll kill you, cousin told girl': Muslim tells of terrifying phone threats," *Daily Mail*, January 19, 2011.
108 "Woman in legal limbo over refusal to cover hair," AFP, November 4, 2013.
109 "Egyptian girl shoots herself to death after refusing to wear hijab," *Al Arabiya*, July 17, 2013.
110 Bryan Littlely, "Teachers at Islamic College of South Australia's West Croydon campus ordered to wear hijab or face sack," *The Australian*, February 11, 2013.
111 Amie Ferris-Rotman, "Russia's Muslim south triples sharia bride price," *Reuters*, July 7, 2010.
112 Amie Ferris-Rotman, "RPT-Women without headscarves targeted in Muslim Chechnya," *Reuters*, August 21, 2010.
113 "Tunisia: Salafites threaten to kill teachers without veil," ANSAmed, December 4, 2013.
114 Qaeda tells Syria schoolgirls to wear Islamic clothes: NGO," AFP, September 28, 2013.
115 "Hamas set to compel Gaza women to wear head covering," *Haaretz*, July 26, 2009.
116 Moni Basu, "Women in Iran march against discrimination," CNN, June 19, 2009.
117 "'Wear a headscarf or we will kill you': How the 'London Taliban' is targeting women and gays in bid to impose sharia law," *Daily Mail*, April 17, 2011.
118 Undercover 2011, "IAmA 21 yr old Muslim girl who wears the headscarf but has led a double-life kept hidden from my family for the last 3 years," *Reddit.com*, November 26, 2011.
119 "Saudi police 'stopped' fire rescue," BBC, March 15, 2002.
120 Robert Snell, "Detroit physician charged with mutilating girls' genitalia," *Detroit News*, April 13, 2017.
121 Brooke Singman, "Michigan doctor, wife arrested for allegedly conspiring to perform female genital mutilation," Fox News, April 21, 2017.
122 Robert Snell, "2nd doctor, wife arrested in genital mutilation case," *Detroit News*, April 21, 2017.
123 Robert Snell, "Detroit physician charged with mutilating girls' genitalia," *Detroit News*, April 13, 2017.
124 Mayra Cuevas and Sonia Moghe, "Prosecutor: 'Brutal' genital mutilation won't be tolerated in US," CNN, April 26, 2017.
125 Ahmed ibn Naqib al-Misri, *Reliance of the Traveller ('Umdat al-Salik): A Classic Manual of Islamic Sacred Law*, Nuh Ha Mim Keller, translator. Amana Publications, 1999, p. xx; Mark Durie, *The Third Choice: Islam, Dhimmitude and Freedom*, Deror Books, 2010, p. 64.

126 Ahmad Ibn Hanbal 5:75; Hamdun Dagher, *The Position of Women in Islam*, Light of Life, 1997. Reprinted at www.light-of-life.com/eng/reveal/r5405efc.htm.
127 Abu-Dawud Sulaiman bin Al-Aash'ath Al-Azdi as-Sijistani, *Sunan abu-Dawud*, Ahmad Hasan, translator, Kitab Bhavan, 1990, no. 5251.
128 Nick Thompson, "Female genital mutilation: Why Egyptian girls fear the summer," CNN, June 25, 2015.
129 Gabrielle Paluch, "Female genital cutting in Thailand's south," *Al Jazeera*, April 2, 2015; Marie Dhumieres, "Female genital mutilation persists in Indonesia," *Global Post*, April 16, 2015.
130 Hajir Sharifi, "Study reveals shocking FGM prevalence in Iran," Rudaw, July 4, 2015.
131 Mohua Das, "Bohra cleric urges female genital mutilation?," *Times of India*, April 29, 2016.
132 Roland Oliphant, "Outrage in Russia after religious leaders back female genital mutilation," *The Daily Telegraph*, August 18, 2016.
133 "AMJA Senior Committee Member: Female Genital Mutilation Is 'an Honor' per Islam," *Translating Jihad*, April 27, 2012.
134 Craig Mackenzie, "Islamic holy man and his wife are jailed for mutilating the genitals of their four daughters," *Daily Mail*, June 3, 2012.
135 Sofia Petkar, "REVEALED: Thousands of Female Genital Mutilations STILL taking place illegally in Britain," *Express*, March 7, 2017.
136 Rachel Baxendale, "Female circumcision is a right, says imam," *The Australian*, December 24, 2012.
137 Ibid.
138 "Female genital mutilation Fact sheet," World Health Organization, February 2017. www.who.int/mediacentre/factsheets/fs241/en/
139 Ibid.
140 Peter Beinart, "When Conservatives Oppose 'Religious Freedom,'" *The Atlantic*, April 11, 2017.
141 Ibid.
142 Linda Sarsour, Twitter, April 21, 2017.

Chapter 4

1 Scott Simpson, "How Pulse Forged a Lasting Partnership Between Muslims and LGBTs," *The Advocate*, June 12, 2017.
2 Will Reisman, "San Francisco Muni buses getting more anti-Islamic ads, this time with anti-gay message," *San Francisco Examiner*, March 19, 2013.
3 Ibid.
4 Thom Senzee, "HBO's *VICE* Uncovers Gay Iranians Forced to Surgically Change Gender," *The Advocate*, April 11, 2015.
5 Sasha von Oldershausen, "Iran's Sex-Change Operations Provided Nearly Free-Of-Cost, *Huffington Post*, June 4, 2012.

6 Chris Stedman, "Stop Trying to Split Gays and Muslims, *Salon*, April 2, 2013.
7 Ibid.
8 Bella Waddle, Twitter, March 18, 2017.
9 Andrew E. Kramer, "Chechen Authorities Arresting and Killing Gay Men, Russian Paper Says," *The New York Times*, April 1, 2017.
10 Ibid.
11 Ibid.
12 Ibid.
13 Ibid.
14 Bella Waddle, Twitter, April 1, 2017.
15 Bella Waddle, Twitter, March 13, 2017.
16 Thomas Burrows, "Chechnya opens world's first concentration camp for homosexuals since Hitler's in the 1930s where campaigners say gay men are being tortured with electric shocks and beaten to death," *MailOnline*, April 10, 2017.
17 Loaa Adel, "Photos: Islamic State stones a youth accused of homosexuality in Mosul," *Iraqi News*, March 27, 2017.
18 Leith Fadel, "ISIL throws Iraqi man off roof of building for alleged crime of 'homosexuality,'" *AMN*, January 9, 2017.
19 Afdhere Jama, "5 Muslim Nations Where Gay is Legal," *LGBT Muslims*, December 5, 2014.
20 Max Bearak and Darla Cameron, "Here are the 10 countries where homosexuality may be punished by death," *Washington Post*, June 16, 2016.
21 Ibid.
22 Jonathan Easley, "DNC boots candidate from chairmanship race for criticizing Ellison's Islamic faith," *The Hill*, January 31, 2017.
23 Abu-Dawud Sulaiman bin Al-Aash'ath Al-Azdi as-Sijistani, *Sunan abu-Dawud*, Ahmad Hasan, translator, Kitab Bhavan, 1990, no. 4462.
24 Jonathan Easley, "DNC boots candidate from chairmanship race for criticizing Ellison's Islamic faith," *The Hill*, January 31, 2017.
25 Ibid.
26 Ibid.
27 Raheem Kassam, "'Behead, Burn, And Crush Gays' Islamic Preacher To Deliver 10 Days Of Lectures In London," *Breitbart*, October 4, 2016.
28 Robert Spencer, "Britain Capitulates to Jihad," *Jihad Watch*, June 26, 2013.
29 Nick Gutteridge, "Fury as watchdog says it's OK to send gay people death threats—but only if you're Muslim," *Express*, December 3, 2016.
30 Ibid.
31 Ibid.
32 Scott Campbell, "Migrants 'slaughter gay man, dress him in women's clothes and wrap snake round his neck,'" *Express*, December 18, 2015.
33 "Across Europe, gay refugees facing abuse in asylum shelters," Associated Press, February 22, 2016.

34 Ibid.
35 Ibid.
36 Oliver JJ Lane, "'People Like You Should Be Shot': Muslim Taxi Driver Beat Up Gay Couple For Kissing In His Cab," *Breitbart*, March 8, 2016.
37 Ibid.
38 Frank le Duc, "Man arrested after 'gay-bashing' attack on Brighton seafront," *Brighton & Hove News*, May 11, 2016.
39 Ibid.
40 "Vice-President Of Hungarian Muslim Community: Homosexuals Are The Filthiest Creatures," Middle East Media Research Institute (MEMRI), July 10, 2015.
41 Ibid.
42 "2 suburban Chicago men arrested on terrorism charges," Associated Press, April 12, 2017.
43 Dominic Holden, "Police Arrest Musab Mohamed Masmari in Neighbours Arson Case," *SLOG News & Arts*, February 1, 2014.
44 James Queally, "Seattle man says he killed 4 in Wash., N.J. to gain revenge against U.S.," *Los Angeles Times*, August 20, 2014.
45 Shayna Jacobs, "Man who bashed gay couple over their heads with chair at Dallas BBQ gets nine years in prison," *New York Daily News*, September 15, 2016.
46 Ibid.
47 Ibid.
48 Omar Mateen, 9/11 call transcripts, June 12, 2016. info.publicintelligence.net/FL-OmarMateenTranscripts.pdf
49 Ibid.
50 Ibid.
51 Ibid.
52 Tim Hains, "Lynch: 'Partial Transcript' Of Orlando 911 Calls Will Have References To Islamic Terrorism Removed," *RealClearPolitics*, June 19, 2016.
53 Ibid.
54 Ibid.
55 Ibid.
56 Ibid.
57 Ibid.
58 Kevin Johnson, "Justice Dept. reverses course on redacting transcript of Orlando gunman," *USA Today*, June 20, 2016.
59 Ibid.
60 Ibid.
61 Alex Pfeiffer, "The SPLC Considers The Most Deadly Islamic Terror Attack Since 9/11 A Right-Wing Plot," *The Daily Caller*, December 8, 2016.
62 "Terror from the Right," Southern Poverty Law Center, November 1, 2015.

63 Fox News, "Professor: Islamophobia plays pivotal role in terrorism," YouTube, November 30, 2016.
64 Rick Moran, "Study: Right Wing Extremists a Bigger 'Threat' to US than Islamic Terrorists?," PJ Media, June 24, 2015.
65 Alex Griswold, "White Americans Are Biggest Terror Threat in U.S. Once You Exclude The Death Of 3,000 Americans," *Mediaite*, June 24, 2015.
66 Scott Shane, "Homegrown Extremists Tied to Deadlier Toll Than Jihadists in U.S. Since 9/11," *The New York Times*, June 24, 2015.
67 Julia Craven, "White Supremacists More Dangerous To America Than Foreign Terrorists, Study Says," *Huffington Post*, June 24, 2015.
68 "Right-Wing Extremists More Dangerous Than Islamic Terrorists In U.S.," National Public Radio, June 24, 2015.
69 "White Right-Wing Terrorists Are Biggest Threat to Americans, Study Finds," *TruthDig*, July 30, 2015.
70 Thomas D. Williams, "Florida Bishop Blames Orlando Massacre on Catholic 'Contempt' for Homosexuality," *Breitbart*, June 14, 2016.
71 Ibid.
72 Ibid.
73 Emily Thode and Melissa Mecija, "Craigslist ad threatens Orlando-style massacre in San Diego," KGTV, June 14, 2016.
74 "Iranian doctor's planned talk on Islam and homosexuality outrages some in Sanford," WFTV.com, March 29, 2016.
75 Dylan C. Robertson, "Trudeau government under fire for ending LGBT Iranian refugee program," *Daily Xtra*, February 10, 2017.
76 Ibid.
77 Ibid.
78 Ibid.
79 Ibid.
80 Ian Austen, "Canada Closes Tehran Embassy and Orders Iran Envoys to Leave," *The New York Times*, September 7, 2012.
81 Daniel Lak, "Canada and Iran Ease into a New Friendship," *Al Jazeera*, January 27, 2016.
82 Benjamin Weinthal, "Shots fired as Iran arrests over 30 gay men in violent raid," *The Jerusalem Post*, April 20, 2017.
83 Ibid.
84 Jonathan D. Halevi, "Toronto principal: 'Homosexuals are cursed by Allah', LGBTQ 'not permissible,'" *CIJ News*, January 15, 2017.
85 Ibid.
86 Rosa Brooks, "Can Gay Marriage Defeat the Islamic State? A few—admittedly sappy—thoughts on the power of #LoveWins," *Foreign Policy*, June 26, 2015.
87 Ibid.
88 Ibid.
89 Ibid.

Chapter Five

1 "Stop Islamization of America (SIOA), Anti-Defamation League, 2013. www.adl.org/sites/default/files/documents/assets/pdf/civil-rights/stop-islamization-of-america-2013-1-11-v1.pdf
2 Abraham H. Foxman, "Norwegian attacks stem from a new ideological hate," *Washington Post*, July 29, 2011.
3 "A Joint Statement Regarding Robert Spencer's Visit to Calgary," Islamic Supreme Council of Canada, April 27, 2016.
4 David Bell, "U.S. blogger Robert Spencer draws hundreds in Calgary as critics call him anti-Muslim, 'dangerous' speaker," CBC News, April 28, 2016.
5 Stephen Collinson, "Trump condemns anti-Semitism but can't stop questions about his motives," CNN, February 21, 2017.
6 "Copenhagen imam accused of calling for killing of Jews," *BBC News*, May 11, 2017.
7 Imam Muslim, *Sahih Muslim*, Abdul Hamid Siddiqi, translator, Kitab Bhavan, revised edition 2000, no. 6985.
8 "Copenhagen imam accused of calling for killing of Jews," *BBC News*, May 11, 2017.
9 "Ibid.
10 "Imam prædiker om jødedrab:—Jeg tror ikke, han mener noget ondt med det," *Nyheder*, May 11, 2017.
11 Ibid.
12 Ibid.
13 "Copenhagen imam accused of calling for killing of Jews," BBC News, May 11, 2017.
14 Giulio Meotti, "Disappearing Jewish Symbol Reveals Europe's Submission to Islam," *The Geller Report*, March 1, 2017.
15 Simon Kent, "Jewish Student Driven Out of Berlin School by Threats and Violence from Muslim Classmates," *Breitbart*, May 28, 2017.
16 Ibid.
17 Ibid.
18 Ibid.
19 Ibid.
20 Giulio Meotti, "Disappearing Jewish Symbol Reveals Europe's Submission to Islam," *The Geller Report*, March 1, 2017.
21 "French intellectuals accuse authorities of covering up Jewish woman's slaying by Muslim neighbor, *JTA*, June 9, 2017.
22 Ibid.
23 Ibid.
24 Harvey Day, "Man is held by police in north London after roaming through heavily Jewish area shouting 'Allah Allah' and 'I'm going to kill you all,'" *Mailonline*, June 8, 2017.

25 Ibid.
26 "As Gaza Fighting Continues, Egyptian Clerics Intensify Antisemitic Statements; Columbus, Ohio Muslim Scholar/Leader Dr. Salah Sultan: Muhammad Said That Judgment Day Will Not Come Until Muslims Fight the Jews and Kill Them; America Will Suffer Destruction," Middle East Media Research Institute, December 30, 2008.
27 "AAH Demands Congressman Keith Ellison Denounce Islamist Group Or Resign," Americans Against Hate Press Release, June 6, 2007.
28 James Osborne, "Clinton Invites Controversial Muslim Leader on Conference Call," FoxNews.com, June 8, 2009.
29 Daniel Mael, "Boston Islamist: The Jews Better Learn How to Swim, Moses Ain't Coming [VIDEO]," *Truth Revolt*, July 25, 2014.
30 Danielle Avel, "CAIR-Affiliated Protest: 'We Are Hamas!,'" *Breitbart*, July 23, 2014.
31 Ibid.
32 "Michigan Activist Lina Allan Lambasts People who Prohibit Stabbing of Jews by Palestinians: It's Like Defending Animal Rights at Best," Middle East Media Research Institute (MEMRI), December 28, 2015.
33 Kyle Olson, "Thousands chant 'Allahu Akbar' for Farrakhan in Detroit," *The American Mirror*, February 20, 2017.
34 "Washington D.C. Imam Abdul Alim Musa: Zionists Brought Trump, Like Hitler, to Power; We Have to Rescue the Poor Dumb Americans," Middle East Media Research Institute (MEMRI), November 18, 2016.
35 Ibid.
36 Ibid.
37 Ibid.
38 Nicole Perez, "Local man accused of threatening to kill President Obama," KSAT, December 24, 2016.
39 Lea Spyer, "'Stuff Jews in the Oven' Among Antisemitic Social Media Posts Flooding Pages of University of Texas-Arlington Students, Covert Campus Watchdog Finds," *Algemeiner*, February 15, 2017.
40 Daniel Mael, "Student Leader: '*Hamas & Shariah Law* Have Taken Over UC Davis,'" *Truth Revolt*, January 30, 2015.
41 Blake Neff, "Meet The Brilliant Harvard Student Who Called A Jewish Politician 'Smelly,'" *The Daily Caller*, April 21, 2016.
42 "A Statement on Recent Anti-Semitic Comments," *Harvard Law Record*, April 18, 2016.
43 Blake Neff, "Meet The Brilliant Harvard Student Who Called A Jewish Politician 'Smelly,'" *The Daily Caller*, April 21, 2016.
44 "Oren heckled at US College," *The Jerusalem Post*, February 9, 2010.
45 Ibid.
46 Lauren Williams, Nicole Santa Cruz and Mike Anton, "Muslim Students Found Guilty of Disrupting Speech," *Los Angeles Times*, September 24, 2011.

47 Ibid.
48 Ibid.
49 Daniel Mael, “Temple Univ. Jewish Student Punched In Face And Called ‘Kike’ In Anti-Semitic Attack,” *Truth Revolt*, August 20, 2014.
50 Ibid.
51 Ibid.
52 Hannah Broad, “‘F**k Israel, long live the Intifada’ angry mob screams at Jewish UC student,” *The Jerusalem Post*, May 22, 2016.
53 Ibid.
54 Ibid.
55 Ibid.
56 Shlomo Greenwald, “Critics Slam CUNY Response to Campus Anti-Semitism,” *Jewish Press*, March 16, 2016.
57 Ibid.
58 Ibid.
59 Matt Lebovic, “‘Apartheid Week’ Really Does Threaten Israel, Some Experts Warn,” *The Times of Israel*, March 18, 2016.
60 Ibid.
61 Ibid.
62 Daniel Mael, “On Many Campuses, Hate is Spelled SJP, *The Tower*, October 2014.
63 Michael Melia, “Educators Update Anti-Bullying Messages to Protect Muslims,” Associated Press, March 5, 2016.
64 Alec Dent, “Muslim Student Association Demands All ‘Islamophobic Speech’ Be Punished,” *The College Fix*, December 28, 2015.
65 Ibid.
66 Ibid.
67 Adam Kredo, “‘K-I-L-L-I-N-G,’” *The Washington Free Beacon*, August 21, 2014.
68 Pamela Geller, “Unapologetic Muslim Prof Denounces ‘Dirty Jewish Zionist Thugs,’” *Breitbart*, August 12, 2015.
69 Benjamin Weiser, “Convictions in Synagogue Bombing Plot Upheld,” New York Times, August 23, 2013; Trevor Aaronson, “Inside the Terror Factory,” *Mother Jones*, January 11, 2013.
70 Ibid.
71 Maxine Bernstein, “Portland teen accused of threatening to blow up NE Portland deli ‘in the name of Allah,’ court records say,” by Maxine Bernstein, *The Oregonian/OregonLive*, January 12, 2015.
72 Aaron Feis, “Thugs rough-up Jewish couple, drive off flying Palestinian flags,” *New York Post*, August 26, 2014.
73 Russ Bynum, “‘I am an American’: Man who was ‘ready for jihad’ before attempting to join ISIL sobs as he’s given 15 years prison,” Associated Press, July 28, 2015.

74 Muslim accused of threatening to cut off heads of Jewish congregation denies allegations," WSVN, March 10, 2015.
75 Ibid.
76 Ibid.
77 "Sources: FBI foils terror attack at Aventura synagogue; 1 arrested," WSVN, May 1, 2016.
78 "Arizona man charged with plotting terror attack also eyed Jewish center, FBI says," Associated Press, July 20, 2016.
79 "1 arrested in fires at Jewish center in central Las Vegas—VIDEO," by Michael Shoro, *Las Vegas Review-Journal*, May 9, 2017.
80 Ibid.
81 "West Miami-Dade Temple Vandalized With Swastika," NBC Miami, September 9, 2014.
82 Ibid.
83 Ibid.
84 Andrea Cavallier, "NYPD steps up patrols after two 'suspicious' men attempt to enter multiple synagogues in Brooklyn," WPIX, March 8, 2015.
85 Myles Ma, "Man pleads not guilty to tossing firecrackers outside synagogue," *NJ.com*, August 31, 2015.
86 Mark Hirshberg, "NYPD: Bottle Caps Thrown at Jewish Mom From Mosque in Brooklyn," *JP Updates*, October 11, 2015.
87 Hezki Ezra, "Muslim NYC cabbie attacks Jewish passenger," *Israel National News*, November 15, 2015.
88 Ari Soffer, "New York: Attacker shouts 'f– you Jews,' punches man in face," *Israel National News*, December 1, 2015.
89 Mark Hirshberg, "Shirtless Man Who Threatened Jewish Man in Crown Heights May Face Hate Crime Charges," *JP Updates*, April 4, 2016.
90 Rocco Parascandola, Dale W. Eisinger, and Larry Mcshane, "Meat cleaver madman, a Palestinian, was in Midtown to appeal deportation order before he sliced cop," *New York Daily News*, September 16, 2016.
91 Mark Hirshberg, "NYPD Seeking to Question Muslim Woman Caught On Video Taking Photos From Jewish School," *JP Updates*, October 1, 2016.
92 Julian Robinson, "'Dress up like a Jew and make sure you have plenty of weapons under your coat': ISIS fanatics issue chilling call to 'terrorise' Jewish people in the West," *Daily Mail*, February 28, 2017.
93 Debra Rubin, "Muslims, Jews break bread at shul event," *New Jersey Jewish News*, March 7, 2016.
94 Ibid.
95 Ibid.
96 "Non-Muslims entering the mosque," Islam Question and Answer, July 19, 1999.
97 Itamar Marcus and Nan Jacques Zilberdik, "Little girls on PA TV: Jews are the 'most evil among creations, barbaric monkeys, wretched pigs,' condemned to 'humiliation and hardship,'" *Palestinian Media Watch*, July 7, 2013.

Chapter Six

1 Qasim Rashid, "ISIS Violates The Consensus Of Mainstream Islam By Persecuting Christians," *Huffington Post*, August 27, 2015.
2 Imam Muslim, *Sahih Muslim*, Abdul Hamid Siddiqi, translator, Kitab Bhavan, revised edition 2000, no. 4294.
3 Mark Mueller, "Bashing liberals, Muslims and millennials: Has this pro-Trump priest gone too far?," *NJ.com.*, February 8, 2017.
4 Rebecca Atkins and Soyoung Kim, "Parents accuse Belen priest of making discriminatory comments against Muslims," KRQE, March 30, 2017.
5 Ibid.
6 Ibid.
7 "Catholic priest stands by 'Muslims will cut your head off' statement," KOAT, March 31, 2017.
8 Ibid.
9 Ibid.
10 Ibid.
11 Ibid.
12 Jonas Romea, "Letter of Apology from Father Jonas Romea," April 12, 2017. www.scribd.com/document/346794317/Fr-Jonas-Romeo-Apology
13 David Romero, "Belen priest removed from Archdiocese of Santa Fe," KRQE, May 1, 2017.
14 Clara Garcia, "Father Jonas Romea terminated from Our Lady of Belen, archdiocese, amid allegations of inappropriate conduct," *News-Bulletin*, May 3, 2017.
15 "Catholic Men's Conference Opens Ticket Sales," *Catholic Free Press*, February 8, 2013.
16 Harry Farley, "Bishop Michael Nazir-Ali Condemns Koran Reading At Anglican Cathedral Epiphany Service," *Christianity Today*, January 9, 2017.
17 Kelvin Holdsworth, "Keeping the faith," What's in Kelvin's Head? The weblog of Kelvin Holdsworth, Provost of St Mary's Cathedral, Glasgow, January 31, 2017.
18 Christopher Mathias, "Teacher Gave 6th-Grade Students Reading That Called Islam 'Immoral And Corrupting,'" *Huffington Post*, April 19, 2017.
19 Ibid.
20 Ibid.
21 Ibid.
22 Ibid.
23 Ibid.
24 Kyle Shideler, "Georgetown's Bridge Initiative Partners with Think Tank linked to Al Qaeda, Islamic Jihad and Hamas," *CounterJihad*, July 24, 2015.
25 Ibid.
26 Georeen Tanner, "Christian persecution: How many are being killed, where they are being killed," Fox News, April 14, 2017.

27 Laurie Goodstein, "Christian Leaders Denounce Trump's Plan to Favor Christian Immigrants," *The New York Times*, January 29, 2017.
28 Miranda Devine, "We rush to condemn Islamophobia. What about anti-Christian attacks?," *The Daily Telegraph*, April 8, 2017.
29 Ibid.
30 Ibid.
31 Ibid.
32 Abbot Tryphon, "Orthodox Cathedral Burned," The Morning Offering, September 11, 2016.
33 Philip Chrysopoulos, "Vandals On the Island of Crete Set Church on Fire, Write 'Allah is Great,'" *Greek Reporter*, December 18, 2016.
34 Mattias Albinsson, "Aggressiv man slog sönder kyrka i Malmö," *Fria Tider*, June 27, 2016.
35 Virginia Hale, "France: Anti-Christian Attacks Rise 245 Percent," *Breitbart*, February 7, 2017.
36 "French Public Right in Doubting Authorities, Media on Migrant Crime - EU MP," *Sputnik*, April 20, 2016.
37 David Chazan and James Rothwell, "Live / Normandy siege: knifemen 'shouted Daesh and slit 84-year-old priest's throat' after taking nuns hostage in church before being shot dead," *The Daily Telegraph*, July 26, 2016.
38 Una Brankin, "Normandy horror attack priest's church donated land to build mosque, reveals Down monk who knew Fr Jacques Hamel," *Belfast Telegraph*, July 28, 2016.
39 Ibid.
40 Ibid.
41 Daniel Hamiche, "Vivonne : le portrait du tueur de Nice sur l'autel de l'église!," *L'Observatoire de la Christianophobie*, August 19, 2016.
42 Melissa Eddy, "Refugee's Arrest Turns a Crime Into National News (and Debate) in Germany," *The New York Times*, December 9, 2016.
43 Nick Hallett, "Parish Centre Vandalised, Islamist Slogans Written on Walls," *Breitbart*, January 13, 2017.
44 Virginia Hale, "France: Anti-Christian Attacks Rise 245 Percent," *Breitbart*, February 7, 2017.
45 Tom Heneghan, "Growing concern for German churches: Muslim refugees harassing Christians," *Deseret News*, June 3, 2016.
46 Chris Tomlinson, "Muslim Migrants Converting To Christianity Fear Murderous Islamic Retaliation In Europe," *Breitbart*, April 15, 2016.
47 Chris Tomlinson, "40,000 Christians Persecuted By Muslims In Germany," *Breitbart*, May 10, 2016.
48 Tom Heneghan, "Growing concern for German churches: Muslim refugees harassing Christians," *Deseret News*, June 3, 2016.
49 Katie Mansfield, "Migrant 'attacked in German refugee camp for converting to Christianity,'" *Express*, July 15, 2016.

50 Chris Tomlinson, "Muslim Migrants Converting To Christianity Fear Murderous Islamic Retaliation In Europe," *Breitbart*, April 15, 2016.
51 Chris Tomlinson, "Priest: Muslim Migrants Ruthlessly Bully Christian Kids," *Breitbart*, November 29, 2016.
52 Virginia Hale, "Christians Forced to Hide Bibles Amid Migrant Muslim Death Threats," *Breitbart*, August 11, 2016.
53 Ibid.
54 Ibid.
55 Ibid.
56 Stoyan Zaimov, "743 Christian Refugees, Converts Attacked by Muslims in German Camps, Persecution Report Finds," *The Christian Post*, October 19, 2016.
57 Ibid.
58 Ignacio Murillo, "El juez considera un ataque islamista la quema de la iglesia de Fontellas e impone al autor el alejamiento de edificios católicos," *Navarra.com*, September 10, 2016.
59 Joey Millar, "Muslim migrant who wanted to destroy Christian symbols sets fire to church Nativity scene," *Express*, January 3, 2017.
60 Sam Webb, "Son of extremist imam arrested over ISIS terror plot to attack Christians in a shopping centre with chainsaws," *Mirror*, September 7, 2016.
61 May Bulman, "Prince Charles issues veiled warning over Donald Trump and return to 'dark days of 1930s,'" *The Independent*, December 22, 2016.
62 Joanna Rothkopf, "'It's beyond stupid': Bill Maher responds to backlash against Islam views," *Salon*, December 5, 2014.
63 Christopher Hitchens, "Free Exercise of Religion? No, Thanks. The taming and domestication of religious faith is one of the unceasing chores of civilization," *Slate*, September 6, 2010.
64 May Bulman, "Prince Charles issues veiled warning over Donald Trump and return to 'dark days of 1930s,'" *The Independent*, December 22, 2016.
65 Ibid.
66 Ibid.
67 Hollie McKay, "Churches take new security measures in face of terror threats," Fox News, August 9, 2016.
68 Ibid.
69 Ibid.
70 Ibid.
71 Ibid.
72 Ibid.
73 Ibid.
74 Catalin Cimpanu, "Church Website Defaced with Ominous Jihadi Message," *Softpedia*, April 25, 2016.
75 Ibid.
76 Gilad Shiloach, "Exclusive: ISIS Puts Out Holiday Attack List Of U.S. Churches," *Vocativ*, December 22, 2016.

77 Ibid.
78 Anthony Joseph and Richard Spillett, "World on terror alert: Security ramped up in major cities over Christmas after Berlin lorry tragedy sparks fears of another attack on the West," *Mailonline*, December 20, 2016.
79 John Hayward, "7 Terror Attacks and Plots Foiled This Christmas Season," *Breitbart*, December 24, 2016.
80 Susan Berry, "Exiled Archbishop of Mosul: 'I Have Lost My Diocese to Islam; You in the West Will Also Become Victims of Muslims,'" *Breitbart*, August 18, 2014.
81 Ibid.
82 Ibid.
83 Sixteen Hurt in Christmas Eve Blast at Catholic Church in Philippines," *Reuters*, December 24, 2016.
84 Melissa Eddy, "Refugee's Arrest Turns a Crime Into National News (and Debate) in Germany," *The New York Times*, December 9, 2016.

Chapter 7

1 Matea Gold, "Bannon film outline warned U.S. could turn into 'Islamic States of America,'" *Washington Post*, February 3, 2017.
2 Ibid.
3 Art Moore, "Did CAIR founder say Islam to rule America?," *WND*, December 11, 2006.
4 Ibid.
5 *Minneapolis Star Tribune*, April 4, 1993, quoted in Daniel Pipes and Sharon Chadha, "CAIR: Islamists Fooling the Establishment," *Middle East Quarterly*, Spring 2006.
6 Mohamed Akram, "An Explanatory Memorandum on the General Strategic Goal for the Group in North America," May 22, 1991, Government Exhibit 003-0085, U.S. vs. HLF, et al. P. 7 (21).
7 Robert Spencer, "DC Imam wants to establish an 'Islamic State of North America no later than 2050,'" *Jihad Watch*, November 9, 2007.
8 Matea Gold, "Bannon film outline warned U.S. could turn into 'Islamic States of America,'" *Washington Post*, February 3, 2017.
9 "New Muslim Brotherhood Leader: Resistance in Iraq and Palestine is Legitimate; America is Satan; Islam Will Invade America and Europe," Middle East Media Research Institute Special Dispatch Series No. 655, February 4, 2004.
10 Mohamed Akram, "An Explanatory Memorandum on the General Strategic Goal for the Group in North America," May 22, 1991, Government Exhibit 003-0085, U.S. vs. HLF, et al. P. 7 (21).
11 Ibid.
12 David K. Shipler, "Pamela Geller and the Anti-Islam Movement," *The New Yorker*, May 12, 2015.

13 Patrick Poole, "Pulitzer Prize Winner Hawks 'Protocols of the Elders of the Anti-Islam Movement' in the *New Yorker*," *PJ Media*, May 13, 2015.
14 Ibid.
15 Ibid.
16 Ibid.
17 Ibid.
18 "Civilization Jihad:" Debunking the Conspiracy Theory," Bridge Initiative, February 26, 2016.
19 John L. Esposito, "Islam and the Challenge of Democracy," *Boston Review*, April 1, 2003.
20 *John Esposito: Defending Radical Islam*, Investigative Project on Terrorism, n.d.
21 Daniel Pipes, "John Esposito and Me," DanielPipes.org, September 10, 2007.
22 John L. Esposito, "Islam and the Challenge of Democracy," *Boston Review*, April 1, 2003.
23 Martin Kramer, "Ask Professor Esposito," *Sandbox*, September 26, 2002.
24 "The Bridge Initiative's failed attempt to 'debunk' Federal evidence," Center for Security Policy, March 8, 2016.
25 Ibid.
26 Ibid.
27 Ibid.
28 Ibid.
29 Imam Muslim, *Sahih Muslim*, Abdul Hamid Siddiqi, translator, Kitab Bhavan, revised edition 2000, no. 30.
30 Brennan Neill and Stephen Smith, "Imam calling for Jews to be killed in sermon at Montreal mosque draws police complaint," CBC News, March 23, 2017.
31 Ibid.
32 Ibid.
33 Imam Muslim, *Sahih Muslim*, Abdul Hamid Siddiqi, translator, Kitab Bhavan, revised edition 2000, no. 6985.
34 Alex Matthews, "Hate crime probe after leaflets saying those who insult Islam must be killed 'were handed out at London mosque,'" *Mailonline*, October 7, 2016.
35 Jacob Bojesson, "Germany Moves To Ban Child Marriages After Finding 1500 Cases Among Refugees," *The Daily Caller*, April 5, 2017.
36 "Kurdish Refugee Killed by Arabs in Germany for Smoking during Ramadan," *BasNews*, June 2, 2017.
37 Chris Pleasance, "Number of migrant criminal suspects in Germany soared by more than 50% in 2016, as minister warns the number of crimes has 'increased disproportionately'" *Daily Mail*, April 24, 2017.
38 Gareth Davies, "Somalian asylum seeker 'rapes two elderly disabled men in a care home before murdering one of the victims' wives' in Germany," *Daily Mail*, April 3, 2017.

39 Ibid.
40 Ibid.
41 "Syrian held in Germany over Berlin suicide attack plan," BBC, May 30, 2017.
42 "Police attacked by 150 people inside migrant ghetto," 10News, May 24, 2017.
43 Robert Spencer, "Video from Italy: Muslim migrants assault female reporter live on the air," *Jihad Watch*, May 6, 2017.
44 Virginia Hale, "14 Wounded After Illegal Migrants Storm Town Hall to Protest France's Immigration Laws," *Breitbart*, April 19, 2017.
45 Romina McGuinness, "Afghan father who called son 'Jihad' jailed for threatening to kill French judges," *Express*, March 13, 2017.
46 "Moroccan girl, 14, 'whipped by parents,'" *ANSA*, April 5, 2017.
47 Ibid.
48 Ibid.
49 Vincent Wood, "'Afghan national smashes 59-year-old cyclist on the head with a HAMMER in random assault,'" *Express*, March 26, 2017.
50 Ibid.
51 Gareth Davies, "Somalian asylum seeker 'rapes two elderly disabled men in a care home before murdering one of the victims' wives' in Germany," *Daily Mail*, April 3, 2017.
52 Hannah Al-Othman, "Two Afghan migrants who allegedly raped a woman in Sweden as their friend laughed and livestreamed it over Facebook are charged over the assault," *MailOnline*, March 15, 2017.
53 Joshua Nevett, "Five 'Arab migrants' gang-rape little girl, SEVEN, at refugee centre," *Daily Star*, March 19, 2017.
54 Gareth Davies, "Somalian asylum seeker 'rapes two elderly disabled men in a care home before murdering one of the victims' wives' in Germany," *Daily Mail*, April 3, 2017.
55 Nicolai Sennels, "Sweden: Muslim driving instructor says: 'If it wasn't Ramadan, I would have F**CKED THE SH*T out of you,'" *Jihad Watch*, June 4, 2017.
56 Ibid.
57 "Swiss monitor 500 people for online jihadist propaganda," Swissinfo.ch, March 14, 2017.
58 Lizzie Dearden, "Germany 'spent more than €20bn on refugees in 2016' as crisis outstrips state budgets," *The Independent*, March 10, 2017.
59 Tom Michael, "Simmering Hatred: Refugee camp translator reveals how German migrants 'despise' Christians and want to 'Islamise' the country," *The Sun*, November 17, 2016.
60 Ibid.
61 Cleve R. Wootson Jr., "Pope Francis called refugee centers concentration camps. A Jewish group says there's no comparison," *Washington Post*, April 23, 2017.

62 Oliver JJ Lane, "Cologne Police Reveal 'Cover Up' Of New Year's Eve Rape Attacks Ordered By Government," *Breitbart*, April 6, 2016.
63 Ibid.
64 Ibid.
65 Gareth Davies, "Somalian asylum seeker 'rapes two elderly disabled men in a care home before murdering one of the victims' wives' in Germany," *Daily Mail*, April 3, 2017.
66 Liam Deacon, "Claim: Dutch Police Bribe Newspaper to Bury Data on Criminal Asylum Seekers," *Breitbart*, May 4, 2017.
67 Ibid.
68 Ibid.
69 Donna Rachel Edmunds, "Swedish Police Stop Reporting Suspects' Ethnicity For Fear of Being Branded Racist," *Breitbart*, January 15, 2016.
70 Ibid.
71 Virginia Hale, "Swedish Pensioner Prosecuted for 'Hate' for Accusing Migrants of Torching Cars on Facebook," *Breitbart*, May 14, 2017.
72 Gareth Davies and Sara Malm, "Revealed: Just one in five foreign rapists in Sweden are ever deported to their home countries," *MailOnline*, March 11, 2017.
73 Ibid.
74 "Tvingade 14-åring till sex—frias för våldtäkt eftersom han har 'misstänkt ADHD' och inte kan 'tolka' ett nej," *Fria Tider*, April 21, 2017.
75 Ibid.
76 Allan Hall, "German politicians were warned that Berlin Christmas market attacker was plotting carnage NINE MONTHS before the massacre," *MailOnline*, March 26, 2017.
77 "Stockholm attack suspect 'was ordered deported,'" BBC, April 9, 2017.
78 Gareth Davies, "Somalian asylum seeker 'rapes two elderly disabled men in a care home before murdering one of the victims' wives' in Germany," *Daily Mail*, April 3, 2017.
79 Ibid.
80 Keith Ellison, "Rep. Keith Ellison: The mistake in my past, and the case for my DNC candidacy," Star Tribune, December 5, 2016; "Keith Ellison Reneges on Islamist Event; MEF Had a Role," Middle East Forum, December 22, 2016.
81 John Rossomando, "Muslim Scholar: Group That Sponsored Ellison's Hajj a 'National Security Threat,'" *IPT News*, December 19, 2016.
82 Mitch Anderson, "Ellison: Hajj was transformative," *Star Tribune*, December 18, 2008.
83 Steven Emerson, "IPT Exclusive: In Private Fundraiser, Ellison Blasted Israeli Influence Over U.S. Policy," *IPT News*, November 29, 2016.
84 Ibid.
85 Ibid.
86 Ibid.

87 Ibid.

88 Ibid.

89 Noreen S. Ahmed-Ullah, Sam Roe and Laurie Cohen, "A rare look at secretive Brotherhood in America," *Chicago Tribune*, September 19, 2004.

90 Noreen S. Ahmed-Ullah, Sam Roe and Laurie Cohen, "A rare look at secretive Brotherhood in America," *Ikhwanweb*, March 10, 2006.

91 al-Husein N. Madhany, "Re: [Muslim Justice League] Fwd: President Obama: 'Ground Zero' Mosque Project: Muslim and Interfaith Leaders Respond," August 16, 2010. www.investigativeproject.org/documents/misc/912.pdf

92 Sam Stein and Jessica Schulberg, "Witness At Ted Cruz Hearing Accuses Congress' Two Muslim Members Of Muslim Brotherhood Ties," *Huffington Post*, June 28, 2016.

93 "ISNA Admits Hamas Ties," *IPT News*, July 25, 2008.

94 "List of Unindicted Co-Conspirators and/or Joint Venturers," United States of America vs. Holy Land Foundation for Relief and Development, n.d., www.investigativeproject.org/documents/case_docs/423.pdf.

95 Patrick Poole, "Rep. Keith Ellison Rewrites History on his Muslim Brotherhood, CAIR Ties," *PJ Media*, July 21, 2012.

96 "DOJ: CAIR's Unindicted Co-Conspirator Status Legit," IPT News, March 12, 2010.

97 "CAIR's Ayloush Gives Dishonest, Bullying Answer to Hamas Question," *IPT News*, November 18, 2013; Robert Spencer, "CAIR's Hussam Ayloush refuses to condemn Hamas and Hizballah as terrorist organizations," Jihad Watch, April 11, 2007; "CAIR's Nihad 'Awad Refuses to Condemn Hamas," *Translating Jihad*, January 24, 2011.

98 Patrick Lion and Caroline Mortimer, "'White supremacist's' chilling rant hours before he 'murdered Good Samaritans defending Muslim girls from racist abuse on Portland train,'" *Mirror*, May 29, 2017.

99 Patrick Lion and Caroline Mortimer, "'White supremacist's' chilling rant hours before he 'murdered Good Samaritans defending Muslim girls from racist abuse on Portland train,'" *Mirror*, May 29, 2017.

100 Matthew Haag and Jacey Fortin, "Two Killed in Portland While Trying to Stop Anti-Muslim Rant, Police Say," *The New York Times*, May 27, 2017.

101 Amy B Wang, "'Final act of bravery': Men who were fatally stabbed trying to stop anti-Muslim rants identified," *Washington Post*, May 27, 2017.

102 "'I call it patriotism': Man accused of murdering two people during anti-Muslim rant defiant in court," *The Daily Telegraph*, May 31, 2017.

103 Derek Hawkins, "Portland mayor asks feds to bar free-speech and anti-sharia rallies after stabbings," *Washington Post*, May 30, 2017.

104 Ibid.

105 Ibid.

106 Ibid.

107 Ibid.

108 Ibid.
109 Jaime Adame, "UA professor suspended after speech cancellation a scapegoat, author says," *Arkansas Online*, May 5, 2017.
110 Ibid.
111 Richard Landes, "Prof. Phyllis Chesler disinvited from honor killings conference," *Israel National News*, April 14, 2017.
112 Ibid.
113 Winston Churchill, *Churchill by Himself: The Definitive Collection of Quotations*, Richard Langworth, editor, PublicAffair, 2008. P. 574.
114 "Democracy or Theocracy? Robert Spencer vs. Anjem Choudary & Abu Izzadeen," YouTube, November 17, 2011.

Chapter Eight

1 Benazir Bhutto, *Reconciliation: Islam, Democracy and the West*, Harper, 2008, pp. 245-246.
2 Robert Spencer, editor, *The Myth of Islamic Tolerance*, Prometheus, 2004.
3 Mohammed Kloub, "Yes, there is such a thing as a secular Muslim," *The Seattle Globalist*, March 30, 2016.
4 Ibid.
5 Ibid.
6 Charles M. Sennott, *The Body and the Blood: The Holy Land's Christians at the Turn of a New Millennium—A Reporter's Journey*, Public Affairs, 2001, p. 422.
7 Muhammed Ibn Ismaiel Al-Bukhari, *Sahih al-Bukhari: The Translation of the Meanings*, translated by Muhammad M. Khan, Darussalam, 1997, vol. 9, book 88, number 6922.
8 Ahmed ibn Naqib al-Misri, *Reliance of the Traveller ('Umdat al-Salik): A Classic Manual of Islamic Sacred Law*, Nuh Ha Mim Keller, translator. Amana Publications, 1999, o8.1, o8.4.
9 Robert Spencer, "Death to the Apostates," FrontPageMagazine.com, October 24, 2006.
10 Bethan McKernan, "Man 'sentenced to death for atheism' in Saudi Arabia," *The Independent*, April 26, 2017.
11 Jon Boone, "Liberal newspaper Express Tribune cowed into silence by Pakistani Taliban," *The Guardian*, February 28, 2014.
12 Ibid.
13 "Secular Islam: The St. Petersburg Declaration," Center for Inquiry, April 5, 2007. www.centerforinquiry.net/secularislam/
14 "'Secular' Islam," IqraSense.com, n.d., www.iqrasense.com/islam-and-media/secular-islam.html
15 Ibid.
16 Kim Smith, "Killer of Tucson imam gets 25-to-life prison term," *Arizona Daily Star*, January 29, 2013.

72 Zoie O'Brien, "'No evidence' Westminster terrorist Khalid Masood linked to ISIS – Met Police," *Express*, March 27, 2017.
73 Kim Sengupta, "Last message left by Westminster attacker Khalid Masood uncovered by security agencies," *The Independent*, April 27, 2017.
74 Robert Spencer, "Islamic State: 'We will conquer your Rome, break your crosses, and enslave your women, by the permission of Allah,'" *Jihad Watch*, September 21, 2014.
75 Robert Snell, "Detroit terror suspect strikes deal in federal court," Detroit News, March 30, 2017.
76 Frank Jordans, "German court sentences extremist to life over bomb plot," Associated Press, April 3, 2017.
77 "US teen pleads guilty to IS-inspired plot to kill pope," *Agence France-Presse*, April 3, 2017.
78 "'Can I criticize Islam without fearing for my life?,'" *CIJ News*, February 26, 2017.
79 Ibid.
80 Ibid.
81 Ibn Ishaq, *The Life of Muhammad: A Translation of Ibn Ishaq's Sirat Rasul Allah*, translated by Alfred Guillaume, Oxford University Press, 1955, p. 675.
82 Ibn Ishaq, *The Life of Muhammad: A Translation of Ibn Ishaq's Sirat Rasul Allah*, translated by Alfred Guillaume, Oxford University Press, 1955, p. 676.
83 Ibid.
84 Muhammed Ibn Ismaiel Al-Bukhari, *Sahih al-Bukhari: The Translation of the Meanings*, translated by Muhammad M. Khan, Darussalam, 1997, vol. 5, book 64, no. 4037.
85 Ibid.
86 Ibid.
87 Ibid.
88 Muhammed Ibn Ismaiel Al-Bukhari, *Sahih al-Bukhari: The Translation of the Meanings*, translated by Muhammad M. Khan, Darussalam, 1997, vol. 9, book 88, no. 6922.
89 Yusuf al-Qaradawi, "Apostasy Major and Minor," Islam Online, April 13, 2006.
90 Nonie Darwish, "If They [Muslims] Had Gotten Rid of the Punishment for Apostasy, Islam Would Not Exist Today," Gatestone Institute, February 5, 2013.

Chapter Nine

1 Diane Daniel, "Flying While Muslim: A Civil Rights Advocate on Travel Right Now," *The New York Times*, September 28, 2016.
2 Ibid.
3 Ibid.

4 Conor Shine, "Southwest says passenger who overheard college student's remarks also spoke Arabic," *Dallas Morning News*, April 18, 2016.
5 Ibid.
6 Home Office, Letter to Robert Spencer, June 25, 2013; Robert Spencer, "Britain capitulates to jihad," *Jihad Watch*, June 26, 2013.
7 "Remarks by President Trump to the People of Poland," WhiteHouse.gov, July 6, 2017.
8 Ibid.
9 Ibid.
10 Christian Borys and Oskar Górzyński, "Trump in Poland: A Clash of Civilizations Battle Cry, or, Reality TV as Policy," *The Daily Beast*, July 6, 2017.
11 Walter Shapiro, "Donald Trump's warning about 'western civilisation' evokes holy war," *The Guardian*, July 7, 2017.
12 Sarah Wildman, "Trump's speech in Poland sounded like an alt-right manifesto," *Vox*, July 6, 2017.
13 Jamelle Bouie, "A New Warsaw Pact," *Slate*, July 6, 2017.
14 Brian Lombardi, "27 Ways to Be a Modern Man," *The New York Times*, September 29, 2015.
15 Ibid.
16 Ibid.
17 Ibid.
18 Ibid.
19 Ibid.
20 Mary McCarthy, *Between Friends: The Correspondence of Hannah Arendt and Mary McCarthy, 1949-1975*, Harcourt, 1995, pp. 11-12. Italics in the original.
21 Ben Guarino, "Reza Aslan, host of CNN's 'Believer,' catches grief for showcasing religious cannibals in India," *Washington Post*, March 6, 2017; Jessica Chia, "CNN drops 'Believer' host Reza Aslan days after he called Donald Trump a 'piece of s***' for his response to the London Bridge terror attacks," *Dailymail*.com, June 9, 2017; Gregg Roman, "Celebrity Prof Reza Aslan Brings His 'Islamophobia' Show To Penn," *The Daily Caller*, March 10, 2017.
22 Gregg Roman, "Celebrity Prof Reza Aslan Brings His 'Islamophobia' Show To Penn," *The Daily Caller*, March 10, 2017.
23 Ibid.
24 Arnie Cooper, "Is Islam 'Worse' Than Any Other Religion?," *Miller-McCune*, December 3, 2010.
25 Ben Guarino, "Reza Aslan, host of CNN's 'Believer,' catches grief for showcasing religious cannibals in India," *Washington Post*, March 6, 2017; Jessica Chia, "CNN drops 'Believer' host Reza Aslan days after he called Donald Trump a 'piece of s***' for his response to the London Bridge terror attacks," *Dailymail*.com, June 9, 2017; Gregg Roman, "Celebrity Prof Reza Aslan Brings His 'Islamophobia' Show To Penn," *The Daily Caller*, March 10, 2017.

26 Robert Spencer, "Reza Aslan rebuked: 'Those abusive emails you sent [to Robert Spencer] were far below what most educated people would expect,'" *Jihad Watch*, April 8, 2013.
27 Dan Arel, "Islamic apologist Reza Aslan lied about his academic credentials," *Patheos*, August 13, 2015.
28 Jeremy Carl, "Liberal Bullies Threaten Free Speech," *National Review*, May 24, 2017.
29 Jeremy Carl, "Liberal Bullies Threaten Free Speech," *National Review*, May 24, 2017.
30 Faiz Siddiqui, "The Koran-burning preacher has been driving for Uber, *Washington Post*, February 4, 2017.
31 Stephanie Saul, "The Conservative Force Behind Speeches Roiling College Campuses," *The New York Times*, May 20, 2017.
32 Ibid.
33 Ibid.
34 "Manchester bombing latest: Investigation making 'immense' progress as police 'get hold of' large part of terror network," *The Daily Telegraph*, May 26, 2017.
35 Fraser Moore, "MI5 reveal 'up to 23,000 jihadis living in Britain' ahead of Bank Holiday security boost," *Express*, May 27, 2017.
36 "UK to deploy troops after attack, risk now 'critical': May," *Reuters*, May 23, 2017.
37 Victoria Friedman, "Tommy Robinson Arrested for Contempt of Court After Trying to Film Alleged Rapists Outside Canterbury Court," *Breitbart*, May 10, 2017; "May's speech to the Conservative Friends of Israel—full text," *Conservative Home*, December 12, 2016; Samuel Westrop, "UK: Isolating Britain's Phony Moderates 'Leaders of the Muslim Community,'" Gatestone Institute, February 2, 2015; Jamie Doward, "Revealed: preachers' messages of hate," *The Observer*, January 7, 2007.
38 "May's speech to the Conservative Friends of Israel—full text," *Conservative Home*, December 12, 2016.
39 Alex Matthews, "Hook-handed hate cleric Abu Hamza launches legal fight to return from US jail to UK cell because our prisons are softer," *Mailonline*, October 8, 2016.
40 Shiv Malik and Alice Su, "Abu Qatada cleared of terror charges by Jordan court and released from jail," *The Guardian*, September 24, 2014.
41 Gordon Blackstock, "Mosque leaders dump plans to host controversial hate preacher exposed by Sunday Post," *Sunday Post*, December 11, 2016.
42 Raheem Kassam, "'Behead, Burn, And Crush Gays' Islamic Preacher To Deliver 10 Days Of Lectures In London," *Breitbart*, October 4, 2016.
43 Iram Ramzan, "Clerics who hailed killer at mosque," *Oldham Evening Chronicle*, August 16, 2016.

44 Tom Porter, "Pakistani 'hate preacher' who glorifies Islamist murder welcomed by Archbishop of Canterbury," *International Business Times*, July 21, 2016.

45 Harry Yorke and Edward Malnick, "Exclusive: Islamist preacher who compared Jews to 'fleas' to speak at Palestine Expo event in government building," *The Daily Telegraph*, July 7, 2017.

46 Caroline Wheeler, "Britain BANS heroic bishops: Persecuted Christian leaders from war zones refused entry, *Express*, December 4, 2016.

47 Robert Spencer, "Spencer and Geller Banned from Britain for Supporting Israel," *FrontPageMagazine.com*, December 3, 2013.

48 Ian Cobain, Frances Perraudin, Steven Morris, and Nazia Parveen, "Salman Ramadan Abedi named by police as Manchester Arena attacker," *The Guardian*, May 23, 2017.

49 Rebecca Camber and Stephen Wright, "Bomber from a red brick semi who 'knew an ISIS recruiter': British-born Manchester United fan is the son of refugees, 'chanted Islamic prayers in the street' and was known to MI5 after 'terrorism training in Libya,'" *Daily Mail*, May 23, 2017.

50 Trista Sullivan, "Demand Truman State University Cancel Robert Spencer Event," Care2 Petitions, n.d.

51 A. Prince, "NO STUDENT FEES FOR HATE! PRIORITIZE THE SAFETY OF ALL STUDENTS!," Change.org, n.d.

52 Anthony Wagner, "Opinion: President Riggs should immediately rescind the right of Robert Spencer to speak at Gettysburg College," The Gettysburgian, May 1, 2017.

53 Paul Fontaine, "Known Islamophobe To Hold Conference At Grand Hotel, Protest Likely," *Reykjavik Grapevine*, May 2, 2017.

54 "Islamophobe US lecturer believes he was poisoned by Icelandic man in Reykjavik," *Iceland Monitor*, May 16, 2017.

55 U.K. Home Office, Letter to Robert Spencer, June 25, 2013; Robert Spencer, "Britain capitulates to jihad," Jihad Watch, June 26, 2013; Robert Spencer, "Spencer and Geller Banned from Britain for Supporting Israel," *FrontPageMagazine.com*, December 3, 2013; Acts 17 Apologetics, "On the Radicalization of Anders Behring Breivik," YouTube, August 6, 2011.

56 Andrew Berwick (Anders Behring Breivik), *2083: A European Declaration of Independence*, p. 948.

57 Ralph Ellis, Ashley Fantz, Faith Karimi and Eliott C. McLaughlin, "Orlando shooting: 49 killed, shooter pledged ISIS allegiance," CNN, June 13, 2016; "French jihadist murders police couple at Magnanville," BBC, June 14, 2016; Kate Brady and Samantha Early, "Several injured in attack on train near Würzburg, southern Germany," *DW*, July 18, 2016; Frederik Pleitgen, Tim Hume and Euan McKirdy, "Suicide bomber in Germany pledged allegiance to ISIS leader," CNN, July 26, 2016; "France church attack: Priest killed by two 'IS militants,'" BBC, July 26, 2016; Max Blau, Emanuella Grinberg and Shimon Prokupecz, "Investigators believe Ohio State attacker was inspired by ISIS,"

CNN, November 29, 2016; Justin Huggler, James Rothwell, Louise Burke, "Berlin terror attack: Horrifying dashcam video shows truck speeding into Christmas market," *The Daily Telegraph*, December 23, 2016; Kim Pilling and Eleanor Barlow, "Manchester attack: Salman Abedi's explosive 'designed to kill and maim indiscriminately,'" *The Independent*, June 10, 2017; Steve Almasy, Ralph Ellis, Natalie Gallon, and Steve George, "London terror attack: Seven victims killed, three suspects shot dead by police," CNN, June 4, 2017.

58 "Robert Spencer Vs. Antifa in Stuttgart - German Subtitles," YouTube, June 5, 2011.

59 Eugène Ionesco, *Rhinoceros and Other Plays*, Derek Prouse, translator, Grove Press, 1960, p. 107.

60 Ibid.

61 Ibid.

62 Xavier Ternisien, "Archive: A 'Charlie Hebdo', on n'a 'pas l'impression d'égorger quelqu'un avec un feutre,'" *Le Monde*, September 20, 2012.